LEGACIES OF

SPACE AND

INTANGIBLE

HERITAGE

LEGACIES OF SPACE AND INTANGIBLE HERITAGE

ARCHAEOLOGY, ETHNOHISTORY, AND THE POLITICS OF CULTURAL CONTINUITY IN THE AMERICAS

EDITED BY
Fernando Armstrong-Fumero
and Julio Hoil Gutierrez

UNIVERSITY PRESS OF COLORADO
Boulder

© 2017 by University Press of Colorado

Published by University Press of Colorado
5589 Arapahoe Avenue, Suite 206C
Boulder, Colorado 80303

All rights reserved
Printed in the United States of America

 The University Press of Colorado is a proud member of
The Association of American University Presses.

The University Press of Colorado is a cooperative publishing enterprise supported, in part, by Adams State University, Colorado State University, Fort Lewis College, Metropolitan State University of Denver, Regis University, University of Colorado, University of Northern Colorado, Utah State University, and Western State Colorado University.

∞ This paper meets the requirements of the ANSI/NISO Z39.48-1992 (Permanence of Paper).

ISBN: 978-1-60732-571-0 (cloth)
ISBN: 978-1-60732-659-5 (paperback)
ISBN: 978-1-60732-572-7 (ebook)

Library of Congress Cataloging-in-Publication Data

Names: Armstrong-Fumero, Fernando, editor. | Hoil Gutierrez, Julio, editor.
Title: Legacies of space and intangible heritage : archaeology, ethnohistory, and the politics of cultural continuity in the Americas / edited by Fernando Armstrong-Fumero and Julio Hoil Gutierrez.
Description: Boulder : University Press of Colorado, [2017] | Includes bibliographical references and index.
Identifiers: LCCN 2016056647| ISBN 9781607325710 (cloth) | ISBN 9781607326595 (pbk) | ISBN 9781607325727 (ebook)
Subjects: LCSH: Cultural landscapes—America—Case studies. | Cultural property—Protection—America—Case studies. | Cultural property—America—Management—Case studies. | Historic sites—Conservation and restoration—America—Case studies. | Historic sites—America—Management—Case studies.
Classification: LCC GF500 .L44 2017 | DDC 973—dc23
LC record available at https://lccn.loc.gov/2016056647

An electronic version of this book is freely available, thanks to the support of libraries working with Knowledge Unlatched. KU is a collaborative initiative designed to make high-quality books open access for the public good. The open access ISBN for this book is 978-1-60732-700-4. More information about the initiative and links to the open-access version can be found at www.knowledgeunlatched.org.

Front-cover photographs: Taperinha Plantation (top), Cavern of the Painted Rock, Monte Alegre (bottom), courtesy of Anna C. Roosevelt.

Contents

List of Figures   **vii**

List of Tables   **ix**

CHAPTER 1. INTRODUCTION
Fernando Armstrong-Fumero and Julio Hoil Gutierrez   **3**

CHAPTER 2. SETTLEMENT PATTERNS, INTANGIBLE MEMORY, AND THE INSTITUTIONAL ENTANGLEMENTS OF HERITAGE IN MODERN YUCATÁN
Fernando Armstrong-Fumero and Julio Hoil Gutierrez   **15**

CHAPTER 3. HOPISINMUY WU'YA'MAT HISAT YANG TUPQA'VA YEESIWNGWU (HOPI ANCESTORS LIVED IN THESE CANYONS)
Maren P. Hopkins, Stuart B. Koyiyumptewa, Saul L. Hedquist, T. J. Ferguson, and Chip Colwell   **33**

CHAPTER 4. DESIGNS ON/OF THE LAND: COMPETING VISIONS, DISPLACEMENT, AND LANDSCAPE MEMORY IN BRITISH COLONIAL HONDURAS
Christine Kray, Minette Church, and Jason Yaeger   **53**

CHAPTER 5. CULTIVATING COMMUNITY: THE ARCHAEOLOGY OF JAPANESE AMERICAN CONFINEMENT AT AMACHE
Bonnie Clark **79**

CHAPTER 6. INDIGENOUS HOUSE PLANS AND LAND IN MEXICO CITY (SIXTEENTH CENTURY): REFLECTIONS ON THE BUYING AND SELLING, INHERITANCE, AND CONFLICTS SURROUNDING HOUSES AND LAND
Keiko Yoneda (translated by Hannah Becker) **97**

CHAPTER 7. THE ARCHAEOLOGY OF PLACE IN EBTÚN, YUCATÁN, MEXICO
Rani T. Alexander **131**

CHAPTER 8. NAMES, NAMING, AND PERSON REFERENCE IN QUIAHIJE CHATINO
Emiliana Cruz **163**

CHAPTER 9. A CULTURESCAPE BUILT OVER 5,000 YEARS, ARCHAEOLOGY, AND VICHAMA RAYMI IN THE FORGE OF HISTORY
Winifred Creamer, Jonathan Haas, and Henry Marcelo Castillo **189**

CHAPTER 10. INTERPRETING LONG-TERM HUMAN-ENVIRONMENT INTERACTION IN AMAZONIA
Anna C. Roosevelt **209**

Contributors **239**
Index **241**

Figures

3.1.	Hopitutskwa as imagined as a pilgrimage route	36
3.2.	Hopi Reservation in relation to Black Mesa, Glen Canyon, and US Highway 160	41
3.3.	Hopi project participants and anthropologists at Glen Canyon	43
3.4.	Toko'navi (Navajo Mountain)	44
3.5.	Pictograph at ancient site in GLCA	46
3.6.	Warrior images at GLCA	47
3.7.	Sample of places with Hopi names on Highway 160	47
4.1.	British Honduras in late nineteenth and early twentieth centuries	54
4.2.	Valentín Tosh and Ementerio Cantún of San José Nuevo	57
4.3.	Fragment of incendiary rocket	60
4.4.	Jamaica Ginger bottles	62
4.5.	Ceramics from San Pedro Siris	63
5.1.	War Relocation Authority camps	80
5.2.	Amache showing internee landscaping	84
5.3.	Block 9L at Amache	85
5.4.	Garden Plot in Block 9L	86

vii

viii FIGURES

5.5.	Excavation crew chief and former internee volunteer talk	91
6.1.	Plan 9	99
6.2.	Plan 9 bis	107
6.3.	Toponymic glyph	110
6.4.	Architectural complex at Cholula	111
6.5.	Plan 7	113
6.6.	Plan 18	115
7.1.	Map of Eastern Yucatán	134
7.2.	Census document from Kaua in 1841	138
7.3.	Shrine at Tzaab	148
7.4.	Cenote at Bubul	150
8.1.	Kitchen interaction	165
8.2.	Cieneguilla seen from San Juan	165
8.3.	Map of location-based names	167
8.4.	The first plane that landed in Cieneguilla	168
8.5.	Map of Cieneguilla and San Juan Quiahije	169
8.6.	Map of San Juan Quiahije, Cieneguilla, and Juquila	170
9.1.	Map of the Norte Chico region	191
9.2.	Maize, yuca, and pepino	193
9.3.	Huancas	194
9.4.	Figure of a woman	195
9.5.	Photo of U-shaped layout of Caballete	198
9.6.	Pageant at Fortress of Paramonga	202
10.1.	Tropical forest at Taperinha	212
10.2.	Floodplain and floodplain forest, Monte Alegre	214
10.3.	Santarem period cultural black soil	218
10.4.	Cavern of the painted rock	220
10.5.	Paleo-Indian camp layer, Cavern of the Painted Rock	221
10.6.	Taperinha Plantation	223
10.7.	Cultural Forest, Marajó Island	224
10.8.	Anthropic acai grove, Marajó Island	232
10.9.	Paleo-Indian point curated by Cayapo community	233

Tables

7.1.	Maya social organization	136
7.2.	Population distribution in the study area	140
7.3.	Household change in 1841, 1883, and 1890	141
7.4.	Comparison of household size	142
7.5.	Most numerous male surnames in 1841	144
7.6.	Marriage patterns in 1841	144
7.7.	Most Numerous Male Surnames in 1883	145
7.8.	Marriage patterns in 1883	146
8.1.	Teknonymy	173
8.2.	Consanguinity terms	175
8.3.	Coparenthood	177
8.4.	Autonym	177
8.5.	Ethnonym	177
8.6.	Names derived from Spanish	179
8.7.	Distribution of family names and place-names	180
8.8.	Tones	183
8.9.	Place-names	183

LEGACIES OF
SPACE AND
INTANGIBLE
HERITAGE

I

Introduction

FERNANDO ARMSTRONG-FUMERO AND JULIO HOIL GUTIERREZ

Whether on the scale of a household, of a community, or of a much larger regional environment, spaces of human habitation are both historical records of our past and a key element in reproducing the knowledge and values that define our lives in the present. This process of cultural reproduction can be endangered when migration, displacement, or changes in property regimes limit communities' access to sites where they have important historical connections. Around the world, formal legal statutes, grassroots organizations, and local acts of resistance can play different roles in reasserting these connections between people and place. Accordingly, the claims that contemporary stakeholders make on archaeological sites and related landscape features extend beyond the simple desire for conservation or site preservation and include the rights to visit, inhabit, and even alter the physical composition of these spaces.

The essays in this volume are an interdisciplinary exploration of these intersections between the study and management of physical sites and the reproduction of intangible cultural legacies. Some chapters focus on more abstract theoretical insights into societies' relationship to different places and how this relationship figures in the reproduction of cultural continuities amidst processes of social change. Other essays turn to more pragmatic ways in which these insights figure in contemporary negotiations through which different groups seek greater access or control over culturally significant sites and landscapes. As a group, they are meant to provide a comparative body of case studies that explore the different ways in which

DOI: 10.5876/9781607325727.c001

place is mediated by social, political, and ecological processes that have deep historical roots and that continue to effect the politics of heritage management today.

The close relationship between physical space and more ephemeral manifestations of culture and social organization are a common thread joining diverse currents of anthropological and archaeological research. Since the rise of New Archaeology in the 1960s and 1970s, archaeological research has focused on reconstructing long-term patterns of culture and social structure. Working "up" from the material traces of human behavior, the processualists and their various intellectual successors and competitors have been keenly attuned to the intimate and dynamic relationship between the materiality of space and the more intangible dimensions of human behavior and experience. In cultural and linguistic anthropology, a number of theoretical currencies that focus on the intersections of space and culture gained prominence in the 1990s and 2000s. These range from studies of the spatialization of collective memory that were inspired by the work of Pierre Norá (1989), to linguistic analyses of the intimate relationship between patterns of reference and the social organization of space (Hanks 1990), to studies of environment that focus on the intimate ties between evolving ecosystems and patterns of settlement and subsistence (Ford and Nigh 2015; Gordillo 2004; Wright 2014).

Many of the theoretical currencies that we listed above figure in the essays in this volume. But the case studies presented here are also joined by an overarching concern for stakeholders' access to culturally significant spaces. "Accessibility" becomes a question of crossing boundaries that are defined by regimes of private property, heritage legislation, and the eminent domain of modern nation-states. In this regard, these essays touch upon questions of spatial justice that figure in the tradition of cultural geography associated with Henri Lefebvre (1992), and later Anglophone authors such as David Harvey (1996) and Edward Soja (2011). These authors adapted the dialectical analysis of Western Marxism to explore the dynamic historical relationship between space and the social organization of human labor. Space was never simply an inert material template on which human social processes were enacted but was also a *product of* and *agent in* the processes of human history. Thus, landscapes were both a record of previous human interactions with the material world and an ontic component of ongoing processes through which society recreates itself. This dynamic relationship between the social and the spatial had important ramifications for the questions of social justice that were at the heart of this critical human geography. Full enjoyment of what it means to be in the world hinges on the equitable distribution of access to and stewardship over the spaces that define our historical experience.

As the essays in this volume show, these questions of accessibility and stewardship are becoming a guiding political and ethical concern for archaeologists and other scholars studying heritage sites and landscapes. Increasingly, international policy instruments and national legal reforms are granting recognition to the rights that diverse human communities have to preserve and publicly perform elements of their cultural heritage. However, when it comes to the role of designated heritage sites in promoting cultural continuities, researchers, stakeholders, and activists often face a series of legal and political tensions (Aikawa-Faure 2003; Gilman 2010).

Many of these tensions emerge from the fact that different legal principles tend to crosscut the concatenation of material, social, and cultural processes that constitute the heritage of different groups. That is, the formal regimes of property and political jurisdiction that govern the management of heritage rarely account for the intimate relationship between physical space and more intangible forms of heritage that shape the lives of diverse stakeholders. These tensions become particularly evident when scholars and activists try to reconcile statutes for the physical management with a contemporary tendency to view the preservation of intangible heritage as a human right. While the former tend to be deeply rooted in state-sanctioned regimes of land tenure and eminent domain, the latter have a more recent origin in a body of international policy instruments. For our purposes here, it is worth turning to UNESCO's influential 2003 Convention for the Safeguarding of Intangible Cultural Heritage. It defines "intangible cultural heritage" as ". . . the practices, representations, expressions, knowledge, skills—as well as the instruments, objects, artifacts and cultural spaces associated therewith—that communities, groups and, in some cases, individuals recognize as part of their cultural heritage. This intangible cultural heritage, transmitted from generation to generation, is constantly recreated by communities and groups in response to their environment, their interaction with nature and their history, and provides them with a sense of identity and continuity, thus promoting respect for cultural diversity and human creativity."

Most scholars and heritage professionals recognize that physical access to culturally important places is an essential mechanism for reproducing this sort of heritage. However, turning this recognition into a generalized practice for heritage stewardship can be more complicated. Culturally significant access to a site or landscape can be something as simple as visiting places that evoke different elements of collective memory. In this case, the practices to which stakeholders can claim an inalienable right are not materially different from those engaged in by tourists and other casual visitors. But culturally significant access can also involve transformations of space that range from the practice of traditional agriculture to recycling the architectural remains of previous occupations. While visits to sites that are materially similar to those of tourists are easy to reconcile with the operation of legally protected heritage sites, these latter forms of interaction challenge forms of stewardship that stress the in situ preservation of structures and artifacts with minimal alteration by contemporary human activity.

What emerges from the diverse case studies that we highlight in this volume is that different political and historical contexts provide very different outcomes when it comes to stakeholder communities' interaction with the places that figure in the reproduction of their identity and customs. For example, when compared to most indigenous groups in Latin America, Native American tribes in the United States have a long history of nominal legal recognition of their sovereignty in the management of tribal properties, notwithstanding pervasive impingements by nontribal federal and state governments (Wilkins and Kiiwetinepinesiik Stark 2010). This legacy is evident in a number of legal and political victories that allow tribal stakeholders to control elements of tangible heritage in ways that have few precedents in Latin America. For example, the application of the Native American Graves Protection and Repatriation Act has led to the repatriation of human remains and accompanying artifacts to native communities, who, in some cases, bury or otherwise steward these materials in ways that preclude future study by academic institutions. In this case, the protection of indigenous ceremonial practices and notions of the sacred can trump the preservationist mandate of secular heritage institutions. Likewise, as in the case discussed in this volume by Maren P. Hopkins et al. in chapter 3, sacred sites that meet the criteria of tangible cultural heritage remain under the jurisdiction of tribal political entities or are granted special status that limits their use by public or private development.

This poses a sharp contrast to most parts of Latin America. Few indigenous ethnic groups in Latin America have as long a history of formally recognized political and territorial jurisdiction as do tribes currently located within the United States. In most of these countries, the protection of heritage sites ranging from pre-Hispanic ruins to colonial churches is treated as an eminent domain of federal agencies whose authority usually trumps that of local groups who seek greater access to or control over sites. Cases in which federal heritage agencies in Latin America have tried to make archaeological sites accessible to descendant communities underscore the precedence of state-sanctioned heritage practice over local forms of intangible heritage. In the early 2000s, for example, Guatemalan heritage authorities made a concession to pan-Maya cultural activists by creating spaces in which rituals could be performed in the ancestral ruins of Iximché. But these activities are restricted to specially designated areas that were built with this purpose in mind by state heritage institutions on the periphery of sites, and required forms of official licensing that many traditional ritualists found to be too restrictive (Frühsorge 2007).

Seen within a larger temporal context, the state-managed formalization of indigenous ritual at Iximché highlights a fundamental tension between the legal protection of tangible heritage and the historical formation of intangible heritage. In pre-Hispanic times, ritualism at Maya sites involved continuous construction activity through which earlier structures were eventually dismantled or covered by newer ones. Colonial churches that figure in the syncretic religion of modern Maya people were likewise often built on or with the ruins of pre-Hispanic structures, and other forms of architectural recycling are fundamental to patterns of landscape use that have largely defined Mayan peoples' relationship to their territory. These intimate links between the reproduction of cultural heritage and the material transformation of space are ultimately irreconcilable with attempts to compromise between tangible and intangible heritage that segregate the materiality of space from a presumably "immaterial" living culture.

Developing alternative approaches poses both a pragmatic challenge for heritage professionals and stakeholders and a more general conceptual problem for theorizing culture and heritage. Are there separate substances that exist in physical objects and human practices that justify their being treated as qualitatively different forms of "heritage"? Or, following authors such as Bruno Latour (2004), can we think of heritage as a political terrain constituted through a more dynamic interplay of human and nonhuman actors? There may be no single answer to these questions that applies to all cases in which the reproduction of living cultural legacies comes into conflict with the physical preservation of sites and artifacts. But a closer examination of the different kinds of relationships between human beings, objects, and the reproduction of cultural legacies is useful in thinking through this complex theoretical and ethicopolitical terrain. This sort of comparative analysis is the ultimate goal of the diverse case studies presented here.

CASE STUDIES: COMMON THEMES AND DIFFERENCES OF SCALE

The case studies presented in this volume are not only a diverse sample of distinct regional experiences, but also reflect a range of different temporal and geographical scales on which societies' relationship to territories and landscapes unfold. Although a number of possible arrangements of the case studies were possible, we have chosen to present the chapters under four rubrics that illustrate different moments in the complex relationship between local communities, spatialized identities, and state-sanctioned regimes for the management of property and cultural heritage. Chapters 2 and 3 explore *the state of the question*, with two case studies of present-day negotiations between state-sanctioned heritage institutions and communities that seek to exercise more control over sites that figured in migrations that shaped their livelihood and cultural heritage. Chapters 4 and 5 explore the *roots of displacement*, focusing on the immediate aftermath of the historical traumas that distance communities from the places that define their collective identity and experience. Tracing different processes of *continuity and adaptation*, chapters 6 through

8 examine how marginalized peoples have adopted different legal frameworks, notions of territoriality, and elements of culture that have been imposed on them from above as a means of reproducing their own control and perspective on space. And finally, a pair of chapters that we characterize as *expanding the boundaries of heritage* look to models of stakeholdership that expand the temporal and spatial scale of territorial identities far beyond the intimate environs and local histories of closely bounded communities.

We open with two chapters that highlight how distinct historical, political, and legal contexts shape the encounter between state-sanctioned regimes of heritage management and descendant communities' relationships to ancestral landscapes. Based on examples from Mexico's Yucatán Peninsula and the southwestern United States, chapters 2 and 3 focus on two different indigenous communities that seek to preserve livelihoods and identities that have been affected by histories of migration and displacement. However, the distinct legal contexts of indigenous politics and heritage management in the United States and Mexico yield very different outcomes to the communities' attempts to establish claims on culturally significant territories and practices.

In chapter 2, we document how governmental institutions that seek to preserve archaeological sites and artifacts find themselves at odds with the practices through which local communities have used the same sites and objects. Yucatec Maya-speaking subsistence cultivators today share a knowledge of the regional landscape that includes thousands of named sites, the locations and features of which have been transmitted orally during hundreds of years of ecologically and politically motivated migrations. This process of cultural transmission is intimately tied to the physical labor of agriculture, which includes activities that federal heritage authorities consider to be a threat to the survival of archaeological sites. In the specific examples that we highlight, Yucatec Maya communities have relatively few formal mechanisms with which to advance claims that can successfully contest the preservationist mandate of federal heritage institutions.

In the case of the Hopi Tribe, which is discussed in chapter 3 by Hopkins et al., there is a more congenial relationship between the intangible heritage of living tribal members and the work of federal authorities. Working with archaeologists, members of the Hopi Tribe have enjoyed a number of key successes in securing protected status for sites outside of tribal lands, whose cultural role is documented in oral histories and ritual activities. In the Yucatec Maya case, the state's mandate to preserve antiquities with minimal alteration is understood to trump territorial claims made in the name of more localized identity groups. In the Hopi case, federal intervention for the preservation of sacred sites becomes a viable means of reproducing the collective identities and value systems that Hopi people associate with their historical landscape.

Despite their very different political outcomes, the cases discussed in chapters 2 and 3 are both linked by a common experience of indigenous and minority peoples the world over. In both cases, fostering a collective relationship to culturally significant places means negotiating regimes of land tenure and geopolitics that emerged when colonization and other forms of violence disarticulated older forms of territoriality. The following two sections, composed of chapters 4 through 8, look more closely at these moments of disarticulation and their different aftermaths.

Whereas the Hopi and Yucatec Maya examples show people coping with the impacts of events that happened a century or more in the past, chapters 4 and 5 deal with traumatic events that occurred within the lifetime of some of the stakeholders in question. In chapter 4, Christine Kray, Minette Church, and Jason Yeager trace the exodus of Yucatec Maya people who fled from parts of Mexico that were ravaged by the Caste War in the mid-nineteenth century, only to be displaced from various settlements in twentieth-century British Honduras. Tensions between traditional agriculture and the interests of major logging concerns led to the eviction of these communities from the Yalbac Hills area and to their forcible resettlement in regions that were less ecologically suitable. This displacement is recalled by survivors as more than just the loss of land. Those who lived through the eviction often relate negative health effects of the move and a diminished sense of well-being as they were forced to assume alternative subsistence strategies. What results is a collective identity that is tied to a place and lifestyle that are currently inaccessible to the descendants of the Yalbac Hills Maya.

In chapter 5, Bonnie Clark discusses how Japanese American inmates at the internment camp of Amache used different techniques of gardening and cooperation to make the carceral environment socially and aesthetically livable. Former internees and their descendants testify to the difficulty of adapting to an environment that was both physically alien and associated with the experience of racial discrimination. The implementation of Japanese landscape principles on the grounds provides a material testimony to how ethnic identity was written into the site in an attempt to create a sense of community amidst adversity. Clark also documents how collaboration between archaeologists and former internees and their descendants becomes a successful convergence of work to document and preserve tangible heritage and the reproduction of a more intangible collective memory that has been marginalized within the official historical narratives of the United States.

Just as the internees at Amache struggled to reconstitute a culturally specific sense of well-being through the limited materials that were offered by federal authorities that imprisoned them, other societies adapt to displacement and social trauma by incorporating and transforming elements of the regimes that have been imposed on them. After generations of survival and resilience, these adaptations can become seamlessly integrated into the fabric of everyday life and in the constitution of culturally significant place. This process is evident in different ways in chapters 6 through 8, all of which focus on different regions of present-day Mexico. In these cases, legal or bureaucratic procedures that were imposed by the Spanish colonial state and its nineteenth- and twentieth-century successors become a tool for the long-term survival of different elements of indigenous culture.

In chapter 6, Keiko Yoneda discusses visual representations of lands that were inherited, bought, and sold in the Valley of Mexico in the sixteenth century. These texts reflect the translation of indigenous forms of land use and family structure into the idiom of Spanish legalism. As Yoneda argues, this was not a case of Western notions of household space and organization being superimposed onto indigenous properties but of Nahua-speaking communities adopting a colonial legal framework that allowed them to retain a degree of control over ancestral properties and their use. Legal disputes that are recorded from the sixteenth century demonstrate the complex layers of meaning and ownership that exist within the deceptively simple label of "house." Comparing these texts with the ethnography of contemporary Nahua communities provides a longer historical context for how the inheritance and adaptation of family properties over time has contributed to the reproduction of kinds of social and spatial organization that are at the heart of indigenous communities today.

In chapter 7, Rani T. Alexander follows a parallel track in tracing the cultural and political identity of Maya-speaking agriculturalists in Yucatán through the history of interactions between traditional subsistence practices and different state-sponsored regimes of land tenure. In this case, population displacements caused by the Caste War of 1847 produce a demographic rupture that separates colonial populations from present-day ones. Ebtún, the community on which Alexander focuses, was essentially depopulated in the mid-nineteenth century. However, a new wave of settlers was able to establish a viable community by mediating between their own subsistence needs, older land titles, and opportunities offered by twentieth-century agrarian reforms. The resulting dialog between state-sanctioned land tenure and local forms of family structure and subsistence practices converges in a deeply rooted identity centered on what Alexander refers to as "smallholder resilience."

Whereas Yoneda and Alexander's chapters focus on the material implications of different regimes of ownership and land tenure, Emiliana Cruz examines how territoriality is expressed in the more abstract idiom of personal reference in chapter 8. That is, she explores different forms of person reference among Chatino speakers in the Oaxacan town of San Juan Quiahije, the more recently settled village of Cieneguilla, and various other communities to which people travel to live and work. In everyday conversations, subtle differences in terms of reference or the pronunciation of Spanish names help to situate individuals and places within the larger history of the community's relationship to the physical landscape, nonindigenous Mexicans, and different groups within the town. Cruz notes that situating individuals in social and physical space is particularly important given the history of migration and neocolonial interventions from the state that have marked the modern Chatino experience. Like negotiations with formal regimes of land title, framing the realities of contemporary political geography in distinctly Chatino forms of reference is a key mechanism in the reproduction of collective identities and values.

The inheritance of family properties, smallholder resistance, and the reproduction of indigenous forms of spatial reference embody forms of cultural continuity that can constitute clearly defined descendant communities. That is, chapters 6, 7, and 8 each present cases in which written records and collective memories can document the transmission of territories and cultural practices within specific descendant groups. But what happens when living stakeholders make claims to territorial identities that cannot be documented through the same chain of continuous transmission? Or when this territorial identity is tied to processes that take place on a geographical scale that cannot be contained within the landscape of a single community or well-documented migration route?

These more expanded communities of people who identify with different spatialized pasts present some important conceptual and ethicopolitical challenges. Many of the formal policies that stakeholder groups have used to assert control over ancestral sites and remains rely on documented ancestral ties, for example, the formal statutes of tribal membership for federally recognized Native American nations in the United States (see Wilkins and Kiiwetinepinesiik Stark 2010). But as Ian Hodder (2003) and others have observed, nontraditional stakeholders such as New Age religious practitioners have emerged as significant players in debates over the use of heritage sites. These different models of stakeholdership and use rights challenge the idea that cultural heritage is reproduced within self-enclosed communities that maintain consistent and more-or-less homogeneous "traditions" over time. The two final chapters of this book examine cases in which more dispersed communities make claims to territorial identities that touch on these expanded notions of stakeholdership.

Turning to the Norte Chico region of Peru in chapter 9, Winifred Creamer, Jonathan Haas, and Henry Marcelo Castillo situate the early history of social complexity within more recent traditions of mythology and public celebration. Although thousands of years separate the origins of agriculture and social hierarchy from the seventeenth-century myth of Vichama Raymi, this widely known narrative represents an indigenous interpretation of history that parallels the work of archaeological research. Today, the revival of the myth in state-sponsored pageantry provides contemporary populations with a means of celebrating their own relationship to this landscape and the agricultural heritage of its earliest human populations. Although this represents a tradition of narrative and ritual that is distinct from what we see in the intimate spaces of communities such as San Juan Quiahije or the Maya settlements of Yucatán, it is playing a parallel role in turning contemporary residents of the Norte Chico into stakeholders in the interpretation of a deep history that is written into their coastal landscape and the various resources that it offers.

In chapter 10, A. C. Roosevelt speaks to a similar reclamation of deep historical processes, though on the much larger geographical scale of the Amazonian basin. Like other archaeologists of her generation, Roosevelt revised an earlier vision of tropical forest societies as being determined by fairly static ecological constraints to recognize the concatenation of natural and anthropogenic factors that shaped Amazonian ecosystems and the different forms of agency through which human societies could adapt to them. A concurrent process involved the emergence of diverse and wide-ranging Amazonian populations as stakeholders in archaeological research, both as regards discussions of sustainable resource use and in reclaiming ancient iconographic traditions that embody cosmological principles that have survived into the present day. New collaborations between archaeologists and indigenous people are providing a means through which diverse and geographically separated descendant communities are imagining a shared pan-Amazonian heritage with roots in the very long-term processes that shaped the ancient forest environment.

FINAL COMMENTS

As a group, the nine case studies in this book offer different perspectives on the substances that embody the relationship between people and places and on the scale at which these substances are reproduced and contested over time. But all touch on something that is a common reality for archaeologists and other heritage workers. The spaces and landscapes that we study are never simply a record of the past. They are also part of an ongoing dialog between living societies and space. This dialog is mediated through things such as agricultural knowledge, cosmology, collective memory, and collective strategies for interacting with legal and political institutions.

This particular confluence of human populations, historical landscapes, and the cultural practices that situate people in places resonates with broader questions facing archaeologists today. An evolving body of scholarly and policy literature on intangible heritage is granting the cultural legacies that mediate between people and places more formal legal and political status. Along with a range of theoretical currencies that have emphasized dialog with stakeholders, the growing importance granted to intangible heritage challenges archaeologists and other heritage workers with finding new ways of incorporating the cultural legacies that link societies to place into the work of research and stewardship.

Cases of the type presented in this volume raise important empirical and conceptual issues for facing these challenges. One of the most important involves developing working definitions of heritage that bridge or blur the conceptual differences between current frameworks of protecting tangible and intangible legacies. Such a concept of heritage would better reflect the histories of peoples and places discussed in these essays and the relationship of different stakeholders and tangible heritage sites the world over. What if the sites that play the most significant role in reproducing the intangible heritage of living communities were granted the same kind of protection as famous World Heritage sites? Turning these considerations into more of an institutional priority would bring more official attention to seemingly mundane places such as the mountaintops that surround the Chatino communities of Quiahije and Cieneguilla, or to places such as the ruins of the internment camp at Amache, which have been intentionally marginalized within the narratives of official historiography.

This expanded dialog between the discourses of tangible and intangible heritage involves its own challenges. As a number of the chapters in this book show, the reproduction of intangible heritage often involves manipulating natural and anthropogenic landscapes in ways that differ significantly from the strict emphasis on preservation that pervades most policy on tangible heritage. But these case studies also highlight the diverse strategies with which even colonized peoples and other disadvantaged minorities have negotiated politics of place imposed on them from above. These strategies range from engagements with the Spanish legal system by sixteenth-century Nahuas, to uses of agrarian reform by Yucatec Maya settlers, to the present-day successes that the Hopi Tribe has enjoyed in attaining federal recognition and protection of historical sites. Cases like this highlight how turning formal regimes of heritage protection into a tool for preserving the intangible legacies of minority groups is not simply a question of reforms articulated from above, but one in which agendas, strategies, and outcomes are often successfully defined by the stakeholders themselves.

REFERENCES

Aikawa-Faure, Noriko. 2003. "From the Proclamation of Masterpieces to the *Convention for the Safeguarding of Intangible Heritage*." In *Intangible Heritage*, ed. Laurajane Smith and Natsuko Akagawa, 13–44. New York: Routledge.

Ford, Anabelle, and Ronald Nigh. 2015. *Maya First Garden: Eight Millennia of Sustainable Cultivation in the Tropical Woodlands*. Walnut Creek, CA: Left Coast Press.

Frühsorge, Lars. 2007. "Archaeological Heritage in Guatemala: Indigenous Perspectives on the Ruins of Iximche.'" *Archaeologies* 3 (1): 39–58. http://dx.doi.org/10.1007/s11759-007-9001-4.

Gilman, Derek. 2010. *Understanding Cultural Heritage*. Cambridge: Cambridge University Press.

Gordillo, Gaston. 2004. *Landscapes of Devils*. Durham: Duke University Press. http://dx.doi.org/10.1215/9780822386025.

Hanks, William. 1990. *Referential Practice: Language and Lived Space among the Maya*. Chicago: University of Chicago Press.

Harvey, David. 1996. *Justice, Nature and the Geography of Difference*. New York: Blackwell.

Hodder, Ian. 2003. "Archaeological Reflexivity and the 'Local' Voice." *Anthropological Quarterly* 76 (1): 55–69. http://dx.doi.org/10.1353/anq.2003.0010.

Latour, Bruno. 2004. *The Politics of Nature*. Cambridge, MA: Harvard University Press.

Lefebvre, Henri. 1992. *The Production of Space*. New York: Wiley-Blackwell.

Norá, Pierre. 1989. "Between Memory and History: Les Lieux de Memoire." *Representations (Berkeley, Calif.)* 26 (1): 7–24. http://dx.doi.org/10.1525/rep.1989.26.1.99p0274v.

Soja, Edward. 2011. *Postmodern Geographies*. 2nd ed. London: Verso.

Wilkins, David E., and Heidi Kiiwetinepinesiik Stark. 2010. *American Indian Politics and the American Political System*. New York: Rowman and Littlefield.

Wright, Shelley. 2014. *Our Ice Is Vanishing / Sikuvut Nunguliqtuq: A History of Inuit, Newcomers, and Climate Change*. Alberta: McGill-Queen's University Press.

2

Settlement Patterns, Intangible Memory, and the Institutional Entanglements of Heritage in Modern Yucatán

FERNANDO ARMSTRONG-FUMERO AND JULIO HOIL GUTIERREZ

Heritage scholars have written at length about how institutional criteria of "worth" tend to privilege artifacts and customs that are valued by some stakeholders over those which are valued by others (Aikawa-Faure 2009; Gillman 2010). Here, we will discuss the agricultural landscape of rural Yucatán as one specific case in which laws governing archaeological sites tend to disqualify certain traditional practices—and by extension, the people who engage in these practices—from the terrain of "legitimate" cultural heritage. In treating the physical deposition and manipulation of archaeological remains as the exclusive terrain of trained scholars and museums, state-sponsored institutions in Mexico tend to marginalize the vernacular practices through which pre-Hispanic artifacts become relevant to Mayan descendant communities. This process is further complicated by the fact that indigenous forms of territoriality and landscape use do enjoy certain official protections, both through recent charters for the defense of intangible heritage and more traditional forms of municipal and agrarian governance. When heritage practices that are applied to pre-Hispanic sites sideline these Yucatec Maya forms of territoriality and landscape, they create a hierarchy between different ways of interacting with the past and generate conflict around the ambiguous boundaries between local and translocal political jurisdictions. The striking parallels between two very different examples that we will discuss next reflect how both factors have deep historical roots in the experience of local communities.

The first of these incidents involves the early collecting efforts of a regional institution originally known as the Museo Yucateco. This museum was originally

DOI: 10.5876/9781607325727.c002

chartered as a state-level institution in 1864 and passed through a number of different incarnations before falling under the purview of the federal National Institute of Anthropology and History, or INAH, in the mid-twentieth century. At the time of its foundation, Museo Yucateco's mandate was defined as collecting those objects that were deemed "worthy of preservation" (*dignos de preservar*) and preventing their loss through local neglect or removal from national soil. By delegating the work of historical preservation to this specialized institution, and not to existing territorial units in which heritage objects were located, the government of Yucatán set a precedent for a series of jurisdictional conflicts that continue to play a role in the politics of archaeology and historical preservation.

In the autumn of 1877, Juan Peón, the director of the Museo Yucateco, wrote to the governor of Yucatán, asking him to direct Xavier Santa María, the *jefe político* of the municipality of Ticul, to cooperate in an upcoming expedition. Together with Juan Peón, this municipal official was to supervise the transfer of a colonial monument from the town of Maní to the Museo Yucateco. The artifact in question was a carved stone included in the wall of the colonial town hall and bearing the crest that the Spanish crown had granted to the sixteenth-century Maya ruler Tutul Xiu. This monument held particular historical relevance for the state capital of Mérida, and a slightly different series of historical resonances for the residents of Maní. The conquest of the Yucatán Peninsula was an especially drawn-out process. Fighters and colonists led by two generations of the Montejo family struggled to establish a permanent foothold on the peninsula for twenty years after the conquest of the Mexica at Tenochtitlan. The alliance of Tutul Xiu with the newly founded settlement of Mérida in 1541 marked a turning point, as the collective effort of Spanish and Xiu forces against the powerful Cocom family ultimately secured the permanence of European settlement. But if Juan Peón and other intellectuals in Mérida saw Tutul Xiu as a key figure in the establishment of Christian civilization on the peninsula, residents of Maní could look to him as a more distinctly regional figure. Maní was the traditional seat of the Xiu family, whose feud with the Cocom had begun more than a century before the foundation of Mérida. In contrast to Juan Peón's celebration of Tutul Xiu as a Yucatecan figure, the sixteenth-century ruler's connection to Maní embody a distinct set of microregional loyalties that have historically fragmented any sense of an overarching "Maya" identity in the Yucatán Peninsula (Armstrong-Fumero 2013; Gabbert 2004; Restall 1999).

Shortly after his first visit to Ticul, Juan Peón sent a telegraph to the governor in which he mentioned that the building in which the monument was placed was in ruins and that he was prepared to remove the stone. However, this was soon followed by a telegraph from the municipal official, Xavier Santa María. Santa María observed that the old municipal building was, in fact, being repaired, and that these repairs would be compromised by the removal of the carved monument (Archivo General del Estado de Yucatán [AGEY] 30.10.1877). Later that same day, he wrote a letter in which he described how a group of sixty local men had appeared in his office to protest the removal of the monument. One complaint was that this was a public, not a private, building, and that considerable money had already been spent from the municipal coffers for its reconstruction. These public funds had been supplemented by another significant sum raised from private subscriptions among the town's principal citizens. To underscore the gravity of the situation, Santa María added that the large population of "Indian race" in the municipality was motivated by strong localist feelings and was likely to impede the removal of the monument with force (AGEY 31.19.1877).

The governor does not seem to have made an immediate reply. Whether or not Santa María made these same arguments to Juan Peón, the museum director persisted in his efforts to remove the monolith. The following day, the fears of violence seem to be fulfilled when a crowd of 300 people that Santa María identified as "Indians" arrived in Maní to remove the monument, which they then hid in the bush before dispersing to their own hamlets.

It's debatable whether the Maní riot of 1877 was a spontaneous popular uprising or if it had been orchestrated by wealthy families who had invested cash in the restoration of the old municipal building. Drumming up public unrest was a common tool through which local elite factions pressured state and federal officials in late nineteenth century Mexico (see Wells and Joseph 1996). However, there was also a persistent tradition of popular resistance in rural Yucatán in the decades before and after the Caste War (Eiss 2010). In either case, the rioters were essentially defending the political imperatives of a municipal government to control an element of the local built landscape against the collecting efforts of an institution that had been tasked with protecting a more abstractly defined "Yucatecan" heritage. Although the correspondence between Peón, Santa María, and the governor gives only a vague sense of how the people of Maní understood their relationship to the arms of Tutul Xiu, the raising of funds through subscription suggests that local elites were willing to make material investments in preserving a building associated with him and his descendants. It's possible that Peón and Santa María rioters identified as "Indians" were mobilized by patronage networks headed by these local elites. But it's also feasible that they were choosing to defend a historical artifact that they considered to be the public property of Maní against a Mérida-based institution that few of them would ever visit.

On the surface, this conflict seems like the result of a local population defending a historical memory that was coded in their local built environment against the more artificial construction of a regional history by a state-sponsored institution (see Nora 1989). But there is also a more basic question regarding the role of different formal governmental institutions whose respective jurisdictions and roles were ambiguously defined. Although the museum had an official claim on Tutul Xiu's crest as a historical artifact that was "worthy of preservation," removing this object would have led to the defacement of public property that was managed by the municipal government of Maní. This tension between federal institutions and more localized governments is especially important in understanding the heritage politics of Yucatán. Although the internal structure and legal prerogatives of community-level governments had changed significantly in the centuries since the Spanish conquest, there are important continuities in the tendency of units such as the municipality to embody desires for local autonomy that is defended against control from larger-order political entities (see Armstrong-Fumero 2013; Eiss 2010; Gabbert 2004). This continues to be a factor in similar conflicts today: rural Maya speakers often have reason to assume that there are valid legal arguments for asserting local control over objects that fall under the bailiwick of heritage institutions.

In theory, the ambiguous relationship between the mandate of heritage institutions and local authorities was addressed by an evolving body of laws and regulations that attained greater enforceability over the course of the late nineteenth century and twentieth century. Under the direction of Mexico's INAH, founded in 1941, these laws developed into a coherent body of legal protocols that hinged on the assumption that antiquities are an eminent domain of the state that is comparable to other subsurface resources such as petroleum. But moving to and from most archaeological sites, and organizing peripheral activities such as the clearing of bush, usually require negotiations with local municipal and agrarian institutions whose members have a different sense of their own territorial prerogatives. Other factors limit the sense of exclusive control over heritage sites that the letter of the law grants to the INAH. In the Yucatán Peninsula, the expansion of archaeological tourism has generated an especially broad range of stakeholders with concrete economic as well as moral claims on sites. As Lisa Breglia (2006) and others have observed, the control of antiquities is complicated by the confluence of a range of nonfederal and civil society actors, particularly in the wake of neoliberal reforms that developed in the last decades of the twentieth century (see also Armstrong-Fumero 2013; Castañeda 1996).

This new role of civil society actors, along with the persistent tensions between local and translocal levels of government, figures in contemporary conflicts that mirror many elements of the Maní riot of 1877. Our second example took place several years ago, when one of us (Julio) was asked to play a mediating role in a disagreement between INAH archaeologists based at Chichén Itzá and the residents of the village that we will refer to as Chanmul. The modern archaeological zone of

Chichén Itzá was developed in the 1920s as a "showcase" for Yucatán's Maya culture (see Castañeda 1996) and has emerged as a dense intersection of federal and state institutions, big and small business, and civil society organizations. In this sense, it is simultaneously a museum that stewards heritage objects for the nation and a nexus of a regional economy that incorporates a diverse range of nongovernmental stakeholders.

A community of around 500 in a rural municipality that we will refer to as Holtunich, Chanmul lies on the periphery of Chichén's economic influence. The village was settled at the very end of the nineteenth century, and in 1928 Mexico's federal agrarian bureaucracy granted the settlers official land title.[1] This title took the form of an *ejido*, or tract of land to be managed under collective tenure. As a municipal territory, Chanmul is a satellite of the municipal seat of Holtunich, on which it depends for infrastructural funds and law enforcement. But the people of Chanmul have de facto autonomy in the management of their lands, which are titled through a federal bureaucracy and managed by a village-level committee. In principle, these are federal lands to which the local community receives usufruct rights. But in speeches made by local political leaders during public events in rural Yucatán, it is common to hear the local agriculturalists referred to as *yumilo'ob eejido*, or the "owners of the *ejido*," a phrase that reflects the sense of collective local ownership that is common in these communities.

By extension, the *ejidatarios* of Chanmul consider themselves to be owners of lands that contain several small archaeological sites that fall within the boundaries of their original ejido grant. That is, they understand the law as granting them a valid claim on archaeological objects that parallels their right to the exploitation of wild animal and vegetable resources and to mine building material within the ejido. As far as the letter of the law goes, and notwithstanding the ejidatarios' usufruct rights over the surface of their lands, any heritage objects that are found in or protrude from this surface are an eminent domain of the federal government and fall under the jurisdiction of the INAH. Regulations of the INAH strictly prohibit ejidatarios from engaging in any activity that would lead to an "alteration of the characteristics" (see INAH 1975) of these artifacts (see also Breglia 2006). The people of Chanmul are far from naive about these legal complexities, as they have had extensive interactions with archaeologists in different capacities. Many of the ejidatarios have provided labor to INAH-sponsored excavations, during which they applied many of the same skills involved in agriculture to the physical work of archaeology (see Armstrong-Fumero 2012; Armstrong-Fumero and Hoil Gutiérrez 2011). But familiarity with the legal jurisdiction claimed by the INAH is not necessarily the same as a surrendering local claims over objects found in the ejido.

The ejidatarios' sense of having a physical claim to archaeological remains was bolstered when the INAH decided to make use of the symbolically powerful space of the village's ejido committee building by moving a number of carved monuments there, where they have remained in safekeeping. Tensions first became evident in the 2000s, when the Yucatán regional office of the INAH seemed determined to move the monuments into more permanent storage at Chichén Itzá. At that point, the ejidatarios rejected the idea that the federal government had a right to move locally unearthed objects to a site that was not only outside the boundaries of their ejido but in a neighboring municipality that was already blessed with a wealth of marketable tourism resources. In effect, they considered the monuments to be found objects that—like firewood, game animals, and medicinal plants—should provide moral and material benefits to the owners of the land in which they existed. During one of the initial attempts to have the ejidatarios hand over the monuments, debate became heated enough that a nervous archaeologist decided to make a hasty retreat from Chanmul.

Several years ago, we were both present at a more cordial, if only slightly more successful, meeting between the municipal and ejido leadership of Chanmul and two representatives of a state-level agency called the Instituto para el Desarrollo de la Cultura Maya del Estado de Yucatán (INDEMAYA). In Yucatán, INDEMAYA works to promote the welfare and culturally sensitive economic development in rural Maya communities, primarily by serving as intermediaries for the implementation of federal initiatives. Legally speaking, there was virtually no way in which the ejidatarios could have advanced a claim on the ultimate deposition of the monuments that trumped INAH's. But it was possible that INDEMAYA could help the ejidatarios to secure a range of resources for developing a local museum project that would meet the standards set by the INAH and therefore justify the monuments' remaining within the community. However, this project implied a separate set of problems. Any funds for building a museum would have to follow the same lines of authority as any other nonagrarian federal programs. That is, they would have to be channeled through the municipal seat of Holtunich. This was a tough pill for the ejidatarios to swallow. As far as they were concerned, the ruins from which the archaeologists removed the monuments lie within the ejido of their village, which they consider to be a sovereign territory of Chanmul. They were concerned that the municipal authorities might approve the construction of a museum to house and display the valuable stones . . . in Holtunich!

Here, the parallels with the Maní riot of 1877 are significant. The archaeological complex of Chichén Itzá is a mere twenty kilometers or so from Chanmul, much closer than the distance from Maní to Mérida. But it is socially and politically distant in a number of ways. Although their status as Mexican citizens entitles them to benefit from the INAH's educational mission, few people from Chanmul visit the site as tourists. There is also the question of who will draw tangible benefits from objects that were extracted from the soil that the federal government granted to their ancestors in usufruct and that they see themselves as "owning." Tourism at Chichén Itzá provides work and sales venues to individuals from a range of different communities in the area. But given limitations of transport or lack of fluency in Spanish and foreign languages, few of the people who actively till the soil in Chanmul have been able to derive direct benefits from this tourism. What's more, many of the jobs and informal sales venues at Chichén are dominated by people of the town of Pisté who, though usually Maya speakers themselves, often treat people such as the ejidatarios of Chanmul as cheap and exploitable labor (see Armstrong-Fumero 2013). Even if the small archaeological sites within their own ejido will never transform Chanmul into a major tourist destination, the sentiment among the ejidatarios seemed to be that the only way in which they would enjoy an equitable relationship to these heritage objects were if they remained within their local territory.

In the years that followed, a private business made another unsuccessful attempt at partnership with the ejidatarios of Chanmul. There are relatively few grassroots NGOs dealing with Maya cultural politics in this part of Yucatán, but there are a number of nonprofits organized by such businesses. This particular outfit, which had previously been designated as an "auxiliary organ" of the INAH, offered to front the money to create furnishings that would facilitate the display of the stones in the village. We're not entirely certain why this particular collaboration failed to materialize, but the experience of other communities involved in the tourist business might suggest that the ejidatarios had good reason to question motivations of businessmen who run nonprofits. A number of the corporate-funded nonprofits operating on the periphery of Chichén Itzá employ a rhetoric of sustainability that explicitly derides subsistence practices such as the harvesting of hardwoods for production of handicrafts, a practice that competes directly with stores operated by larger hotels. Even more disturbing is the potential confluence between this business-oriented civil society sector and real estate developers who have taken advantage of a 1992 constitutional reform to purchase ejido lands near lucrative tourist destinations.

Several neighboring communities have sold their ejido lands to private investors for touristic development. But the people of Chanmul have made a collective decision to retain theirs and to continue a lifestyle that still relies on substantial amounts of subsistence maize production even as most families also participate in wage labor at Chichén and elsewhere. As of this writing, the carved stones are hidden from public view in the municipal house that embodies this agrarian institution, and there does not seem to be any plan to develop a local museum. But short of bringing in a detachment of armed police—and generating bad publicity that institutions such as the INAH can ill afford—it is unlikely that the archaeologists will be able to unilaterally secure their transfer to Chichén Itzá.

LANDSCAPE, COMMUNITY HERITAGE, AND RIGHTS

Despite the vast historical, social, and political gulf that separates 1877 Maní from present-day Chanmul, there are important continuities. In both cases, members of rural communities understand the prerogatives of local government—be they municipal or ejidal—as including control of heritage objects that are officially considered to be the purview of higher-order political dependencies. Although the claims on these objects that are made by community members are only weakly sustained by the letter of the law, we think that scholars and heritage professionals have an obligation to consider them as part of the larger terrain of heritage management.

We don't make this argument as a simple appeal to help the more disadvantaged social groups or because of the ethnic status of the ejidatarios as descendants of the ancient Maya. Rather, the arguments of the ejidatarios reflect assumptions about territoriality that are consistent with a body of vernacular knowledge and quotidian practices that have defined how generations of rural Maya speakers relate to the landscape that they inhabit. This in turn places their claims within a terrain of intangible heritage that enjoys certain protections under Mexico's heritage laws, particularly as relates to Mexico's ratification of the International Labor Organization (ILO) Indigenous and Tribal People's Convention in 1990. The importance of places such as the bush around Chanmul or the town landscape of Maní rests in their subsistence value and in the historical and symbolic content that is attributed to them by living Maya people. According to the late Guillermo Bonfil Batalla, a central figure in the development of modern indigenous rights discourse in Mexico, this kind of landscape knowledge embodies "the memory of ethnic territory that historically belonged to each people and whose recuperation is a constant object of indigenous struggle" (Bonfil Batalla 2012:240). Reconciling this sort of intangible heritage with the traditional bailiwick of archaeology is not always easy, but offers some promise for creating more equitable approaches to heritage in a multicultural and neoliberal Mexico.

In this context, local governments such as the municipality or the ejido play an especially important role, since they provide the formal institutional context that promotes the survival and development of indigenous patterns of subsistence, social organization, and worldview. Although the specific title held by the residents of Chanmul and other people stems from the twentieth-century agrarian reform, the original formalized territorial claims that the local community had already established by other means. In the decades that followed, local customs and knowledge of landscape shaped Chanmul's particular iteration of the federal ejido law. A similar process occurs in the formalization of different forms of community government through federal laws for the management of municipalities. In this sense, the ejido, the municipality, and other such institutions are a hybrid of the liberal political structures embodied in the Mexican Constitution and indigenous forms of political organization and land tenure.

Bonfil observed that "there was no rupture, or negation of indigenous history as a result of European invasion" (Bonfil Batalla 2012:241). In some senses, his insistence on the integral continuity of a "deep Mexico" amidst the institutions of the modern state seems like a romantic oversimplification of processes of cultural change and adaptation that marked centuries of colonial and postcolonial interaction. But there is something to the assertion that different means of cultural transmission tended to reproduce indigenous patterns of landscape use and perception that existed parallel, if not always in direct opposition, to the official regimes of colonial and postcolonial states. We would argue that the case of landscape memory and territoriality in the rural Yucatán illustrates an especially powerful mechanism for this reproduction. By extension, rural Yucatecans' stake in archaeological sites stems from a larger body of collective memory that is embodied by named places in the physical landscape and reproduced through the narratives and subsistence practices of local communities.

Toponyms play an especially important role in this process. The names of thousands of places in the Yucatecan bush have been preserved over long periods of time despite the fact that many of these places have been abandoned and resettled over the course of centuries (Armstrong-Fumero 2013; see also Solari 2013). This naming is particularly striking given the high historical levels of illiteracy in the region and the fact that many of these named places have not been recorded in written sources that would have been readily available to subsequent generations of agriculturalists. The cultural transmission of place-names occurred in tangent with, but often independently from, the formation of documentary records that constituted official land titles. This process points to the fact that oral narratives associated with agriculture and other subsistence practices reproduced knowledge of the landscape across the generations of Mayan agriculturalists, even as they experienced changes in the state-sponsored institutions of land tenure.

One of the historical ironies of the northern Maya lowlands is that the same processes that have worked against the long-term residence of specific communities in specific locations have also contributed to the reproduction of detailed knowledge of the larger landscape over time. Central to this are a series of short-term and long-term populations movements conditioned by the exigencies of swidden maize agriculture and a history of colonial control, local resistance, and large-scale violence. Some of these same demographic movements will be discussed in depth by Rani Alexander in chapter 7 (this volume) and Kray et al. in chapter 4. Here, we introduce them very briefly to focus on how the confluence of territorial politics with subsistence practices and collective memory of the local landscape have contributed to continuities in some forms of occupying and using space.

As Alexander will discuss in more detail, many settlements that had existed at the time of the Spanish conquest were abandoned due to forced resettlement policies imposed by colonial authorities to concentrate the population in large towns (Quezada 1993:81–101). Despite being deprived of the right to live in their traditional lands, it is evident that many families retained formal and informal usufruct rights over them and used them for agriculture, hunting, and other subsistence activities. In many cases, the people forced to live in larger settlements continued to hold titles to their original lands that were recognized by the indigenous authorities of the new towns. This was the case with the towns of Tixcacalcupul, Tekom, Cuncunul, and Ebtún, to the north and east of Chanmul. For example, the residents of the settlements Kulha, Kankabdzonot, Hulmal, and Yaxoy were moved to the town of Tekom. Texts in the *Titles of Ebtun* record the names of the various lineages of Tekom and the title that they held to lands that they had inhabited at the time of the Spanish conquest (Roys 1939:73–81).

From the perspective of landscape history, these titles establish two important things. First, resettled kinship groups continued to be closely identified with particular stretches of land. As Amara Solari (2013) has discussed in her analysis of the *Book of Chilam Balam* and related texts, the commemoration of different places through which groups had migrated in the past was important to defining collective identities and territoriality for colonial-era Maya speakers. Second, this commemoration was reflected in legal documentation, since the survival of ancestral titles contributed to the remembrance of toponyms such as Kulha, Kankabdzonot, Hulmal, and Yaxoy, even though the lands to which they referred were essentially uninhabited.

There was more than just identity bringing Maya people back to their ancestral settlements; this form of memory also played a distinct subsistence role. The itinerant forms of cultivation that are most adaptable to swidden agriculture, combined with tribute pressures applied by the colonial administration, often induced people to cultivate lands far from their formal place of residence. In this sense, the remembrance and repopulation of abandoned settlement sites involved an integration of cultural memory with a series of environmental and productive factors that were essential to the survival of Yucatec Maya communities.

There is evidence that relocation to distant settlements expanded toward the end of the eighteenth century. Social and economic changes that were prompted by the Bourbon reforms, and which accelerated after independence from Spain, included policies that contributed to the annulment of indigenous title and the purchase of land by nonindigenous Yucatecans who competed for the production of maize and cattle. It's telling that a number of historians have characterized this period as a "second conquest" of the Yucatecan landscapes whose effects on indigenous land tenure were more devastating than what had occurred in the sixteenth century (Farris 1984:539). Sources, including a regional census from 1841, suggest that many Maya people reacted to these processes by occupying abandoned lands. Akulá, Hulmal, Kancabdzonot, and other sites that had been depopulated since the sixteenth century, and whose residents had been resettled in Tekom, were all repopulated late in the eighteenth century.

This resettlement also involved changing political jurisdictions and seems to have continued through the first decades after Mexico's independence from Spain. For example, Akulá, a site that was historically associated with people who had been resettled in Tekom, was designated as a hamlet with twelve residents in 1841, and was then subject to the political jurisdiction of Muchukux. This change indicates that the older tie to Tekom was ruptured and that the families that resettled the site retained the old toponym, even if the specific jurisdictions to which these places corresponded shifted.

These same places experienced a new series of dislocations during the Caste War of 1847 and the endemic violence of the succeeding four decades. If the events of the late eighteenth century contributed to the dispersal of population, the aftermath of the Caste War was marked by a strong pull toward places that guaranteed better security. This movement involved the abandonment of even relatively large communities. Muchukux, for example, had had 714 inhabitants in 1841 and was abandoned along with Akulá by 1888. Tihosuco and Tela, had 3,500 and 5,000 residents respectively. Both were abandoned between the 1870s and 1890s, and Tihosuco was only resettled between 1920 and 1930.

The Mexican state's defeat of the powerful rebel polity of Chan Santa Cruz in 1900 greatly diminished the risks associated with living and growing crops in the east of Yucatán and prompted a renewed movement of population out of larger towns. As had happened a century earlier, families were returning to abandoned sites whose names and particular features had been preserved in collective memory in spite of the fact that they had been abandoned for a generation. So, for example, the town of Muchukux was reoccupied at the beginning of the twentieth century. The letters written by the residents of this new settlement hint at the degree to which the place had not lost its social and cultural status during the period that it was uninhabited.[2] A document filed in 1931 detailed the history of the site that had been gleaned from the stories of its current inhabitants and observed that "this settlement has existed for many years, though for unknown reasons, it had been de-populated, and was not re-populated until the last thirty years." In effect, the idea that Muchukux was an old site with deep historical roots had not faded from historical memory, even if the exact reasons why the site had been abandoned had.

This particular series of letters comes from the archives of Mexico's agrarian bureaucracy and marks a process that strengthened the claims that different groups had had to elements of the landscape, even as the bureaucracy transformed the region's political geography. As we noted earlier, ejido grants provide communities with collective usufruct rights of lands that are titled by the federal government. Dialogs between the residents of rural settlements and urban engineers and notaries gave formal status to many sites that were represented through passing references in the spotty documentary record or simply through oral narrative. At the same time, this redrawing of land title tended to disrupt some older territorial divisions.

So, for example, Muchukux received an ejido grant in 1929 that consisted of 7,433 hectares that corresponded to the lands that were used by the settlers that arrived around 1900. However, these lands did not include all of the places that had been associated with the pre–Caste War community of Muchukux. Some ultimately fell into the ejido donation of Xcalakdzonot, a community where we conducted ethnographic and ethnoarchaeological research for a number of years.

The process of creating Xcalakdzonot's ejido reflects the evolving relationship between traditional forms of landscape knowledge and the formal institutions of the agrarian reform. What became Xcalakdzonot was, in fact, a collection of several different named sites that had been resettled around 1900 (Armstrong-Fumero 2013; Armstrong-Fumero and Hoil Gutiérrez 2011). One of these was Akulá, which we first encountered in the colonial period as lands associated with kinship groups that had been resettled in Tekom, and again in the nineteenth century as a dependency of pre–Caste War Muchukux. The settlers who came in the early twentieth century were people from the towns of Cuncunul, Kaua, and Ebtún, some thirty kilometers to the north, who had historical awareness of these sites but had not resided there before. In order to raise the number of households above the number required to receive official title, the residents of these different settlements relocated to the site of Xcalakdzonot to solicit lands as group. Through this donation of land, Xcalakdzonot emerged as a formal political and territorial entity for the first time.

It is important to underscore how this "new" political entity came about through a twentieth-century iteration of the same kind of political and cultural process that has preserved the distinct relationship that Yucatec Maya people have had to their landscape for many generations. Knowledge of the location and geophysical qualities of abandoned settlements and agricultural sites has been central to the subsistence and territorial identity of these communities. Earlier, we described how the name of Akulá has been preserved in the collective memory of rural Yucatecan people despite the fact that it was repeatedly abandoned and resettled. The same can be said for thousands of other named places in the region. If the agrarian reform gave many of these places a formal juridical status, this act of bureaucratic naming was anticipated by a far older series of material and symbolic processes through which Maya agriculturalists stake claim to territory. This is very much the status of the ejido today: it is a formal institution that provides for the subsistence of rural communities and for the preservation of the intangible cultural heritage of landscape knowledge. This is a form of intangible heritage in which pre-Hispanic remains play a persistent, and often important, role.

PRE-HISPANIC ARTIFACTS BETWEEN TANGIBLE AND INTANGIBLE HERITAGE

Which brings us back to the claims on pre-Hispanic artifacts made by the ejidatarios of Chanmul. As far as many in the INAH and other federal institutions are concerned, the ejido grant is simply a usufruct right over the surface of lands that in no way impinges on federal jurisdiction over subsurface archaeological remains. But for rural Maya agriculturalists, the institution of the ejido has been incorporated into an older series of practices that imbue sites that have been abandoned and settled repeatedly over the course of several generations. Thus, the ejido and all of the organisms and objects found within it accrue a series of material and moral features that have been a part of Yucatec Maya society for generations.

In essence, archaeological sites are traces of previous settlement in a landscape that Maya-speaking agriculturalists already assume has been settled and abandoned many times, both in pre-Hispanic antiquity and the more recent past. In some ways, as Solari (2013) has shown, the return to such sites echoes a time-honored practice of pilgrimage or ritual circuits. Conditioned by patterns of fallowing, abandonment, and resettlement that reflect the ecological and agricultural particulars of the Yucatán Peninsula, these returns are also marked by subsistence concerns. This dual nature of resettlement is evident in the uses of different objects that are found in the ruins of ancient pyramids or recent house sites. Some objects, such as clay figurines or stone bas reliefs, are imbued with a special aura of antiquity and "otherness" and are used ritually or avoided altogether. Other artifacts that are discovered during the process of founding new settlements are quite familiar and integral parts of the quotidian material culture of Maya agriculturalists. Objects from grindstones to ceramics are often repurposed in modern kitchens, and before industrial building materials such as cinderblock were widely available, it was common to see facing stones from pre-Hispanic ruins used in modern vernacular architecture.

Sacred or profane, the use of pre-Hispanic stone is often characterized as "vandalism" by the INAH and related authorities. But it could also be argued that the reuse of vestiges of these earlier occupations, whether they be historical house sites or pre-Hispanic ruins, has often been an important feature of the process of reclaiming these spaces for human habitation (Armstrong-Fumero 2012; Armstrong-Fumero and Hoil Gutiérrez 2011). As such, it is part of the living heritage of landscape use that links the Maya agriculturalists who work the bush today to a deep historical tradition.

In making this argument, we are not claiming that institutions such as the INAH should abandon their mandate to protect historical artifacts or that the right of rural communities to practice traditional forms of reclaiming and recycling named places always trumps the interest of archaeological research or touristic development. In many respects, this reuse of stones is far less of an issue today than it would have been generations ago. As cinderblock and other industrial materials became more accessible, vernacular architectural traditions were altered in ways that diminished the need for precut stones that were once mined from pre-Hispanic and historical sites. What's more, given the importance of archaeological tourism in the area, rural people are more likely to value the preservation of architecture in situ as potential attractions.

Still, as an ethicopolitical question, there are lessons to be learned from the difficulty of reconciling policy that treats tangible heritage objects as an eminent domain of the state whose physical characteristics cannot be legally altered with a form of intangible heritage that entails the physical alteration of those same objects. For one, the conflict can lead us to question the degree to which "multivocality," the celebration of the right of different groups to narrate their own version of different places and historical events (Armstrong-Fumero 2011, 2014), is the best model through which to think about the inclusion of indigenous stakeholders in the management of heritage. For generations of rural Maya-speaking agriculturalists, objects found within territorial units such as the ejido are part of a larger complex of goods that contribute to subsistence. From this perspective, well-intentioned projects that constitute "inclusion" of indigenous perspectives as being independent from questions of subsistence (see McAnany and Parks 2012) tend to intentionally sidestep the values that many stakeholders ascribe to these places.

Furthermore, the economic and moral primacy that Yucatec Maya ideas of place grant to the physicality of found objects involves far more than controversial practices such as the recycling of building material. This confluence of subsistence and morality is evident in a particularly poignant oral tradition in which pre-Hispanic are said to have been built by a bygone generation of human beings, the *uchben maako'ob*, who were destroyed by God for some transgression. In some versions, these beings were dull-witted hunchbacks known as the *p'uso'ob* (see Burns 1983). In others, they were a primordial people known simply as the Itza, who lived before the creation of the sun and saw in the dark with eyes like those of cats. Almost all versions of this story are in agreement regarding the indolence of the ancients, the fact that their use of magical whistles or receiving favors directly from God spared them the pains of labor that marked the lives of modern peasant families. In some versions of the story, the sin that led to the death of the uchben maako'ob was the creation of the *castillo* at Chichén Itzá, which some Maya speakers associated with the tower of Babel. In some versions that we have recorded, the fact that the buildings at Chichén Itzá survived the death of their builders is a moral counterpoint to the sloth and pridefulness of the uchben maako'ob. A merciful God left the buildings behind so that the hardworking generations who inherited the land could derive benefit from the work of their sinful predecessors (Armstrong-Fumero 2014).

In these stories, it is the ability to work the ruins that validates living people. In essence, ruins are activated by the same act of usufruct that defined the granting of ejido lands in the early twentieth century and that marked the process through which earlier generations had reclaimed abandoned spaces through migration and the creation of new settlements. This is also a moral economy that is especially difficult to reconcile with the idea that an abstractly defined nation has eminent domain over artifacts that exist beneath the soil that other people are "working."

In one sense, the intangible heritage of landscape use that is embodied in these traditions presents a challenge to archaeology, since it forces us to consider a complex, and potentially contradictory, ethicopolitical relationship between archaeologists, communities, and heritage objects. But in this sense, it also offers an opportunity. The kind of joint stewardship that was imagined by the ejidatarios of Chanmul when they insisted on the monument being displayed in a locally controlled museum would allow INAH officials to meet their mandate of preserving antiquities while also fostering institutions—in this case, the ejido—that preserve the intangible heritage of descendant communities. Doing so might involve challenging traditional hierarchies between local memory and national history. But in so doing, archaeologists would engage the landscape values of Yucatec Maya people on a terrain that they have always occupied, negotiating highly mutable territorial jurisdictions against a more durable backdrop of known and named places.

NOTES

1. These documents were filed in the Registro Agrario Nacional in Mérida as RAN. They are currently being digitized in Mexico City.

2. AGEY, Padrón general del pueblo de Muchucux, caja 40, volumen 3, expediente 35, May 6, 1841. RAN, Dotación del pueblo de Muchucux, Toca, File 23/213, carpeta 1, foja 2; 23 of January 1931.

REFERENCES

Aikawa-Faure, Noriko. 2009. "From the Proclamation of Masterpieces to the *Convention for the Safeguarding of Intangible Heritage.*" In *Intangible Heritage*, ed. Laurajane Smith and Natsuko Akagawa, 13–44. New York: Routledge.

Armstrong-Fumero, Fernando. 2011. "Words and Things in Yucatán: Poststructuralism and the Everyday Life of Mayan Multiculturalism." *Journal of the Royal Anthropological Institute* 17 (1): 63–81. http://dx.doi.org/10.1111/j.1467-9655.2010.01669.x.

Armstrong-Fumero, Fernando. 2012. *Tensiones entre el patrimonio tangible e intangible en Yucatán, México: La imposibilidad de re-crear una cultura sin alterar sus características.* Guest-edited volume of *Chungara: Revista de Antropología Chilena* 44 (3): 435–43.

Armstrong-Fumero, Fernando. 2013. *Elusive Unity: Factionalism and the Limits of Identity Politics in Yucatán, Mexico.* Boulder: University Press of Colorado. http://dx.doi.org/10 .5876/9781607322399.

Armstrong-Fumero, Fernando. 2014. "A Tale of Two Mayan Babels: Vernacular Histories of the Maya and the Limits of Inclusion." *Ethnohistory (Columbus, Ohio)* 61 (4): 761–84. http://dx.doi.org/10.1215/00141801-2717858.

Armstrong-Fumero, Fernando, and Julio Hoil Gutiérrez. 2011. "Community Heritage and Partnership in Xcalakdzonot, Yucatán." In *Handbook of Postcolonial Archaeology*, ed. Uzma Rizvi and Jane Lydon, 391–97. Walnut Creek, CA: Left Coast Press.

Bonfil Batalla, Guillermo. 2012. "Historias que no son todavía historia." In *¿Historia para qué?*, 229–45. Mexico City: Siglo Veintiuno Editores.

Breglia, Lisa. 2006. *Monumental Ambivalence: The Politics of Heritage.* Austin: University of Texas Press.

Burns, Allan. 1983. *An Epoch of Miracles: Oral Literature of the Yucatec Maya.* Austin: University of Texas Press.

Castañeda, Quetzil. 1996. *In the Museum of Maya Culture: Touring Chichén Itzá.* Minneapolis: University of Minnesota Press.

Eiss, Paul. 2010. *In the Name of the Pueblo.* Durham: Duke University Press. http://dx.doi .org/10.1215/9780822392798.

Farris, Nancy. 1984. *Maya Society under Colonial Rule: The Collective Enterprise of Survival.* Princeton: Princeton University Press.

Gabbert, Wolfgang. 2004. *Becoming Maya: Ethnicity and Social Inequality in Yucatán since 1500.* Albuquerque: University of Arizona Press.

Gillman, Derek. 2010. *The Idea of Cultural Heritage*. Cambridge: Cambridge University Press.

INAH (Instituto Nacional de Antropología e Historia [México]). 1975. *Ley federal sobre monumentos y zonas arqueológicas, artísticos y históricos*. http://www.cnmh.inah.gob.mx/2001.html.

McAnany, Patricia A., and Shoshaunna Parks. 2012. "Casualties of Heritage Distancing: Children, Ch'orti' Indigeneity, and the Copán Archaeoscape." *Current Anthropology* 53 (1): 80–107. http://dx.doi.org/10.1086/663687.

Nora, Pierre. 1989. "Between Memory and History: Les Lieux de Memoire." *Representations (Berkeley, Calif.)* 26 (1): 7–24. http://dx.doi.org/10.1525/rep.1989.26.1.99p0274v.

Quezada, Sergio. 1993. *Pueblos y Caciques Yucatecos, 1550–1580*. Mexico City: Colegio de México.

Restall, Matthew. 1999. *The Maya World*. Stanford: Stanford University Press.

Roys, Ralph. 1939. *The Titles of Ebtun*. Washington, DC: CIW.

Solari, Amara. 2013. *Maya Ideologies of the Sacred: The Transfiguration of Space in Colonial Yucatán*. Austin: University of Texas Press.

Wells, Allan, and Gilbert M. Joseph. 1996. *Summer of Discontent, Seasons of Upheaval: Elite Politics and Rural Insurgency in Yucatán, 1876–1915*. Stanford: Stanford University Press.

3

Hopisinmuy Wu'ya'mat Hisat Yang Tupqa'va Yeesiwngwu
(Hopi Ancestors Lived in These Canyons)

MAREN P. HOPKINS, STUART B. KOYIYUMPTEWA, SAUL L. HEDQUIST,
T. J. FERGUSON, AND CHIP COLWELL

INTRODUCTION

The Hopi people have strong and abiding cultural ties to the lands where their ancestors lived in ancient times. They recognize these lands as Hopitutskwa (Hopi land), a cultural landscape marked by the numerous archaeological sites and named places that figure into Hopi oral traditions as their metaphorical "footprints." Today much of Hopitutskwa has passed from Hopi ownership into private property and public lands managed by multiple federal agencies. Access to ancestral sites has thus become increasingly restricted, making it difficult for the Hopi people to maintain their historical traditions based on cultural practices embedded in the land.

To address this situation, the Hopi Cultural Preservation Office—the Hopi tribal government's official department that helps manage, preserve, and protect traditional culture—uses the political and regulatory processes provided by the National Historic Preservation Act (as well as other federal and state laws). The tribe draws on this National Historic Preservation Act in particular to identify traditional cultural properties, evaluate their eligibility for the National Register of Historic Places, and document the Hopi history and cultural practices associated with them. Using the research opportunities created by a series of relatively small projects, the Hopi Tribe is building a regional perspective on the tangible sites of its heritage that are associated with the retention and transmission of the tribe's cultural practices and intangible traditions.

DOI: 10.5876/9781607325727.c003

In this chapter we describe how three separate historic preservation projects enabled the Hopi Tribe to trace a physical connection between the Hopi Mesas in Arizona and Glen Canyon in Utah. In collaborative research with archaeological ethnographers, the Hopi Cultural Preservation Office investigated Hopi traditional cultural properties along a pipeline right-of-way, along a highway improvement project, and in the Glen Canyon National Recreation Area. These investigations relate specific historic properties to larger concepts of landscape and cultural identity. The results of these projects serve to elucidate the connections between individual sites in Glen Canyon and the regional context of Hopitutskwa, including clan migrations and narratives of a legendary boy named Tiyo that encompass the Gulf of California.

The intangible heritage of the Hopi people—the traditional cultural beliefs and practices that are important in maintaining their sense of identity and continuity—is intimately linked to historical events that are situated in different locations across the Hopitutskwa landscape. Contemporary Hopi customs, including ceremonies, largely focus on commemorating the places that contributed to the development of Hopi society and religion. Such places retain power that is activated and enlivened through ongoing cultural traditions. In this way, the Hopitutskwa landscape represents a collection of experiences that cohesively binds the Hopi people to the land and to each other. In a managerial context, the articulation of Hopi land and identity is accomplished by the tribe's participation in the national historic preservation program.

The projects we discuss below were designed as collaborative, community-based participatory research to advance Hopi scholarship. In each project, members of the Hopi Tribe and non-Hopi researchers worked jointly to identify ancestral archaeological sites, springs, shrines, landforms, and other tangible places with cultural importance to the Hopi people. Documenting Hopi traditional places has wide-ranging benefits, foremost of which is the preservation of historical and place-related knowledge for use by future generations of Hopis. Furthermore, working within the framework of the National Historic Preservation Act provides a means of communicating the importance of specific Hopi places to non-Hopi audiences, thus facilitating the implementation of culturally sensitive land management strategies.

In this chapter, we reflect on the historical role and contemporary politics of cultural memories of landscape, providing a cultural analysis of community engagement that combines archaeological analyses of space with ethnographic research. These issues are particularly timely given the evolving relationship of Americanist archaeology to heritage policy and identity politics.

HOPI HISTORY AND HOPI LAND

> The land is really important to us because it's our ancestral land. That's where we have been, and I think it's good to make pilgrimage to various places and leave your prayer feathers . . . That's where the spirits live, and that's how we maintain peace. (Alph Secakuku 2011)

Hopis' connection with the southwestern United States extends back to the Motisinom ("First People"), who are the earliest ancestors of the Hopi. According to traditional accounts, other Hopi ancestors later emerged into the Fourth World (the present world) through the Sipapuni, a travertine cone located in the Little Colorado River Gorge near the Grand Canyon. Upon emergence, the people encountered Màasaw, the guardian of the earth, who instructed them to go in search of the Tuuwanasavi, Hopis' spiritual center of the universe. The people formed clans, split apart, and began a long series of migrations toward their ultimate destination at the Hopi Mesas (Courlander 1971, 1982; Crane 1925; Curtis 1922:16–98; Fewkes 1900; Mindeleff 1891:16–39; Voth 1905; Yava 1978:36–40).

During their migrations, these clans came into contact with the Hoopoq'yaqam (Those Who Went to the Northeast), another group of Hopi ancestors who trace their origins to Mesoamerica (Ferguson and Lomaomvaya 1999; Washburn 1995). Upon leaving Mesoamerica, the Hoopoq'yaqam traveled to Palatkwapi (the Red Walled City), where they stayed until floods and social unrest prompted them to continue their migrations northward. They eventually joined the other clans and settled new villages as they journeyed to the Hopi Mesas (Teague 1993). Collectively, these groups are considered to be Hisatsinom, Hopis' ancient ancestors (Ferguson and Colwell-Chanthaphonh 2006:97; Kuwanwisiwma 2004).

Today, the Hopi people are organized as a federally recognized tribe with a reservation in northeastern Arizona, within the core of Hopitutskwa (figure 3.1). Hopis continue to orient themselves with their ancestral lands through oral traditions and ceremonies. From certain religious perspectives, Hopitutskwa encompasses a complex geographical and temporal span that includes all places Hopi ancestors resided in the past (Balenquah 2008; Bernardini 2005; Ferguson et al. 2009; Ferguson and Lomaomvaya 2011:166; Jenkins et al. 1994; Kuwanwisiwma and Ferguson 2009; Lyons 2003). This landscape is dense with culturally important locations, including landforms associated with deities and historical events, sacred springs, rivers, trails, and ancestral sites (Koyiyumptewa and Colwell-Chanthaphonh 2011). The land is remembered through stories, ceremonial reenactments, and pilgrimages. Hopitutskwa remains vital in the daily life of the Hopi people.

As Hopitutskwa passed from Hopi ownership into private property and federally managed land, varying historical representations of Hopitutskwa were developed

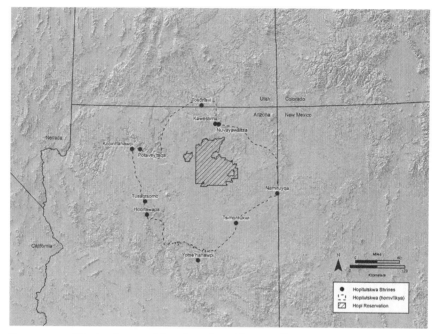

FIGURE 3.1. Hopitutskwa envisioned as a *homviikya*, or pilgrimage route, connecting a series of important Hopi shrines surrounding the Hopi Reservation in northern Arizona.

to respond to political-geographical needs to assert and defend contemporary political and cultural rights. In the early twentieth century, for example, the people of Second Mesa presented a letter to the commissioner of Indian Affairs petitioning for access to traditional lands encompassed by a series of shrines that constitute points along a *homviikya* (pilgrimage route) that is used in ongoing Hopi traditions (Whiteley 1989:7–39). Tribal leaders explained that the land has "been a most vital subject of our people or tribe at present and for generations past" and that they are concerned because surrounding areas are no longer easily accessible because of the encroachment of outsiders. "For centuries the Hopi shrines at the distance points, which borders the Hopi people from every direction, marked and designated the Hopis' tribal land boundary lines. Before the other peoples came the Hopis' essential needs at away places were all obtainable." The Hopis conclude the letter with an appeal for the return of "our land we love so well . . . for the benefit of our future generations" (Hopi Tribe 1930).

Hopi aboriginal lands as determined by the Indian Claims Commission (ICC), a judicial panel established in 1946 that addressed Indian land losses, ultimately did not encompass the entire area claimed by the leaders of Second Mesa. The

ICC reduced the extent of the Hopi claim using a judicial standard of exclusive use and occupancy for the period following the entry of the United States into the Southwest in 1848 (Indian Claims Commission 1970). The area described by Second Mesa leaders, however, has come to be viewed as the extent of Hopitutskwa by many non-Hopis. Meanwhile, Hopi traditionalists maintain that the homvìikya encircles the contemporary core, or "plaza," of the Hopi homeland, while the greater domain of Hopi stewardship extends outward to encompass a much larger area—one that includes all of Hopis' ancestral lands (Hedquist et al. 2014; Jenkins et al. 1994:8; Kuwanwisiwma and Ferguson 2009:92). The area and associated pilgrimage are significant because they demonstrate the ongoing role of the land and its features in contemporary Hopi life (Eggan 1994:15). The preservation of Hopi culture depends in part on continuing the traditional uses of Hopitutskwa, including respecting the ancestral sites it contains.

The Hopi people continue to defend the traditional lands that lie outside their reservation. In recent years, the Hopi Cultural Preservation Office has become increasingly involved in the research needed to implement the National Historic Preservation Act to identify Hopi traditional cultural properties on federally managed land. This approach enables members of the Hopi Tribe to maintain their historical traditions and cultural practices associated with the land and to use scholarly standards in documenting Hopitutskwa at a regional level. Hopis consider all of their ancestral places as integral in understanding the broader picture of Hopi history and religion. The salient features of the Hopi cultural landscape identified during these projects illustrate the depth and complexity of Hopi culture and the role of individual elements in shaping notions of Hopi identity and well-being.

THE NATIONAL HISTORIC PRESERVATION ACT AND THE IDENTIFICATION OF HOPI TRADITIONAL CULTURAL PROPERTIES

The Hopi Tribe never accepted the monetary payment for its aboriginal lands provided by the Indian Claims Commission. Those funds remain in a trust account accruing interest. Many Hopi people feel strongly that they have a moral right to use their traditional lands, even if that right is not formally recognized by the United States. In order to protect its cultural interests in Hopi aboriginal land, the Hopi Tribe has turned to participation in the historic preservation planning process to make sure Hopi cultural sites are considered during federal undertakings.

The National Historic Preservation Act (NHPA) of 1966, as amended, was passed to preserve the historical and cultural foundations of the United States as a living part of community life and development in order to give a sense of orientation to the American people. Section 106 of this act requires federal agencies to make a reasonable and good faith effort to identify historic properties included on or eligible for the National Register of Historic Places (NRHP) prior to any federal undertaking, to assess the potential adverse effects of the undertaking on those historic properties, and to consider how adverse effects can be resolved. Federal agencies are required to consider such properties in planning actions and to consult Indian tribes, interested parties, and the State Historic Preservation Office. Section 110 of the NHPA makes agencies responsible for preserving historic properties owned or controlled by the agency.

Historic properties are eligible for inclusion in the NRHP when they meet one or more of the following criteria set forth in NRHP regulations: (a) association with events that have made a significant contribution to the broad patterns of our history, (b) association with the lives of persons significant in our past, (c) embodiment of the distinctive characteristics of a type, period, or method of construction, or representative of the work of a master, or possession of high artistic values, or representative of a significant and distinguishable entity whose components may lack individual distinction, and (d) history of yielding, or potential to yield, information important in prehistory or history. In order to be eligible for inclusion in the NRHP, properties must also have integrity of location, design, setting, materials, workmanship, feeling, and association.

Traditional cultural properties are historic properties whose significance derives from their association with cultural practices or beliefs of a living community that (a) are rooted in that community's history and (b) are important in the retention and transmission of the cultural identity of the community (Parker and King 1998:1). Hopi traditional cultural properties are important because they comprise the tangible sites and places involved in passing down Hopi culture through generations by oral transmission and practice. As part of their contemporary lifeway, Hopis continue to commemorate thousands of places that are associated with deities, shrines, historical events, water sources, mountains, ancestral villages, and other historical and religious traditions.

Prior to the 1992 amendments to the NHPA, it would have been difficult for tribes to argue the significance of traditional places. However, with these amendments, which formally acknowledged the significance of traditional cultural properties as historic properties, tribes have had greater opportunities to argue for the values of these sites. Nevertheless, the significance of individual properties still has to be determined on a case-by-case basis.

RECONSTRUCTING HOPITUTSKWA: BUILDING A REGIONAL PERSPECTIVE

> I think there's a tendency to lock ourselves into the political boundaries of a
> project area . . . But in terms of good management, [federal agencies] need
> to create a long-term, if not a short-term, goal to sponsor ethnographic
> overviews regionally . . . [Every place] represents a chapter in our history,
> but the regional interest of the Hopi people is really, really huge. During my
> tenure with the office, I've learned to appreciate the breadth of our cultural
> and clan history, and it's our job to try to continue to represent the Hopi
> people's interest regionally. (Leigh J. Kuwanwisiwma, Director of Hopi
> Cultural Preservation Office [Kuwanwisiwma 2011])

The Hopi cultural landscape was created through generations of experience and encounters with the world. Like other communities, members of the Hopi Tribe understand the land in relation to specific events and historical conditions that provide the context for cultural comprehension (Bender 1993:2). In Hopi society, knowledge is privileged and hierarchical, and multiple accounts of history and religion exist. Individual clan histories, gender, and the cultural and religious standing of a person influence the way he or she understands the world. The participation of the Hopi Tribe in cultural preservation projects enables tribal members to identify and reconnect with places on the land that they know through oral traditions, and the Hopi Tribal Council recognizes and encourages the role of villages, clans, and religious societies in their efforts to do this (Hopi Tribe 1994).

The history of Hopi people embedded in the land creates a storied landscape. Features on the land serve as metonyms for cultural concepts; they evoke images of named places, the values associated with them, and the stories embedded in them (Whiteley 2011; Young 1988). In this sense, each place has a far-reaching impact on the Hopi people. Ancestral villages and other archaeological sites represent metaphorical footprints, marking the migrations of Hopi ancestors to the center of the universe on the Hopi Mesas. These ancient footprints continue to provide spiritual strength to the Hopi people, and they are integral in understanding the history of the land (Colwell-Chanthaphonh and Ferguson 2006; Gumerman et al. 2012).

The Hopi Cultural Preservation Office has participated in numerous historic preservation projects as part of the compliance process with the NRHP. Tribal members corroborate traditional knowledge with archaeological information to identify Hopi traditional cultural properties and evaluate their eligibility for the National Register of Historic Places. Here we discuss three projects conducted near the Hopi Reservation, including the Black Mesa Project, the US 160 road improvement project, and a traditional land use study in Glen Canyon National Recreation Area. These three projects identified traditional cultural properties in relation to

Hopi concepts of landscape and cultural identity, elucidating the connections between individual sites and the regional context of Hopitutskwa.

THE BLACK MESA PROJECT

The Black Mesa Project was designed to develop a new source of water for use in conveying coal from the Black Mesa Mine, located north of the Hopi Mesas, to the Mohave Generating Station at Laughlin, Nevada. The Black Mesa Project is a federal undertaking because it requires a permit from the Office of Surface Mining. The proposed undertaking entails several distinct project components (figure 3.2), one of which is the development of a proposed Well Field with up to twelve wells adjacent to Canyon Diablo near Leupp, Arizona. Another component includes the construction of a water supply line, approximately 173 kilometers (108 miles) in length to convey between 6,000 to 11,600 acre feet of water from the Well Field to the Black Mesa Mine. The preferred route for this water supply line runs northward up the Oraibi Wash through the Hopi Reservation, while an alternative route runs entirely through the Navajo Reservation to the west of the Hopi Reservation. In order to pump water uphill to the mine, two pumping stations need to be constructed along the water supply line, requiring the construction of a sixty-nine kilovolt power line along much of the route. The final component of the project is the reconstruction of the coal slurry pipeline of 439 kilometers (273 miles) from the Black Mesa Mine to the Mohave Generating Station.

The Black Mesa Project runs through the heart of Hopitutskwa and includes areas within and around the Hopi Reservation. The Hopi Cultural Preservation Office conducted a study to identify traditional cultural properties in the project area to facilitate compliance with Section 106 of the NRHP and provide environmental information for implementation of the National Environmental Policy Act. A total of fifteen Hopi tribal members participated in fieldwork, representing thirteen clans from seven villages on Second and Third Mesa. The research teams that worked on different project components varied in order to include Hopi consultants knowledgeable about clan interests in different areas (Ferguson and Koyiyumptewa 2007). Interviews were conducted with twenty-eight Hopi tribal members representing thirteen clans from five villages on Second and Third Mesa.

As a result of the study, the Hopi Tribe identified sixty-nine traditional cultural properties, including ancestral sites, pilgrimage routes, farm fields, eagle-collecting areas, plant- and mineral-collecting areas, landforms, shrines, and offering places. A cultural landscape perspective was used to evaluate the results of fieldwork and place individual traditional cultural properties in a broad cultural context. While the land and its features were delineated using traditional cultural properties as

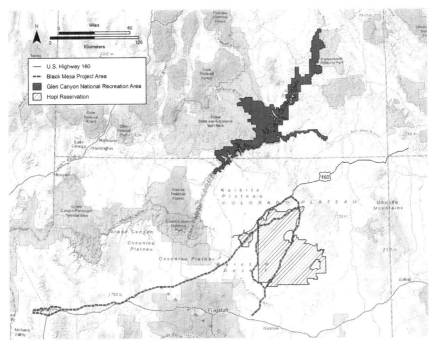

FIGURE 3.2. Location of the Hopi Reservation in relation to the Black Mesa Project, US. Highway 160, and Glen Canyon National Recreation Area.

discrete elements, many Hopis discussed the inextricable relationships between natural landforms, history, animal life, human society, and the spiritual realm. Hopi concerns encompassed both the land itself and how individuals perceive the land given their particular values and beliefs. Hopi cultural advisors recommended for the traditional cultural properties they identified in the project area to be eligible for the NRHP under Criterion A for their association with important events in Hopi history, and under Criterion D for yielding, or having potential to yield, significant information about Hopi history.

US 160

In 2007, the Hopi Cultural Preservation Office participated in a study along a stretch of US Highway 160 slated for improvement from its junction with US 89 to the Four Corners, north of the Hopi Reservation (figure 3.2). This project was conducted in compliance with Section 106 of the NRHP because the highway easement passes through land that is under federal jurisdiction. A total of twelve Hopi tribal members participated in the fieldwork, representing seven clans from eight villages on First, Second, and Third Mesa. Oral interviews were conducted with six Hopi tribal members representing four clans from five villages on Second and Third Mesa.

The US 160 project corridor passes through a region that is culturally significant for the Hopi people, both in the past and the present. During the project, Hopi cultural advisors identified 122 traditional cultural properties, including numerous ancestral sites, eagle-collecting areas, ceremonial collecting areas, hunting areas, pilgrimage routes, and landforms with cultural significance. Sixty-nine Hopi place-names were also documented in the area surrounding the project corridor (Ferguson et al. 2007). As with research conducted during the Black Mesa Project, Hopi cultural advisors discussed the complexity of the cultural geography in the project area and its inextricable relationships with natural landforms, history, animal life, human society, and the spiritual realm. The traditional cultural properties identified in the US 160 corridor were recommended eligible for the NRHP under Criteria A and D by the Hopi Cultural Preservation Office.

The US 160 Hopi traditional cultural property study is important because it demonstrates how ancestral sites, sacred areas, and other places with traditional cultural significance are used in the retention and transmission of Hopi culture. These traditional cultural properties are integral components of the cultural landscapes that figure prominently in Hopi history, ceremonial life, and subsistence practices. When the results of the US 160 project are combined with those of the Black Mesa Project, the richness of Hopis' cultural landscape becomes increasingly evident.

Glen Canyon

A third project, undertaken by the Hopi Tribe in 2011, was sponsored by the National Park Service (NPS) at Glen Canyon National Recreation Area (GLCA) and Rainbow Bridge National Monument (RABR). This project was conducted as part of an ongoing process by the National Park Service to maintain relationships between traditionally associated peoples and park resources. The project was carried out in compliance with Section 110 of the NRHP and other NPS policies. A total of four Hopi tribal members participated in the fieldwork, representing four clans from four villages on First, Second, and Third Mesa (figure 3.3). Oral interviews were conducted with fifteen Hopi tribal members representing thirteen clans from seven villages on Second and Third Mesa (Hopkins et al. 2013).

Glen Canyon National Recreation Area encompasses the area around Lake Powell in Utah and Arizona, covering 1.25 million acres (505,868 hectares) of Colorado Plateau desert (figure 3.3). Approximately 13 percent of GLCA is currently inundated by the waters of Lake Powell as a result of the construction of

FIGURE 3.3. Hopi research participants discuss tribal history and cultural landscapes with anthropologists and National Park Service employees at Defiance House in Glen Canyon National Recreation Area. Photograph by T. J. Ferguson, June 29, 2011.

Glen Canyon Dam on the Colorado River, which was completed in 1966. Rainbow Bridge National Monument covers 160 acres (64.75 hectares) near the southern boundary of GLCA, in the foothills of Navajo Mountain. Hopi ancestors settled the land now encompassed by GLCA and RABR during the time of clan migrations, and many of the sites and topographic features in this region now serve as landmarks commemorating this history.

As a result of the project, Hopi cultural advisors identified ancestral sites, plants, animals, minerals, and landforms with significance in Hopi history and traditions. The study also enriched the scholarly understanding of a cultural landscape related to the story of Tiyo, an oral tradition that entails the migration history of Hopis' Rattlesnake Clan. The landscape described in this story is particularly important because it covers an area that ranges from the southwestern United States to Mesoamerica, revealing the expansiveness of certain understandings of Hopitutskwa (Hopkins 2012).

Toko'navi, or Navajo Mountain, is located at the southern edge of GLCA, east of Rainbow Bridge (figure 3.4). This mountain is an important landmark in the

FIGURE 3.4. Toko'navi (Navajo Mountain) with Colorado River and Lake Powell in the foreground. Photograph by Maren Hopkins, June 29, 2011.

region and is a primary feature of the viewshed in this area. Toko'navi is the location of one of ten shrines delineating the Hopi homvìikya, or pilgrimage route, illustrated in figure 3.1. Several traditions about Hopi clan migrations reference Toko'navi, and prayers and traditions involving this mountain are ongoing. Hopi people recount that the Mountain Lion and the Dove people were among the first to arrive at Toko'navi during ancestral migrations, followed by the Rattlesnake Clan, and the Sand Clan (Stephen 1936:1084). The late Ferrell Secakuku, a member of the Rattlesnake Clan, was taught that Hopi clans initially settled at Toko'navi because of its resemblance to Palatkwapi, (the Red Walled City) a place where many clans lived previously (Secakuku 2006).

Hopi ancestors who lived at Toko'navi are associated with the story of Tiyo, the legend of a boy who traveled the full length of the Colorado River to Mesoamerica, returning with a snake wife, establishing the Rattlesnake Clan, and introducing the Snake Dance into Hopi religion (Anyon 1999; Bourke [1884] 1984:177; Ferguson 1998:107–19; Hopkins 2012; Parsons 1939:975; Secakuku 2006). Oral traditions describe Toko'navi as the place where Tiyo lived before embarking on his journey down the Colorado River (Courlander 1971:82; Fewkes 1900:588–89; Yava 1978:55).

The Colorado River is known to Hopis as Pisisvayu, and it is one of the two principal drainages in GLCA. While looking at the river, one Hopi cultural advisor participating in the project remembered that there were several deities who helped Tiyo during his arduous journey, including Huru'ingwùuti (Hard Objects

Woman), Kòokyangwso'wùuti (Old Spider Woman), and Pöqangwhoya and Palöngawhoya (the Warrior Twins). Viewing the land vividly recalls the spiritual beings associated with it.

Tiyo brought back, Qa'toya, a dragon-like deity, from his journeys to the south. Qa'toya is associated with the Rattlesnake Clan and possesses the powers to make rain. Turkey-like tracks depicted in petroglyphs are said to be the footprints of this deity. A cave located on Toko'navi was once the residing place of Qa'toya. When the Rattlesnake Clan left Toko'navi, the creature flew out of his cave and traveled down the Colorado River to the Little Colorado River, ending up at Wupatki, a Hopi ancestral site located along the Little Colorado River west of the Hopi Mesas. The Rattlesnake Clan followed Qa'toya to Wupatki and stayed there for some time before continuing toward the Hopi Mesas. Rattlesnake Clan members believe that Qa'toya still resides at Wupatki.

A pictograph at an ancient site in GLCA reminded cultural advisors of Qa'toya (figure 3.5). A snake image and a migration symbol were also present at the site, as were the images of anthropomorphic figures holding weapons (figure 3.6). Members of the Rattlesnake Clan today are known as "Hopi warriors," and cultural advisors participating in fieldwork at GLCA believed that these images were all related to this clan's history in the area. Toko'navi, the ancient home of the Rattlesnake Clan, is visible from this site. We found that talking about the land with Hopi research participants provided a meaningful context for talking about Hopi history.

The Glen Canyon study revealed a tangible connection between Hopi history and the resources in GLCA. Equally important were the cognitive associations made by Hopi tribal members between natural and cultural resources of GLCA and distant places known and maintained through Hopi oral traditions.

DISCUSSION AND CONCLUSION

> Those [tracks] are our connections to [our ancestral] places, and we still honor those places today. We make prayer feathers for all of those places and deposit them and give thanks to all the places that we still remember. And those are the reasons why we have shrines around our communities; they become these places that we make our prayers to. (Leonard Talaswaima [Talaswaima 2011])

As access to Hopi traditional lands has become increasingly restricted due to changes in land tenure over time, the Hopi people have struggled to maintain their historical traditions based on cultural practices associated with the land. The Hopi Cultural Preservation Office uses the political processes inherent in compliance

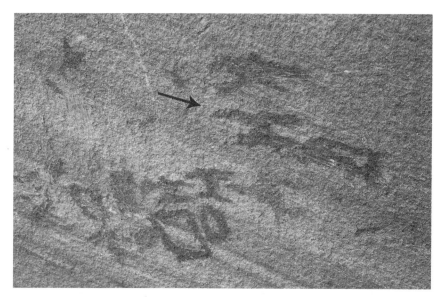

FIGURE 3.5. This pictograph at an ancient site in GLCA is interpreted by Hopi cultural advisors as an image of Qa'toya, a deity associated with Hopis' Rattlesnake Clan. Photograph by Maren Hopkins, June 29, 2011.

with the National Historic Preservation Act and other laws as a way to enable members of the tribe to reconnect with their ancestral lands. By combining archaeological analyses of space with ethnographic research, Hopi tribal members are building a regional perspective on the tangible sites of their heritage and connecting individual sites to larger concepts of landscape and identity. Restoring Hopi place-names on maps helps restore the Hopi history that was erased as non-Indian cartographers imposed alien names on the landforms and watercourses that constitute Hopitutskwa (figure 3.7).

The Hopi Tribe's participation in historic preservation projects for the Black Mesa, US Highway 160, and Glen Canyon National Recreation Area projects has identified numerous traditional cultural properties within and outside the Hopi Reservation. Specific sites and landforms in Glen Canyon articulate Hopi land and identity through their relationship with the story of Tiyo and the Rattlesnake Clan's migration history. As Richard Clemmer (1993:86) noted, "Hopis identify their ancestral dwelling places as much by symbols etched into rock and architectural ruins as by clan legends and traditions. In a sense, knowledgeable Hopis 'read' an archaeological landscape with reference to the fundamental principles of their cosmological system."

FIGURE 3.6. Warrior images depicted on the cliff walls in GLCA are thought by Hopi cultural advisors to be associated with the Rattlesnake Clan's history. Photograph by Maren Hopkins, June 29, 2011.

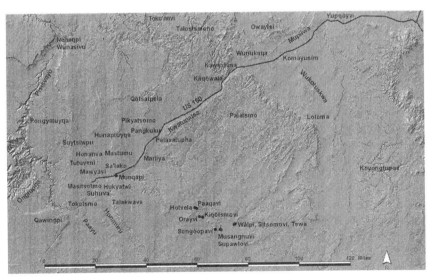

FIGURE 3.7. This sample of locations with Hopi place-names along US Highway 160 demonstrates the deep connections Hopis maintain with their ancestral lands.

The process of linking places through stories, connecting past and present, requires Hopi traditionalists to be present on the land. Visiting places not only reaffirms Hopi responsibilities of land stewardship but can also serve as a process of historic revelation. A comparable moment was recorded in Australia by Howard Morphy (1995), who documented how Narritjin Maymuru, a Yolngu man, discovers that a mythic event had transpired in a place he had never been before. Maymuru knew because he believed that he was not moving into a new country, but that the land was revealing itself to him. In other words, the past—real and tangible—was being transmitted through the physical place. Such processes of blending stories, experience, and landscapes have been documented in other cultural contexts (e.g., Basso 1996; Cruikshank 2005; Wyndham 2011). The Hopis use a similar mechanism. The retention and transmission of Hopi culture depend largely on the Hopis' ability to connect to their ancestral landscape.

REFERENCES

Anyon, Roger. 1999. *Migrations in the South: Hopi Reconnaissance in the Barry M. Goldwater Range.* Tucson: Heritage Resources Management Consultants.

Balenquah, Lyle J. 2008. "Beyond Stone and Mortar: A Hopi Perspective on the Preservation of Ruins (and Culture)." *Heritage Management* 1 (2): 145–62. http://dx .doi.org/10.1179/hso.2008.1.2.145.

Basso, Keith H. 1996. *Wisdom Sits in Places: Landscape and Language among the Western Apache.* Albuquerque: University of New Mexico Press.

Bender, Barbara. 1993. "Landscape: Meaning and Action." In *Landscape: Politics and Perspectives,* ed. Barbara Bender, 1–17. Oxford: Berg.

Bernardini, Wesley. 2005. *Hopi Oral Tradition and the Archaeology of Identity.* Tucson: University of Arizona Press.

Bourke, John G. [1884] 1984. *The Snake-Dance of the Moquis of Arizona.* Tucson: University of Arizona Press.

Clemmer, Richard O. 1993. "Hopi." In *An Investigation of AIRFA Concerns Related to the Fruitland Coal Gas Development Area,* ed. David M. Brugge, 77–90. Albuquerque: Office of Contract Archaeology, University of New Mexico.

Colwell-Chanthaphonh, Chip, and T. J. Ferguson. 2006. "Memory Pieces and Footprints: Multivocality and the Meanings of Ancient Times and Ancestral Places among the Zuni and Hopi." *American Anthropologist* 108 (1): 148–62. http://dx.doi.org/10.1525/aa.2006 .108.1.148.

Courlander, Harold. 1971. *The Fourth World of the Hopis: The Epic Story of the Hopi Indians as Preserved in their Legends and Traditions.* New York: Crown.

Courlander, Harold. 1982. *Hopi Voices, Recollections, Traditions, and Narratives of the Hopi Indians.* Albuquerque: University of New Mexico Press.

Crane, Leo. 1925. *Indians of the Enchanted Desert.* Boston: Little, Brown, and Company.

Cruikshank, Julie. 2005. *Do Glaciers Listen? Local Knowledge, Colonial Encounters, and Social Imagination.* Vancouver: UBC Press.

Curtis, Edward S. 1922. *The North American Indian.* Vol. 12. Norwood, MA: Plimpton Press.

Eggan, Fred. 1994. "The Hopi Indians, with Special Reference to Their Cosmology or World View." In *Kachinas in the Pueblo World*, ed. Polly Schaafsma, 7–21. Albuquerque: University of New Mexico Press.

Ferguson, T. J. 1998. *Öngtupqu Niqw Pisisvayu (Salt Canyon and the Colorado River): The Hopi People and the Grand Canyon. Anthropological Research.* Tucson: Hopi Cultural Preservation Office, The Hopi Tribe.

Ferguson, T. J., G. Lennis Berlin, and J. Leigh Kuwanwisiwma. 2009. "Kukhepya: Searching for Hopi Trails." In *Landscapes of Movement: Trails and Paths in Anthropological Perspective*, ed. James E. Snead, Clark L. Erikson, and J. Andrew Darling, 20–41. Philadelphia: University of Pennsylvania Press.

Ferguson, T. J., and Chip Colwell-Chanthaphonh. 2006. *History Is in the Land: Multivocal Tribal Traditions in Arizona's San Pedro Valley.* Tucson: University of Arizona Press.

Ferguson, T. J., and B. Stewart Koyiyumptewa. 2007. "Hopi Traditional Cultural Properties Investigation for the Black Mesa Project." Tucson: Anthropological Research. Manuscript on file, Hopi Cultural Preservation Office, Kykotsmovi, AZ.

Ferguson, T. J., and B. Stewart Koyiyumptewa, and Chip Colwell-Chanthaphonh. 2007. "Hopi Traditional Cultural Properties along the US 160 Highway Corridor." Tucson: Anthropological Research. Manuscript on file, Hopi Cultural Preservation Office, Kykotsmovi, AZ.

Ferguson, T. J., and Micah Lomaomvaya. 1999. *Hoopoq'yaqam niqw Wukoskyavi (Those Who Went to the Northeast and Tonto Basin): Hopi-Salado Cultural Affiliation Study.* Kykotsmovi, AZ: Hopi Cultural Preservation Office, The Hopi Tribe.

Ferguson, T. J., and Micah Lomaomvaya. 2011. "Nuvatukya'ovi, Palatsmo, niqw Wupatki: Hopi History, Culture, and Landscape." In *Sunset Crater Archaeology: The History of a Volcanic Landscape: Prehistoric Settlement in the Shadow of the Volcano*, ed. M. Elson, 143–186. Anthropological Papers 37. Tucson: Center for Desert Archaeology.

Fewkes, Jesse Walter. 1900. "Tusayan Migration Traditions." In *19th Annual Report of the Bureau of American Ethnology for the Years 1897–1898*, part 2, 573–634. Washington, DC: Government Printing Office.

Gumerman, George, Joëlle Clark, Elmer J. Satala, and Ruby Chimerica. 2012. "Footprints of the Ancestors Reengaging Hopi Youth with Their Culture." *Museums and Social Issues* 7 (2): 149–66. http://dx.doi.org/10.1179/msi.2012.7.2.149.

Hedquist, Saul L., Stewart B. Koyiyumptewa, Peter Whiteley, Leigh J. Kuwanwisiwma, Kenneth C. Hill, and T. J. Ferguson. 2014. "Recording Toponyms to Document the Endangered Hopi Language." *American Anthropologist* 116 (2): 324–31. http://dx.doi .org/10.1111/aman.12088.

Hopi Tribe. 1930. "Petition from Hopi Tribe to Commissioner of Indian Affairs. Plaintiff's Exhibit 279, Vernon Masayesva, etc. Plaintiff, v. Leonard Haskie, etc., Defendant, v. Evelyn James, etc., Intervener, Civil No. 74–842 PHX-EHC," United States District Court for the District of Arizona.

Hopi Tribe. 1994. "Hopi Tribal Council Resolution H-70-94." Kykotsmovi, AZ: The Hopi Tribe.

Hopkins, Maren. 2012. "A Storied Land: Tiyo and the Epic Journey Down the Colorado River." Master's thesis, University of Arizona, Tucson.

Hopkins, Maren, T. J. Ferguson, and Stewart B. Koyiyumptewa. 2013. *Hopisinmuy Wu'ya'mat Hisat Yang Tupqa'va Yeesiwngwu (Hopi Ancestors Lived in These Canyons): Hopi History and Traditions at Glen Canyon National Recreation Area and Rainbow Bridge National Monument*. University of Arizona, School of Anthropology, Colorado Plateau CESU Cooperative Agreement H1200-09-0005. Manuscript on file, Hopi Cultural Preservation Office, Kykotsmovi, AZ.

Indian Claims Commission. 1970. "Opinion and Findings of Fact." The Hopi Tribe, Docket 196, and the Navajo Tribe of Indians, Docket 229 v. The United States of America. 23 Ind. Cl. Comm. 227. Republished in 1974 in *Hopi Indians*, ed. David Agee Horr, 389–424. New York: Garland Press.

Jenkins, Leigh, T. J. Ferguson, and Kurt Dongoske. 1994. "A Reexamination of the Concept of Hopitutskwa." Paper Presented at the Annual Meeting of the American Society for Ethnohistory, Tempe, AZ.

Koyiyumptewa, Stewart B., and Chip Colwell-Chanthaphonh. 2011. "The Past Is Now: Hopi Connections to Ancient Times and Places." In *Movement, Connectivity, and Landscape Change in the Ancient Southwest (Proceedings of the Southwest Symposium)*, ed. Margaret C. Nelson and Colleen Strawhacker, 443–55. Boulder: University Press of Colorado.

Kuwanwisiwma, Leigh J. 2004. "Yupköyvi: The Hopi Story of Chaco Canyon." In *In Search of Chaco: New Approaches to an Archaeological Enigma*, ed. D. G. Noble, 41–47. Santa Fe: School of American Research Press.

Kuwanwisiwma, Leigh J. 2011. *Interviewed by Maren Hopkins at Paaqavi, June 22, 2011. Ms. on file*. Hopi Cultural Preservation Office Archives, Kiqötsmovi.

Kuwanwisiwma, Leigh J., and T. J. Ferguson. 2009. "*Hopitutskwa* and *Ang Kuktota*: The Role of Archaeological Sites in Defining Hopi Cultural Landscapes." In *The Archaeology of Meaningful Places*, ed. Brenda J. Bowser and María Nieves Zedeño, 90–106. Salt Lake City: University of Utah Press.

Lyons, Patrick D. 2003. *Ancestral Hopi Migrations. Anthropological Papers of the University of Arizona No. 68.* Tucson: University of Arizona Press.

Mindeleff, Victor. 1891. "A Study of Pueblo Architecture in Tusayan and Cibola." In *Eighth Annual Report of the Bureau of Ethnology for the Years 1886–1887*, 3–228. Washington, DC: Government Printing Office.

Morphy, Howard. 1995. "Landscape and the Reproduction of the Ancestral Past." In *The Anthropology of Landscape: Perspectives on Place and Space*, ed. Eric Hirsch and Michael O'Hanlon, 185–209. Oxford: Clarendon Press.

Parker, Patricia L., and Thomas F. King. 1998. *Guidelines for Evaluating and Documenting Traditional Cultural Properties. National Register Bulletin 38.* Washington, DC: US Government Printing Office.

Parsons, Elsie Clews. 1939. *Pueblo Indian Religion.* 2 vols. Chicago: University of Chicago Press.

Secakuku, Alph H. 2011. Interviewed by Maren Hopkins at Second Mesa, June 22, 2011. Alph H. Secakuku and Mervin S. Yoyetewa. Manuscript on file, Hopi Cultural Preservation Office Archives, Kiqötsmovi.

Secakuku, Ferrell H. 2006. "Hopi and Quetzalcoatl, Is there a Connection?" Master's thesis, Northern Arizona University, Flagstaff.

Stephen, Alexander M. 1936. H*opi Journal of Alexander M. Stephen*, ed. Elsie Clews Parsons. New York: Columbia University Press.

Talaswaima, Leonard. 2011. Interviewed by T. J. Ferguson and Maren Hopkins at Page, July 1, 2011. Balenquah, Riley and Leonard Talaswaima. Ms. on file, Hopi Cultural Preservation Office Archives, Kiqötsmovi.

Teague, Lynn S. 1993. "Prehistory and the Traditions of the O'Odham and Hopi." *Kiva* 58 (4): 435–54. http://dx.doi.org/10.1080/00231940.1993.11758220.

Voth, H. R. 1905. *Publication 96.* Vol. 8. *The Traditions of the Hopi.* Anthropological Series. Chicago: Field Columbian Museum.

Washburn, Dorothy. 1995. *Living in Balance: The Universe of the Hopi, Zuni, Navajo, and Apache.* Philadelphia: University of Pennsylvania Museum of Archaeology and Anthropology.

Whiteley, Peter M. 1989. *Hopitutskwa: An Historical and Cultural Interpretation of the Hopi Traditional Land Claim. Expert Witness Report for the Hopi Tribe in Masayesva vs. Zah vs. James ('1934 Reservation case').* Phoenix: US District Court.

Whiteley, Peter M. 2011. "Hopi Place Value: Translating a Landscape." In *Born in the Blood: On Native American Translation*, ed. Brian Swann, 84–108. Lincoln: University of Nebraska Press.

Wyndham, Felice S. 2011. "The Semiotics of Powerful Places: Rock Art and Landscape Relations in the Sierra Tarahumara, Mexico." *Journal of Anthropological Research* 67 (3): 387–420. http://dx.doi.org/10.3998/jar.0521004.0067.304.

Yava, Albert. 1978. *Big Falling Snow, a Tewa-Hopi Indian's Life and Times and the History and Traditions of His People*, ed. Harold Courlander, New York: Crown.

Young, M. Jane. 1988. *Signs from the Ancestors*. Albuquerque: University of New Mexico Press.

4

Designs on / of the Land

Competing Visions, Displacement, and Landscape Memory in British Colonial Honduras

CHRISTINE KRAY, MINETTE CHURCH, AND JASON YAEGER

INTRODUCTION

Colonialism is neither fixed in space nor total in its effects, but is perceptible in myriad clashes and acts of force, obedience, subterfuge, and flight. This chapter traces colonial effects in British Honduras from 1847 to 1942 through the lens of *designs on* and *designs of* the land. In the mid-nineteenth century, Yucatec Maya people fleeing from the Caste War in Mexico's Yucatán Peninsula met up with British mahogany crews in the northwestern forests of what would become British Honduras, now Belize. These groups brought with them competing designs on the land in terms of both resource use and land tenure. Some groups settled in and around the Yalbac Hills (figure 4.1).

Although these contests over the land began more than a century ago, they still reverberate strongly in present-day memories of the land, modern designs of the land. Over the span of nearly a century, multiple and competing designs on the land shaped action, reaction, strikes, advances, capitulations, claims, and longings. Present-day designs of the land in the form of landscape memories are tinged with nostalgia for a lost, salubrious land that allowed a community to thrive. While the tangible heritage of the Yalbac Hills towns in large part have been destroyed, the intangible heritage of the Yalbac Hills Maya persists in the knowledge of subsistence milpa techniques and the association of forest living with a healthy life. In this respect, landscape memory itself is part of the intangible heritage of the Yalbac Hills Maya, integral to a moral vision of a good life. This chapter thus reveals the

DOI: 10.5876/9781607325727.c004

53

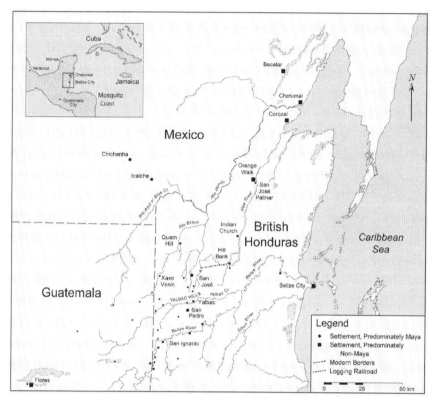

FIGURE 4.1. Northern British Honduras of the late nineteenth and early twentieth centuries.

mutual entailment of land use and imaginings and of landscape memory as a form of resistance.

Throughout the period under examination, at each moment, several competing designs on the land motivated action, and yet at different times and in different places, one gained ascendency, whether through military might, legal strategy, economic force, or simple human occupation. Each design on the land might therefore be envisioned as a tectonic plate, with all in motion, bumping up against one another, sometimes smashing violently, one thrusting upward and submerging another, whose pent-up force reemerges elsewhere. This tectonic metaphor allows us to see the contestation, partialness, and indeterminacy of action, strategy, and policy under the appellation of colonialism. During this time span, several landscape visions emerged, jostled, and subsided. Over the span of a century, land appears as geopolitical territory and a theater of action, a haven and source of subsistence, a source of extractive commodities and rents, private property, hostage, pollutant, homeland, wellspring, commercial farm, and alienable house plot. This chapter explores how these various designs on the land jostled at different times and in different places, with traces of nostalgia and alienation left on Maya historical memory. The story of land in colonial British Honduras is not a stark contrast of British versus Maya or capitalist versus subsistence. Rather, at each stage, multiple visions of land both propelled and constrained action, as "British" and "Maya" groups often obstructed one another. Land was always an object of desire, a utilitarian tool, and a symbol of what might be.

In 1936, the London-based Belize Estate and Produce Company (BEPCO) evicted the Yucatec Maya inhabitants of San José Yalbac (see below for name variants) from lands their ancestors had settled from at least 1862, according to documentary evidence. Archaeological data indicates settlement well before that date, but we know that many came around 1862 seeking a southern refuge away from the fighting and extortionist rents of the Caste War regions to the north. This group was therefore triply displaced, first by the start of the Caste War in the late 1840s, then again roughly a decade later, and a final time in 1936. It is hard not to read this history and imagine deterministic forces, as if the Maya were predestined to be cast off thrice, because of the imperturbable forces of colonialism and capitalism. Yet, that conclusion would be too simplistic. In the end, San José villagers were in the wrong place at the wrong time. In the final dislocation, economic strategies and the momentum of investments converged to focus British Honduran attention on San José in 1935–36. A series of factors—including misinterpretations of survey maps, desperation during the Great Depression, and interpersonal squabbles on the Legislative Council—created a situation in which BEPCO focused all of its attention on mahogany extraction in the Yalbac Hills. Thwarted in various initiatives and feeling fenced in, the company manager doubled down and made the socially unpopular move of evicting the villagers of San José (also called San José Yalbac and San José Viejo). The company manager could not have predicted the irony that American consumers would soon forsake mahogany for walnut, that the secretary of state for the colonies would just a few years later allow BEPCO owners to sell controlling shares to an American buyer, and that the new governor would prioritize commercial agriculture over forestry. In 1936 in the Yalbac Hills, however, there were several hundred square feet of mahogany logs that seemed of tantamount importance to BEPCO's manager, and San José villagers stood in the way.

As always, the unfolding events of history are not predetermined but result from convergences and divergences of interests and actions at certain times and places. The knowledge of actors is forever partial and incomplete. Acting from a standpoint, focus becomes narrowed, heels dig in, and winners and losers emerge, both dirtied in the process. With growing social resentment about the power of BEPCO, the company manager lost in his bid for an elected seat on the Legislative Council, and he headed back to England, tail between legs, and replaced in his post.

This chapter moves backward and forward in time. At its core are neighboring towns of San Pedro Siris (also called San Pedro) and San José Yalbac in the Yalbac Hills; Grant Jones (1977) called the residents of these and smaller satellite villages the San Pedro Maya, after their main settlement. We move backward to trace the routes of their ancestors and then forward to their descendants. Our team brings together archaeological, oral, and documentary data. Minette Church and Jason Yaeger, along with Richard M. Leventhal and Jennifer Dornan, conducted archaeological research at the site of San Pedro Siris, which was abandoned at the turn of the twentieth century; Yaeger and Christine Kray conducted interviews in Spanish and Yucatec Maya with people who had lived in nearby San José Yalbac prior to the eviction in 1936 (figure 4.2);[1] and Dornan and Kray conducted archival research in the Belize Archives (Belmopan) and the National Archives (United Kingdom). This multimethod collaboration has enabled us to trace the movements of generations of people across sites and has also revealed that despite this turbulent history of forced displacement, the intangible heritage persists in the form of subsistence knowledge, moral critique, and landscape memory. This chapter first examines tangible evidence of the competing designs on the land that propelled Maya movements across the region and then examines how narrated memories of the landscape communicate the intangible heritage of subsistence production and a moral vision of the good life.

LAND AS GEOPOLITICAL TERRITORY AND A THEATER OF ACTION

Taking the Yalbac Hills of western Belize as our center, we first tack backward in time to trace the designs on the land that propelled Maya movements across the land. From 1847 through the 1870s, southern Yucatán and northwestern British Honduras were destabilized by visions of land as geopolitical territory and by the theater of military action that resulted. Those who eventually settled in the Yalbac Hills region by 1862 did not settle there straightaway but made stops along the way, including through Chichanha, in search of a safe place to land.

In 1847, Maya and some Mestizo fighters had initiated a large-scale rebellion against descendants of the Spaniards in the Caste War of Yucatán. Although most of the rebels were Maya, over time the factions grew more complicated and shifted, with different Maya groups fighting one another, as well (see Dornan 2004; also Reed 2001). The Caste War rebels were resentful of tax burdens, debt peonage, and liberal land reforms that ushered in widespread disenfranchisement, leaving landless

FIGURE 4.2. Valentín Tosh (a) and Emeterio Cantún (b) of San José (Nuevo) Palmar. Both were residents of San José Yalbac at the time of the 1936 eviction.

peasants open to easy exploitation in an expanding plantation system. Ultimately, Mexican federal forces entered the fray and pushed the rebels back to southern and eastern parts of the Yucatán Peninsula (Reed 2001; Rugeley 1996).

LAND AS SOURCE OF EXTRACTIVE COMMODITIES AND RENTS

To the south, in what is now Belize, thousands of Maya refugees entered a no-man's land simultaneously claimed by Mexico, Guatemala, and Britain. They entered a region that itself was destabilized by competing designs on the land. British buccaneers had been illicitly extracting logwood near the coasts, and in the 1770s, as British demands for mahogany for luxury furniture rose, woodcutters advanced deeper into the forests, where they confronted Maya groups (Bolland 1977b:72).[2] Around the same time that the Caste War fighting spread and factions splintered off, land in the western forests became intensely profitable and desired, as both a source of extractive commodities (primarily, mahogany) and as the leverage by which different Mayan factions extracted rent from British Honduran woodcutters.

Seeking a truce with the Mexican forces, in 1851 and 1853 the rebel Maya group in Chichanha signed peace treaties with Mexico. In so doing, they committed to fight the fiercest of the rebels, the Santa Cruz Maya, or Cruzob, to the east (Bolland 1977b:75–76). They became known in Mexico as *los pacíficos del sur*, "the peaceful ones of the south."

The rebel war with Mexico took on international dimensions as the British were hauled in. Perhaps emboldened by their alliance with Mexico, Maya from Chichanha in 1856 and 1857 attacked the British mahogany camp on Blue Creek, claiming that the woodcutters should pay rent for taking lumber from Mexican territory (Bolland 1977b:76). This set up a four-player game in which the Santa Cruz Maya were fighting the Mexican forces, who were allied with the Chichanha, who then found themselves at odds with the British. Some British Honduran merchants even traded guns and powder to the Santa Cruz Maya, ultimately ensuring that the Caste War stretched over half a century, until 1901.

In 1857, the Santa Cruz Maya attacked Chichanha once again, and half of the village fled south. Ominously foreshadowing future conflicts, British accounts even at this early date noted that Maya swidden farming destroyed valuable mahogany in the forest (Bolland 1977b:76–77).

LAND AS PRIVATE PROPERTY

At the same time as the Chichanha refugees entered the mahogany forests, the British colonial and private sector interests converged, designing a legal strategy to control land as private property. In 1858–61, the Honduras Land Titles Acts drafted in London allowed would-be buyers to purchase lands in the British Honduran settlement even if there were no existing title. Consequently, within a very short period of time, very little land was left for purchase (Bolland 1977a:187). One of the London lawyers who drafted the law also worked for the British Honduras Company (BHC), established precisely in 1858 in London. The attorney general affirmed that the legislation by design was to secure titles for the BHC (Bolland 1977a:185), which subsequently purchased 1 million acres, comprising one-fifth of the area of modern Belize and one-half of the settlement's privately owned land (Luke 1931). Its holdings included the entire Yalbac Hills region (Surveyor General 1929).

Meanwhile, some Maya people fled further to the south. In 1860, the Santa Cruz Maya again attacked and burned Chichanha. The survivors relocated at Icaiche. The group from Chichanha that had left in 1857 moved further south, to evade domination by the Icaiche and conflicts with the Santa Cruz Maya. By 1862, they had settled in the Yalbac Hills area, including in San Pedro and San José (Bolland 1977b:76–77). British woodcutters had only recently entered this region, so it would have seemed relatively safe (Jones 1977). The San Pedro Maya found a land far from the conflicts between the *pacíficos* and the Santa Cruz Maya with mature forests well suited to milpa farming. While it may have appeared to them unclaimed, as it was sparsely inhabited and unused from the perspective of Maya farming, from the British Honduran perspective, the land was private property owned by BHC under the new British laws.

Then, the scheme of land as geopolitical territory resurged with greater force in 1862. British settlers sought to establish political dominion over the region, and the settlement of Belize in the Bay of Honduras reconfigured itself as the colony of

British Honduras. Native *alcaldes* (mayors) were appointed in the western towns and selected from within the communities, but to serve as an extension of the colonial government. Yet even in those early conversations with colonial officials, there were already signs of the British woodcutters and Maya jostling one another, as villagers at San José reported that sometimes woodcutters would chase them out so that they could rob the village and fields (Jones 1977:158). In the following year, 1863, the leader of San Pedro turned to the colonial government for support against Icaiche, which was aligned with Mexico. He also complained that the cattle of the BHC mahogany crews were trampling their fields (Dumond 1997:276).[3] He received ammunition from the lieutenant governor, in return for which he made various promises, including, tellingly, "to respect the mahogany trees" (Dumond 1997:486).

The British were not the only imperial power with an interest in this part of Central America. In 1864, during the short-lived Second Empire of Mexico, the Imperial Commissary of Yucatán claimed all of British Honduras and the Petén for the Mexican Empire (Dumond 1997:274), a fact that apparently emboldened Mexico's pacífico allies at Icaiche in their demands for rents from British woodcutters. In 1866, the Icaiche attacked the BHC mahogany camp at Quam Hill, demanding rent for resources taken from Mexican property. British Honduran officials suspected that the Icaiche and San Pedro Maya were jointly planning more attacks on logging camps.

The relationship between Icaiche and San Pedro was apparently a complicated one. Asunción Ek, *alcalde* (mayor) of San Pedro, appealed to British Honduran officials for protection from Icaiche, yet in December 1866 the Icaiche leader sent a letter to the lieutenant governor, datelined San Pedro, asserting that that area belonged to Yucatán. Although Ek's original intentions are ultimately unknowable, when British Honduran troops marched on San Pedro, San Pedro fighters repelled them, with support from Icaiche (Dornan 2004:114–31).[4]

Seeking retribution, in February 1867 the British sent more troops and burned San Pedro to the ground (Bolland 1977b:78). Accounts of the raid describe the use of early incendiary rockets, fragments of which were recovered during investigations at the site (Church et al. 2011; see figure 4.3). The troops also destroyed San José and other neighboring villages, burning houses, fields, and granaries (Bolland 1977b:78–79).[5]

In the same year that the Yalbac Hills villages were destroyed (1867), the British Honduran government again crafted legal strategies to advance British designs on the land. The lieutenant governor proclaimed that Indians should not occupy or cultivate land without payment of rent to landowner or crown (Bolland 1977b:91); in other words, they were forbidden to own land of their own. In 1868, the lieutenant governor affirmed that many Maya villages in the western area were on land

FIGURE 4.3. Fragment of an incendiary rocket uncovered at San Pedro Siris.

owned by either the BHC or Messrs. Young Toledo and Company. Those living on crown lands should be given space reserved by the crown, though they were not to be issued titles (Bolland 1977b:91). According to Bolland (1987:49), "Apart from a few instances, however, this policy of 'native reservations' was not really implemented, and in the last years of the nineteenth century it was virtually abandoned." The fact that Indians were prevented by law from owning land assured that those in the Yalbac Hills would continue to be unsettled by actors with competing designs on the land.

In 1871, the British colonial government once again used legal maneuvers to advance what were in fact convergent goals of commodity extraction and political dominion. Seeking greater protection against the northern rebels, the Legislative Assembly in the colony ceded governance directly to Britain. British Honduras consequently became a crown colony (Bolland 1977b:92), ultimately enhancing the power of the colonists to pacify the northwestern region.

By 1872, San Pedro and San José had been reoccupied (Jones 1977:153). They remained under the shadow of Icaiche, whose leader appointed the alcaldes, and Icaiche continued to collect rents from British woodcutters (Dumond 1997:342). Until 1898, both Mexico and British Honduras continued to claim dominion over what is now northwestern Belize, emboldening the Icaiche to continue to demand rent payments from woodcutters. Consequently, Maya in the Yalbac Hills region continued to be pulled between Icaiche "protection" and the notion of peace. However, by 1884 the Icaiche were only charging the Belize Estate and Produce Company (the new name for the British Honduras Company, as of 1878) for rents to the north of the Yalbac Hills region (Dumond 1997:383), which probably allowed those in the Yalbac Hills to finally exercise autonomy and feel settled. Their position must have remained somewhat tenuous, however, as the Lacandon Maya to their west in Guatemala continued to charge rents to loggers there throughout this period (Palka 2005).

LAND AS HAVEN AND SOURCE OF SUBSISTENCE

We have seen that groups of Yucatec Maya continually moved further south and deeper into the forest. Their vision (design on the land) appears to have been of land as a safe haven and as a source of subsistence. Joel Palka notes that the dynamics of these "zones of refuge"—where populations disperse into areas not under firm colonial control as a mechanism for survival—are understudied (Palka 2005:30–31). The overall picture painted by the artifact assemblage at San Pedro is an interesting and seemingly paradoxical one, as Maya efforts to find refuge farther south occurred in parallel with their increased access to and participation in the global economy, particularly in terms of their use of manufactured goods. Increasing participation in the cash economy in the nineteenth century seems to have been, perhaps counterintuitively, a way to augment autonomy and local subsistence. A market in nonessential goods tied the villagers of San Pedro to other Maya westward in the Petén as well as to logging camps locally and to San Ignacio and Belize City. Throughout the occupation, however, evidence of the cash economy remains supplemental to evidence of continuing reliance on local resources for the necessities at San Pedro.

The archaeological materials from San Pedro Yalbac reveal a wide variety of subsistence techniques and subsistence resources, only somewhat parallel to Palka's findings among the Lacandon, and for the most part confirmed by interviews with people who lived in San José Yalbac in the 1930s. The Yalbac Hills Maya farmed corn, beans, squash, sweet potato, and jicama. Pollen data from portions of the site of San Pedro, collected by John Gust (2006), indicate slash-and-burn swidden farming, made possible by the steel tools that were common in the assemblage. The pollen data also suggest fruit, spice, and nut (cashew) trees in the vicinity, likely cultivated. There is tentative pollen data for cultivation of tobacco as well, which Joel Palka (2005) cites as an important trade item in the Petén. Excavation yielded smoking pipe fragments embossed "E Roach/London" (manufactured between 1830 and 1860) at San Pedro, at least one of which had residue, indicating local use as well.

The pollen data indicates an area rich and diverse in useful plant resources, generally. Artifacts for exploiting agricultural and wild resources include a high frequency of machete blade fragments, axes and hoes, and perforated cans likely used for holding corn seeds when sowing. Patent medicine and cosmetics bottles (hair tonic and pomades) indicate the villagers at least supplemented local medicinal remedies and cosmetics with commercially available ones.

Oral narratives recount that the Maya in the Yalbac Hills region hunted deer, paca, peccary, squirrel, and a variety of birds, including the wild turkey, dove, pigeon, and quail, and they collected honey. Some of the many small Jamaica Ginger extract (figure 4.4), pepper sauce, and other condiment bottles may have been reused to

FIGURE 4.4. Jamaica Ginger bottles from San Pedro Siris.

store honey from honeybees, as such bottles were in the Petén (Palka 2005). They collected edible freshwater snails called *jute* from the creek that ran through the village, but the shell was also likely burned to make lime, which was essential for softening up corn kernels prior to grinding (Palka 2005). Many of the locally produced earthenware basins at San Pedro had coats of lime on the interiors, presumably from the process of soaking corn (figure 4.5a).

They also used forest materials to fashion a wide variety of items, including their houses, furniture, hammocks, and sandals. This account of a heavy reliance on the forest is confirmed by the faunal assemblage, which includes game animals that remain popular today such as whitetail and brocket deer, *tepescuintle* (paca), agouti, collared and white-lipped peccary, and armadillo (Freiwald n.d.). Cow and pig were present, but these domesticated animals only accounted for approximately one quarter of the remains of commonly consumed mammals found at the site, and peccary remains were roughly twice as common as pig remains (Freiwald n.d.). A relatively common find on the site were roasting pits. Taken together with a remarkable number of cast-iron Dutch oven kettles, they suggest the inhabitants of San Pedro enjoyed traditional Yucatec Maya *pibil* dishes, in which meat is roasted or stews cooked overnight in an earth oven. Fungal spores collected with the pollen data suggest large animal dung, perhaps used as fertilizer (Cummings 2005).

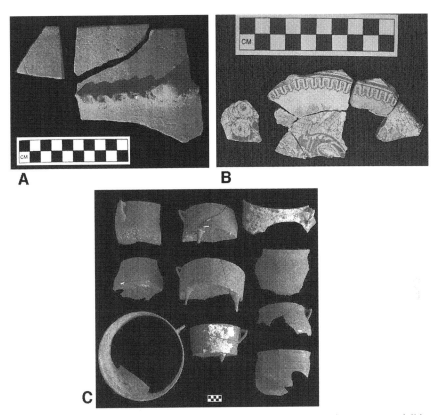

FIGURE 4.5. Locally produced ceramics (a), mulberry transfer ware (1830s to 1850s) (b), and cooking cauldrons (c) from San Pedro Siris.

The archaeological data also show that in addition to subsistence techniques, the San Pedro Maya traded with the British for mostly commercial items, including items for procuring, cooking, and serving food such as machetes, axes, metal cooking vessels, and serving dishes; household items including scissors and buttons; and items for personal leisure, such as porcelain dolls and tobacco pipes. At the same time, though, there is remarkable continuity in subsistence and cooking techniques, reinforcing the conclusion that the period of the late nineteenth century was one in which the Yalbac Maya valued tradition and achieved a degree of cultural autonomy and subsistence through choice and selectivity in acquiring manufactured goods and subsistence self-sufficiency.

For example, the ceramic assemblage at the site included a wide variety of imported decorated serving wares, all of British manufacture (figure 4.5b). Unlike those used by British nationals—which would include many plates, tea cups, and saucers—most of the vessels at San Pedro were deeper forms, such as bowls or tureens. These apparently were more useful for local and preferred cuisine. Cookware largely comprised either iron cauldrons (figure 4.5c) or locally manufactured, large cooking vessels, some with evidence of soaking corn in lime (figure 4.5).

In addition to the possibility that they grew, smoked, and perhaps traded tobacco at San Pedro, a large number of pepper sauce bottles probably indicates rebottling locally produced honey rather than using store-bought products; this they could potentially have traded or sold for cash, as did the Lacandon to the west (Palka 2005). There were also a large number of alcohol bottles including wine, case (whiskey), rum, and various demijohns. Villagers may have consumed alcoholic beverages, or they may have reused these bottles after the contents were gone. One former San José resident indicated in strong terms that San Pedro and San José were dry villages; however, it seems unlikely that so many bottles discarded and broken and swept to the edge of the yard area would have derived only from recycling uses. Sewing machine parts, a bottle of sewing machine oil, and any number of pairs of scissors suggest a cottage industry of some sort, perhaps making *huipiles* (traditional blouses) of Yucatec design. There clearly was access to some luxury items, such as French perfume and costume jewelry, indicating a small cash economy, which may have involved trade with local logging crews, merchants in Cayo, or itinerant traders who were also in the Petén to the west (Palka 2005).

LAND AS HOSTAGE

However, despite an apparent dogged determination for autonomy and self-reliance among the Yalbac Hills Maya, their occupation of those lands was precarious, as the legal framework for their destabilization was already in place. In fact, the combination of British Honduran land tenure laws allowed land to be used as a hostage—to compel desired action on the part of the Maya through blocking their access to it. Because the Honduras Land Titles Act had allowed British forestry companies to purchase almost all of northern and western British Honduras and because the Maya were prohibited from owning land, as the logging crews penetrated the area, the Maya of the Yalbac Hills region were eventually obliged to pay rent on company lands for both house plots and agricultural fields. The burden of rents pushed the Maya to participate more fully in the colonial cash economy perhaps with less choice and to relinquish some self-sufficiency.

The Yalbac Hills Maya must have continued to sell agricultural produce, honey, tobacco, and other handmade items to woodcutting crews working in the area in order to pay rents. By the 1930s, the Creole mahogany crews generally did not have cash on hand at the camps,[6] but this may not have been the case earlier in British Honduras and was not the case in logging camps in the Petén in earlier periods where Lacandon either worked for cash or traded (Palka 2005). The oral narratives of Maya who lived in San José in the 1930s indicate that sometimes the mahogany workers traded their food rations of salt pork and wheat flour to Maya villagers for their agricultural products. Some of this information indicated that men from San José on occasion would travel to Cayo to trade or would trade with itinerant merchants.

People who were children in San José in the 1930s told us that to pay their rents, their fathers worked on support crews for the mahogany companies or in *chicle* (natural gum) bleeding. The *chicleros* often set out for months at a time, sometimes deep into the Petén forest to the west in Guatemala, harvesting the chicle tree's sap to satisfy the growing taste for chewing gum in the United States.[7]

Around 1900, San Pedro was abandoned, for reasons that may have included a drought, a slump in the demand for mahogany (Church et al. 2011:191), and epidemic disease (Jones 1977:151).[8] At this point, San José became the largest town in the Yalbac Hills region.

LAND AS POLLUTANT

Designs on the lands of San José reached a violent climax in the 1930s, symbolized by the transformation of "soil" (Maya: *lu'um*) into "dust" (Spanish: *polvo*), as described below. How the Maya used the land was ever-more circumscribed by the Belize Estate and Produce Company (BEPCO), which was often simply referred to as "The Company."

The centrality of BEPCO in the colony can hardly be overstated. In December 1935, when the company manager, C. S. Brown, was running for a seat on the Legislative Council, he reiterated a line of argument that the company frequently used in bargaining for preferential treatment from the colonial government:

> *The Company's interests are the Orange Walk District's interests. I can go further than that and state that the Company's Interests are the Colony's interests. The Company owns about one-fifth of the Colony. The Company has been the stand-by of the Colony for the past 50–65 years. The Company is the largest taxpayer in the Colony. The Company is the largest and most considerate employer in the Colony. At the present time the Company's lands and works give employment to over 1,000 men. The Company is the largest and most considerate landowner and landlord in the Colony. The Company stands for progress. (Fair Play 1936)*

Mahogany for several decades had been the colony's largest export. In fact, from 1926 to 1935 forest produce (primarily mahogany, and secondarily, chicle) accounted for 83 percent of total exports (Burns 1936a). Repeatedly, the company had been able to leverage its economic importance into favorable government policies.[9] It argued that if it were not for the company, hundreds of people would have been unemployed, there would be no income with which to purchase the imports upon which British Hondurans depended, and the colony's tax base would collapse. As a consequence of the company's importance, one of the appointed ("unofficial") seats on the Legislative Council was generally reserved for the manager of the company (Bolland 2003:162). The company also generally held a seat on the Forest Trust. In fact, in July 1935 the governor reappointed C. S. Brown as a member of the Forest Trust (Government Gazettes 1935).

The company's power extended beyond the tiny Caribbean colony. It was owned by the Hoare brothers in London (Sir Samuel John Gurney Hoare and Sir Oliver Vaughn Gurney Hoare). Sir Samuel Hoare, the First Viscount Templewood, had been elected to the House of Commons in 1910; he was made secretary of state for air in 1922. In 1931, he became secretary of state for India and, finally, in 1935 achieved the position of foreign secretary. The archival documents reveal that when Sir Oliver Hoare wrote to someone in the Colonial Office on Downing Street, he quickly received a personal meeting, and recommendations favorable to the company were sent to the governor in British Honduras (e.g., "Belize Estate and Produce Company" n.d.).

As mahogany stands closer to the coast had become depleted, BEPCO moved its operations westward into the San José area. Its headquarters had been centered at Orange Walk in the colony's northeast. Mahogany logs from the interior were cut, hauled by cattle to the rivers, and floated downstream for export to England and the United States from the mouth of the New River. The company typically had three camps in operation at any one time, the camps being temporary, typically having a life of from one to three years (Whiting 1939). As hardwoods became exhausted in the north, however, BEPCO moved its headquarters from Orange Walk to Hill Bank, on the western edge of the New River Lagoon. In the 1920s, it constructed a logging railway westward from Hill Bank, its endpoint some five miles to the northeast of San José (Surveyor General 1936).[10]

Relations between BEPCO and its Maya tenants came to a head in 1935, for several reasons. First was the matter of the mahogany trees. Although BEPCO tenants were not allowed to burn forest to make milpa in the traditional swidden agricultural practice, so long as the mahogany camps were at a distance, Maya farmers had been able to do so surreptitiously. By the early 1930s, though, BEPCO had established a logging camp next to San José, and the Maya could no longer engage in swidden. The oral narratives reveal that some families tried to farm continuously on the same plot, with diminishing yields; others persisted in burning forest to create new fields, angering the company manager, C. S. Brown. In an apparent effort to defend the company against criticism regarding events in the western forests, in a campaign speech in December 1935, Brown estimated that milpa burning around the Yalbac Hills towns of San José, Yalbac, and Xaxe Venic (also Kaxil Uinic) resulted in mahogany losses to the company estimated at $300,000 (Contributed 1935).[11]

Second was the issue of rent. Maya tenants on BEPCO lands had to pay rents to the company, yet according to the oral interviews, the company regularly rejected cash payments and demanded labor in lieu of payment, typically clearing brush and gathering fodder for the cattle. Some claimed that the amount of labor required was excessive and, further, that the tenants had been denied a deserved refund. Land taxes had been increased in 1928, and the company in turn raised rents. Tensions mounted when it was revealed that the company had paid only a portion of the additional taxes and was several thousands of dollars in arrears. Then in 1935, when the new land tax was repealed, tenants were angered that none of the additional rent they had paid was going to be refunded (Editorial 1935).

The greatest affront was the penetration and pollution of the village sacred and social space, symbolized by the transformation of soil into "dust." Company workers had been using a tractor to haul logs over the road that ran through the center of San José, right in front of the church. They would pile the logs in the space used for cricket and dancing, to which the villagers objected repeatedly. Besides the noise and the danger to children, the hauling of the logs sent up a cloud of dust that wafted into the church. *Lu'um* is a Yucatec Maya word that means both "soil" and "dirt," but in several of the interviews, villagers engaged in code switching and substituted the Spanish word *polvo* (dust) to refer to the dirt kicked up by the tractor and logs. As Mary Douglas (1966:35) notes, dirt is "matter out of place." What, as lu'um is the source of sustenance and abundance, once transformed by the tractor and logs into polvo, becomes a pollutant of the village's central sacred and social spaces.

In April 1935, the brother of the alcalde hit a BEPCO tractor driver with a stick as he hauled logs in front of the church, resulting in a criminal case. The tractor driver asserted that he was hit several times, while the alcalde's brother said that he hit him once to gain his attention because the villagers had told Brown (the manager) that the tractors should not pass in front of the church (Orange Walk Soliloquies 1935).

Several months passed, during which time company and colonial officials deliberated how to resolve the dispute. During this time, C. S. Brown conducted his campaign for an elected seat on the Legislative Council. He lost the race to Robert Turton, the largest chicle supplier to Wrigley's in the colony, but a few weeks later, the governor announced that Brown would be one of the appointed members to the Legislative Council, nonetheless. A letter to the editor stated, "Mr. Brown perhaps is a good man but he is the Manager of the Belize Estate & Produce Company;

and if the people of this Colony fear nothing else they seem to have a tremendous fear for the Belize Estate & Produce Company" (Laing 1936). This letter hints at BEPCO's ability to act with near impunity. In that vein, company management decided to evict the San José villagers. With approval of the governor and the king, BEPCO arranged to transfer some of its lands to the crown as an inalienable "trust" for the villagers, in an area just south of the former BEPCO headquarters in Orange Walk. The new settlement was called San José Palmar (San José of the Palms, but more commonly called San José Nuevo.[12]

In April 1936, San José villagers were loaded into logging railway carts and, following the same route as the mahogany logs that were the source of their conflict with BEPCO, they were taken to Hill Bank on the lagoon.[13] They were put on a barge and sent down river, on a trip lasting three days. They were given temporary residence in a space in Orange Walk known as the "barracks," the site of the former army barracks, then used as communal pasture and playground.[14] The barracks in Orange Walk was the site of the last big Indian attack in the colony in 1872, when a band of Icaiche Maya led by Marcos Canul was repelled and their leader mortally wounded. Placing the San José Maya at the barracks location may have been read by some contemporaries as symbolic of defeat. Employees of BEPCO burned the village of San José, including houses, church, school (which, while administered by the Catholic Church, had been funded by the colonial government), and agricultural fields. In our interviews, many elders were especially distressed that their animals were left behind to fend for themselves or starve. Villagers lived in tents in the barracks for a few months, where they were fed rations of rice while they cleared forest and built new thatch houses at San José Palmar. The eviction did not slow company production that year. In fact, while mahogany exports had experienced a dip early in the 1930s, owing to slumping demand during the Great Depression, between 1935 and 1936 the number of square feet of mahogany logs exported more than doubled (from 1,913 to 4,843 square feet), owing to increased American demand, especially for the large logs of the western limestone region (Burns 1936a).

LAND AS HOMELAND AND WELLSPRING

In the barracks the evictees experienced an immediate health crisis. Back in San José Yalbac, the elevation is relatively high and it is removed from the coast, so malaria is not a problem. Orange Walk is lower and nearer the coast, and malaria is endemic. The year 1936 saw heavy rains and an increase in the mosquito population. The evictees moved into their new village, impoverished, malnourished, and sick. These factors, all of which followed from their dislocation, made them particularly vulnerable to a whooping cough epidemic that spread through the northern districts in mid-1936. The medical officer of the Orange Walk District reported: "The course of the epidemic was attended with the highest mortality in the village of San José. In this small community of 30 families 45 deaths occurred chiefly among infants and children of school age. A combination of factors—increasing poverty with its sequel malnutrition, chronic malaria and ankylostomiasis [hookworm] has lowered the vitality of the people and rendered them highly susceptible to the graver complications of the disease" (Degazon 1936). By way of comparison, in 1936 the infant mortality rate for the whole colony was 152.7 per 1,000 live births; in the Orange Walk District it was 281.4 (up from 247.6 from the previous year) (Annual Medical and Sanitary Report 1936). That year, Orange Walk was the only district to experience a net natural loss (of forty people), attributed to disease (Vital Statistics, 1936). In a report to the secretary of state for the colonies, the governor commented on his August 1936 visit to San José Palmar, indicating that he admonished the villagers for not making greater progress in building their new homes, threatening that if they did not do so, he would not give funding toward their school and he would instruct the district commissioner not to give them jobs working on the district's roads; he acknowledged, though, that the lethargy they exhibited was related to malnutrition and hookworm (Burns 1936b).

The way that San José elders talk about their former village (design of the land) reveals that their landscape memories are a moral discourse—a way in which they encode a vision of the good life and a moral critique of those responsible for their removal. These narratives are therefore a key element of the intangible heritage of the Yalbac Hills Maya and intangible residue of colonialism. According to several of the interviewees, the illnesses and deaths experienced in the aftermath of the eviction were directly related to the insalubrious nature of San José Palmar in comparison with what they call San José Viejo (Old San José). Notably, while official documents recorded the new place-name as San José Palmar (San José of the Palms), elders doggedly refer to it as San José Nuevo (New San José). This appellation underscores that the new town exists only in reference and in comparison to Old San José, the homeland. New San José, through its very name, connotes their dislocation. While the medical officer blamed the deaths of 1936 on whooping cough, hookworm, and malaria, the oral narratives emphasize the contrast between the healthy environment of Old San José and the unhealthy one of New San José. The narrators note that, back in Old San José, they had drunk cool water directly from a clean spring; in New San José there were no wells or springs, so they had to drink brackish water from streams and swamps. In Old San José, they say, the soils were deep and rich; in New San José, the soils sandy and harvests meager.

Perhaps most important, in Old San José they were able to cultivate corn. For millennia, corn has been the mainstay of the Maya diet, and an ancient Maya belief held that the gods fashioned humans from corn dough. As is often remarked by Yucatec Maya speakers in Yucatán, San José elders commented that corn is really the only thing that fills them up. In milpa farming, it is the primary crop and forms the bulk of the diet in the form of tortillas, a variety of corn gruels (*atoles*), thickeners for stews, tamales, corn on the cob, and so on. The archaeological abundance of local ceramics with and without lime residues, as well as the preference for deeper serving and eating vessels of refined British wares at San Pedro—vessels capable of holding stews, beans, corn gruels, and soups—reflects the centrality of corn in the Yalbac Hills diet. Furthermore, the assemblage included virtually no individual settings or pieces of flatware; the only metal spoons were serving spoons. This likely reflects the common Maya practice of using folded pieces of tortilla as a scoop for liquid foods or to pinch off pieces of solid foods such as roasted meat. In Yucatec Maya, the primacy of the tortilla is noted semantically: eating with tortillas is "eating" (*janal*); breakfast, since it does not include tortillas, is just "drinking" (*uk'ul*). Many of the San José elders told us that the rice rations that they were given in the barracks in Orange Walk did not fill them up, contributing to their illnesses. As they were denied food suitable for human beings, they were, by implication, treated inhumanely.

Finally, many noted that sadness itself killed some in the barracks. In Yucatec Maya, *k'oja'anil* (sickness) means both physical sickness and mental or emotional sickness, underlying the connection between body and mind. A body that is *k'oja'an* (sick) from emotional sickness is physically ill, as well. One woman commented that her father died of sadness just eight days after they arrived in the barracks. Overall, the memories of the eviction configure Old San José as homeland and as wellspring, as salubrious land, providing in abundance all of the elements needed to sustain healthy bodies and minds. This particular design of the land (landscape memory) is a biting moral critique of those responsible for their eviction and also honors and celebrates the subsistence lifeways of their ancestors.

LAND AS COMMERCIAL FARM

In the cruelest of ironies, shortly after the eviction, BEPCO's owners gave up on the Yalbac Hills, and the colonial government turned its attention to commercial agriculture. In the early 1930s, as Creoles gained some political traction within the colony and as the Great Depression dropped a bombshell of hunger on the colony ("Conditions in British Honduras [1935]" n.d.; "Unemployment Situation [1934–1935]" n.d.), an alternative design on the land was gaining traction. This emerging view was the land as a plantation, as a large agricultural field on which to grow commercial crops destined for domestic and foreign markets ("Land Settlement [1936]" n.d.). While BEPCO had been angling for hurricane reconstruction funds and tax breaks ("Belize Estate and Produce Company: Future Management of Lands, 1931–1932" n.d.), others in the colonial administration, including the governor, were urgently promoting an alternative design on the land—that of government support for commercial farms ("Agricultural Development, 1932–1933" n.d.), and in 1936 the governor created the colony's first Board of Agriculture (Burns 1936a). By 1938, worldwide demand for mahogany had slumped, due to a preference for steel in railway carriages and furniture and an emerging preference for walnut over mahogany in cabinetry (Whiting 1938).

This new design on the land recast the government's relationship with BEPCO. In 1929, British Honduran Legislative Council members had argued against the sale of BEPCO lands to a US company, Messrs. Mengel ("Belize Estate and Produce Company: Future Management of Lands, 1931–1932" n.d.). Thirteen years later, when BEPCO sold 90 percent of its stock (the controlling share) to Glicksten, a US-based company, the governor and Legislative Council were quiet ("Belize Estate and Produce Company, Ltd., 1941" n.d.). The people of San José Yalbac had been evicted in 1936 in favor of the design on the land of extractive commodities, yet just a few short years later that design was slipping into the background as businessmen chased profits on plantations. Legislative Council members, the governor, and post-Depression social welfare advisers saw commercial agriculture as the key to economic diversification, strength, and social stability.

The Yalbac Hills area was peripheral in this new design on the land. With its hilly topography and soil that is often thin, the area was poorly suited to early mechanized agriculture. The hills were also located far from large permanent settlements that constituted the year-round labor pool needed for commercial agriculture. Further, they were poorly integrated in the developing transportation networks, far both from the ports where cash crops were exported and from markets in the larger settlements.

The logging activities at Hill Bank, San José, Xaxe Venic, and Yalbac have long since ceased and populations dispersed. In the 1930s, though, the company moved in aggressively, displaced settled villages, and moved on again just as quickly. However, no one was left unsullied. In June 1936, C. S. Brown took a six-month leave of absence, returned to England (Happenings and Comments 1936), and was replaced by another manager (Whiting 1938).

LAND AS ALIENABLE HOUSE PLOT

Many of the evictees in New San José and their descendants became wage workers on the expanding sugarcane plantations in the northern districts that were an integral component of this new design on the land. The land set aside for the evictees was never formally recognized as a reserve, and many elders in our interviews remained uneasy that a copy of the trust papers issued by the king was given to the Ministry (of Natural Resources?) and not returned to them. The land beneath their feet felt unsteady. Beginning in the 1980s, some villagers wanted to use house plots as collateral for loans. A committee representing the "San José Palmar Indians" and the Trustee Agent (the Minister of Natural Resources) recommended that the land allotted to them, which had previously been managed as a communal resource, be divided into house plots (Minister of Natural Resources 1996), which as alienable property could be sold. This is the state of land tenure in the community as of our writing.

CONCLUSION

As we have seen, chased out of Yucatán by war and its predations, a group of Yucatec Maya eventually settled in the Yalbac Hills, only to have their descendants evicted from their homes at San José several decades later due to a mahogany extraction scheme, which in turn lost steam a few short years after that. Caught in a maelstrom of desperation, hunger, malnutrition, and political infighting in the Great Depression, San José villagers were removed to a reservation that was ill suited to sustain them, and many succumbed to disease. The village fragmented as one group took its chances on a new life in Santa Familia to the south.

Despite these devastating losses and the rupture of the material connection to the Old San José, certain memories and ways of talking about Old San José are a key element of the intangible heritage of the Yalbac Hills Maya. These landscape memories are the *designs of the land* that persist into the present. Physical distance cannot sever the ties forged by memory. Memories of the homeland arouse the emotions of those who experienced the eviction, as the new settlement is always referred to as "new" and is considered a poor substitute for the favorable environment of the old.

The eviction overwhelms historical memory and identity, and identity is colored by absence. The old, lost place is remembered as salubrious—as providing, as a matter of nature, the elements required for bodily health, including rich soils, corn, safe water, and cool air. The deep forest, its abundant resources for gathering, hunting, fishing, farming, and material culture, and the knowledge of their forebears of how to live well in that environment—these memories are treasured by the older generations. The land that was lost is envisioned and lamented not solely as a place where people lived, but as a place where people thrived. While Belize now looks outward to global tourism and new forms of commercial trade, the colonial primacy of mahogany is long forgotten, except by those who refuse to forget. Landscape memory—-memories of places and their peoples—in this respect is both heritage from the past and a force of agentive action toward an idealized future.

NOTES

1. One group lives in Santa Familia (Cayo District) and another group lives in San José Palmar, or San José Nuevo (Orange Walk District). In 2003, Yaeger interviewed ten in Spanish. In 2005, Kray interviewed the same ten plus four more using Yucatec Maya, though some had become so Spanish dominant that they switched back and forth between languages.

2. "Indian" attacks on woodcutter camps were reported as early as 1788 (Bolland 1977b:72), and fresh attacks in 1847 reignited British fears of "wild Indians." In that year, Maya groups attacked mahogany camps on the Rio Bravo and Belize Rivers, New River Lagoon, and Hill Bank (Bolland 1977b:74). O. Nigel Bolland (1977b:74) suggests that these attacks might have been led by Maya from the Yalbac Hills because that area was equidistant from those three. This scenario may be accurate. Counter to assertions by colonial administrators, archaeological data leads us to conclude that there were people living in San Pedro prior to 1862.

3. In 1865, Marcos Canul of Icaiche demanded rent from the BHC for mahogany taken along the Río Bravo "plus back rent of $2000 for the eight years in which the works had been located there" (Dumond 1997:274). The Río Bravo is north of San Pedro but in relatively close proximity.

4. According to Grant Jones (1977:158), in February 1867 a group from San José had attacked the BHC settlement at Indian Church and demanded that rent be paid to San Pedro or Hill Bank. In contrast, Don Dumond (1997:278) says only that men from San Pedro or San José were suspected as the ones placing the demands.

5. Those fleeing San José created a new settlement called Cerro, which was burned by the British the following month (Jones 1977:158).

6. Although testimony given before the West India Royal Commission in the late 1930s is internally contradictory, all of the testimonials imply that the mahogany crews at the camps would not have had cash for purchases outside of the company store. Kemp indicated that workers were paid in scrip redeemable at the company store and with weekly rations consisting of salt pork and flour (Kemp 1938). The Managing Director of BEPCO reported that the Creole mahogany workers generally insisted on receiving the full amount of their cash payment (outside of their food rations) in an advance contract prior to the season, to leave it in Belize City with their families (Whiting 1939). Then, with little income left, they would buy items on credit at the commissary, leading to a state of perpetual indebtedness that would obligate them to return to work for the company the following year (West India Royal Commission 1941).

7. Chicle bleeding appears not to have become a major economic strategy for Yalbac Hills residents until the second decade of the twentieth century. The first time that *chiclero* is listed as the occupation of a parent of a child born in San José is 1917 ("Cayo District Births, 1885–1931." n.d.).

8. The date of the last births recorded for San Pedro was 1896 ("Cayo District Births, 1885–1931" n.d.).

9. For example, after the devastating hurricane of 1931, the company was able to secure a hurricane reconstruction loan from the colonial government of $200,000, which it used to build a sawmill in Belize City, to export sawn lumber to Europe, which was greatly preferred to whole logs (Whiting 1938).

10. Tellingly, in twenty-six pages of colonial government discussion in 1922 of various proposals to build a railway into the western districts for the purpose of extracting mahogany, no mention was made of people living in the region (Despatches 1922).

11. The document did not specify over what period of time those losses occurred. Colonial Executive Council minutes of January 2, 1935, note that BEPCO had also evicted the people of the Yalbac Hills village of Xaxe Venic in 1929 (Executive Council 1935).

12. The Colonial Office documents regarding the eviction ("Reports the removal . . ." 1936) have been culled ("destroyed under statute") from the National Archives in England. Details are therefore pulled together from oral histories and other archival materials, such as newspaper accounts.

13. A small group of villagers did not want to go to the Orange Walk area and, with family connections, went to Santa Familia (Cayo District) instead.

14. Just prior to this, the Orange Walk District Board wanted to donate the barracks as a government agricultural station because it cost $200 a year to clean and represented a drain on taxpayer resources (Orange Walk Soliloquies 1935).

REFERENCES

"Agricultural Development, 1932–1933." n.d. CO 123/337/8. London: National Archives.

Annual Medical and Sanitary Report. 1936. "Annual Medical and Sanitary Report for the Year Ending 31st December, 1936." In *Administration Reports, 1936–1937*. CO 126/35. London: National Archives.

"Belize Estate and Produce Company, Ltd., 1941." n.d. CO 123/382/6. London: National Archives.

"Belize Estate and Produce Company: Future Management of Lands, 1931–1932." n.d. CO 123/335/6. London: National Archives.

Bolland, O. Nigel. 1977a. *The Formation of a Colonial Society: Belize, From Conquest to Crown Colony*. Baltimore: Johns Hopkins University Press.

Bolland, O. Nigel. 1977b. "The Maya and the Colonization of Belize in the Nineteenth Century." In *Anthropology and History in Yucatán*, ed. Grant D. Jones, 69–99. Austin: University of Texas Press.

Bolland, O. Nigel. 1987. "Alcaldes and Reservations: British Policy towards the Maya in Late Nineteenth Century Belize." *America Indigena* 47 (1): 33–75.

Bolland, O. Nigel. 2003. *Colonialism and Resistance in Belize: Essays in Historical Sociology.* 2nd ed. Cave Hill, Barbados: University of the West Indies Press.

Burns, Governor Alan. 1936a. "Annual Report on the Social and Economic Progress of the People of British Honduras, 1936." CO 123/362/10. London: National Archives.

Burns, Governor Alan. 1936b. "Northern Districts, Governor's Visit to [1936]." CO 123/360/13. London: National Archives.

"Cayo District Births, 1885–1931." n.d. Cen 7. Belmopan: Belize Archives.

Church, Minette C., Jason Yaeger, and Jennifer L. Dornan. 2011. "The San Pedro Maya and the British Colonial Enterprise in British Honduras." In *Enduring Conquests: Rethinking the Archaeology of Resistance to Spanish Colonialism in the Americas,* ed. Matthew Liebmann and Melissa S. Murphy, 173–98. Santa Fe, NM: School for Advanced Research Press.

"Conditions in British Honduras [1935]." n.d. CO 123/352/15. London: National Archives.

Contributed. 1935. "Manager of Company in Political Arena." *Belize Independent* (December 25): 9. Belmopan: Belize Archives.

Cummings, Linda Scott. 2005. "Exploratory Pollen Analysis of Samples from San Pedro Siris, Belize." Paleo Research Institute Technical Report 04-111, Prepared for John Gust. Golden, CO: Paleo Research Institute.

Degazon, D. W. 1936. "Orange Walk District, Medical and Sanitary Report." In "Annual Medical and Sanitary Report for the Year Ending 31st December, 1936." In *Administration Reports, 1936–1937.* CO 126/35. London: National Archives.

Despatches. 1922. "No. 133: Construction of Railway to Tap Mahogany Forests." In *Despatches 1922, Apr.–Jun.* CO 123/311. London: National Archives.

Dornan, Jennifer Lynn. 2004. "'Even by Night We Only Become Aware They Are Killing Us': Agency, Identity, and Intentionality at San Pedro Belize (1857–1930)." PhD diss., Department of Anthropology, University of California, Los Angeles.

Douglas, Mary. 1966. *Purity and Danger: An Analysis of Concepts of Pollution and Taboo.* London: Routledge and Keegan Paul. http://dx.doi.org/10.4324/9780203361832.

Dumond, Don E. 1997. *The Machete and the Cross: Campesino Rebellion in Yucatán.* Lincoln: University of Nebraska Press.

Editorial. 1935. "Land Tax and Rentals." *Clarion* (February 14): 170A. Belmopan: Belize Archives.

Executive Council. 1935. "British Honduras, Executive Council Minutes, 1933–1935." CO 126/31. London: National Archives.

Fair Play. 1936. "Letter to the Editor, Signed 'Fair Play.'" *Daily Clarion* (January 17):1. Belmopan: Belize Archives.

Freiwald, Carolyn. n.d. "Preliminary Analysis of San Pedro Siris Faunal Remains." Unpublished manuscript prepared in 2006, in possession of authors.

Government Gazettes. 1935. *Government Gazettes, British Honduras, 1935.* CO 127/30. London: National Archives.

Gust, John R., III. 2006. "An Investigation of the Catchment and Resource Base of the Historic Period Village of San Pedro Siris, Belize." MA thesis, Applied Geography, Department of Geography and Environmental Studies, University of Colorado at Colorado Springs.

Happenings and Comments. 1936. *The Belize Independent (June 10): 10.* Belmopan: Belize Archives.

Jones, Grant D. 1977. "Levels of Settlement Alliance among the San Pedro Maya of Western Belize and Eastern Petén, 1857–1936." In *Anthropology and History in Yucatán,* ed. Grant D. Jones, 139–89. Austin: University of Texas Press.

Kemp, Luke Dinsdale. 1938. "Memorandum of Evidence: Working People of Belize." For the West Indies Royal Commission, 1938–1989. CO 950/330. London: National Archives.

Laing, E. A. 1936. "Hit or Miss: The Councils." *Daily Clarion* (February 24): 1–2. Belmopan: Belize Archives.

"Land Settlement [1936]." n.d. CO 123 355/5. London: National Archives.

Luke, S. E. 1931. Untitled Colonial Office Memorandum, May 10, 1931. In *Belize Estate and Produce Co., Claims to Lands on Western Frontier [1935].* CO 123/350/3. London: National Archives.

Minister of Natural Resources. 1996. "Cabinet Confidential: Memorandum No. 111 of 1996, San Jose Palmar Lands." Belmopan: Belize Archives.

Orange Walk Soliloquies. 1935. "Hillbank Case." *Clarion* (May 2): 465. Belmopan: Belize Archives.

Palka, Joel W. 2005. *Unconquered Lacandon Maya: Ethnohistory and Archaeology of Indigenous Culture Change.* Gainesville: University Press of Florida.

Reed, Nelson A. 2001. *The Caste War of Yucatán.* Rev. ed. Stanford: Stanford University Press.

"Reports the removal . . . ." 1936. "Reports the Removal of the Maya Village of San Jose to a New Site," dated March 30, 1936, no. 66682 from Gov. 78. Destroyed under statute, but indexed in CO 348/22. London: National Archives.

Rugeley, Terry. 1996. *Yucatán's Maya Peasantry and the Origins of the Caste War.* Austin: University of Texas Press.

Surveyor General. 1929. "Map A of 1929." In *"Belize Estate and Produce Co., Claims to Lands on Western Frontier, 1935."* CO 123/350/3. London: National Archives.

Surveyor General. 1936. "Appendix: Map of British Honduras." In *Forest Trust Report for the Year 1935*. In *British Honduras, Administration Reports, 1934–1935*. CO 126/32. London: National Archives.

"Unemployment Situation [1934–1935]." n.d. CO 123/346/4. London: National Archives.

Vital Statistics. 1936. "Report on the Vital Statistics of British Honduras for the Year 1936." In *Administration Reports, 1936–1937*. CO 126/35. London: National Archives.

West India Royal Commission. 1941. "Labour Conditions for Forest Workers, British Honduras, 1940–1941." CO 318/444/30. London: National Archives.

Whiting, P. E. 1938. Memorandum from BEPC [P. E. Whiting, Managing Director] to the West Indies Commission (Colonial Office, Downing Street), 2 Sept 1938. In *"Memorandum of Evidence: Belize Estate and Produce Co., Ltd.," 1938–1939, for the West India Royal Commission*. CO 950/23. London: National Archives.

Whiting, P. E. 1939. Confidential letter from P. E. Whiting (Managing Director of BEPC) to T.I.K. Lloyd (Secretary to the Commission), 31 May 1939. In *Memorandum of Evidence: Belize Estate and Produce Co., Ltd., 1938–1939, for the West India Royal Commission*. CO 950/23. London: National Archives.

5

Cultivating Community

The Archaeology of Japanese American Confinement at Amache

BONNIE CLARK

Many contributors to this volume explore how the archaeology of landscape is an anthropologically robust avenue for better understanding of place making. In this chapter archaeology yields compelling evidence for the depth of our human need for place even in the unlikeliest of locales: sites of confinement. Incarcerated peoples do not choose the location of their prisons, nor do they design them. Yet modifications made by inmates to their carceral landscapes are common and range from subtle, such as improvements to housing (Casella 2007), to monumental, such as creating parks (Helphand 2006). What these material traces suggest is that investment in place, which has long been of interest to archaeologists, need not be a long-term strategy.

The locales where Americans of Japanese ancestry were incarcerated during World War II provide an especially compelling opportunity for archaeologists to study these phenomena. Communities of people relocated to new environmental settings, these sites have much to contribute to the study of how and why people make places. Occupied just seventy years ago, they are also sites of living memory. As such they are locales where intangible and tangible heritage are irrevocably inter-twined. This chapter interprets the results of collaborative archaeology at Amache, one of the ten Japanese American internment camps in the United States (figure 5.1). It explores not just what we have learned from the tangible remains of the camp but also the ways that our studies contribute to new communities of memory.

The data presented here come from three field seasons at Amache, in 2008, 2010, and 2012. The project is ongoing, so what is presented here is a work in progress.

DOI: 10.5876/9781607325727.c005

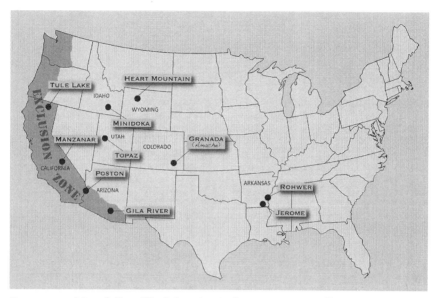

FIGURE 5.1. Map of all ten War Relocation Authority camps, as well as the zone from which Japanese Americans were removed during the war. The official name of the Colorado camp was the "Granada Relocation Center," but it is more commonly known as Amache. Map created by Anne Amati.

Each year we have engaged in intensive pedestrian survey of the blocks where internees were housed. Like all other areas of the site, buildings were removed when the camp was dismantled in 1945. Yet survey reveals significant archaeological remains including surface artifacts, as well as evidence of internee-created landscaping (Clark et al. 2012). Excavations have primarily focused on landscaping elements, especially gardens. These excavations employ intensive garden archaeology techniques with an eye to revealing design, plant materials, and soil management (Clark 2011). Our field and lab analysis call on the expertise of an archaeobotanist, a palynologist, and a soil chemist. Together we have faced the methodological challenges of archaeological research on such a recent cultural landscape, such as the analysis of uncharred seeds (Archer 2009).

The research at Amache was always designed as collaborative, beginning with community consultations years before our first field season. Our conversations with former internees range from informal chats at community events to recorded oral histories. Each field season we have been honored to be joined by former internees who visit the site and some who even work with our crews in the field. The results of "collaborating at the trowel's edge" (sensu Silliman 2008) greatly inform this chapter.

After a brief historic overview, it begins by exploring the variety of internee-created landscaping we find at Amache. These features reveal significant investment in remaking the cultural landscape. Close analysis of materials employed also reveal surprisingly intense networks in this involuntary community. Finally, the chapter explores the importance of this locale for survivors and their descendants, suggesting that prisonscapes remain important, if difficult, heritage sites.

AMACHE: THE PLACE AND THE PEOPLE

In 1942, in the wake of the bombing of Pearl Harbor, just over 120,000 Japanese and Japanese Americans were forcibly removed from the west coast of the United States. Most were imprisoned in internment camps in the country's interior. The rhetoric that justified this action sounds eerily similar to post-9/11 talk about security, terrorism, and divided loyalty. However, Japanese and other Asians in America had long been the target of ire, especially in areas where they lived in large numbers. Hindsight suggests that Japanese American internment was largely driven by racism against an already outsider group who could be visibly linked to an enemy aggressor nation (The Commission on Wartime Relocation and Internment of Civilians 1997).

Amache was designed by the War Relocation Authority (WRA), a civilian administration in charge of the Japanese American removal and internment. These "forced communities" followed a hybrid template of US military outposts and federal experiments in farmworker housing built primarily for migrants moving to California to escape the dust bowl (Horiuchi 2005). What the WRA called the Granada Project (named for the nearby town) encompassed over sixteen square miles, incorporating farmland and ranches to be worked by the internees (Simmons and Simmons 1993). At the center was the camp itself, a square mile surrounded by barbed wire and a series of guard towers manned by armed soldiers. The camp had an urban feel, with buildings laid out in a street grid of military precision. Some specialty community facilities were provided, such as a hospital and a purpose-built high school, but most activities took place in standard, military-issue buildings.

Most of the camp comprised blocks of barracks to house the internees. The twenty-nine such barracks blocks were almost exactly alike. Each held two rows of six barracks flanking two buildings, a mess hall and a combined laundry, a latrine, and a bathhouse. Each block also held a community building that tended to be a recreation hall, but was occasionally a church, and in a few instances it housed a campwide organization. Barrack buildings themselves were divided into six quarters, euphemistically termed "apartments," typically assigned to internee couples or families. Former internees who were children remember that it was terribly easy to get lost in this sea of regimentally laid-out, tarpaper-covered buildings.

The internees at Amache were sent there from primarily three locations: the northern coast of California, its Central Valley, and a neighborhood of southwest Los Angeles known in Japanese as the Seinan (DeWitt 1943). Despite being from different areas of the state, they were united by their occupations. A combination of racially restrictive hiring practices and experience in Japan, pushed the Issei, or first-generation immigrants, into agriculture. Before the war nearly 70 percent of Issei on the west coast had been involved in agriculture or agriculture-related businesses (Helphand 2006:158), a profile that fit those at Amache. The vast majority of internees from the Central Valley were farmers, including residents of three Japanese American farming colonies established before the passage of California laws restricting Asian ownership of land. The Seinan was an ethnically mixed neighborhood, but Japanese Americans predominated. The area held many produce stands, often affiliated with the truck farmers who lived in the neighborhood. On the eve of Pearl Harbor, over 15 percent of the Issei in the greater Los Angeles area were gardeners (Tsukashima 2000), and some of them lived in the Seinan. Other agriculture-related businesses in the area included nurseries, but it was home to other business owners and professionals. The residents from coastal California were of a more mixed professional background, but many were also involved in agriculture or maintenance gardening.

The significant horticultural skills of this population would be put to the test at Amache. Located on the High Plains of Colorado, the area is characterized by wind and little rainfall, and the on-site soil is almost entirely Aeolian-deposited sand. The region had been hard hit by the dust bowl and at the beginning of World War II was just beginning to recover. Despite the delicate nature of the soil, the WRA bulldozed the entire site prior to construction. As a result, the internees arrived in a moonscape devoid of any vegetation and characterized by nearly constant, gritty winds. Lili Sasaki recalled her arrival at Amache: "Everybody was shocked because there was nothing but sand and sandstorms and tumbleweeds. Not a thing to see" (cited in Helphand 2006:161).

GARDENS OF INGENUITY

Internees almost immediately set to changing the situation. Trees were transplanted from the Arkansas River, located three miles north of camp, or later purchased from an enterprising local nursery, which sold them to internees for fifty cents each. Thomas Shigekuni, whose family had owned a nursery, recalled that he and his brother took the lead in planting scores of trees in their block, 12G. Because of their training, they insisted the nursery also provide peat moss to better encourage the transplants in Amache's arid setting (personal communication, Shigekuni, 2011).

Evidence of their hard work remains, especially near the 12G mess hall, where a row of trees continues to thrive seventy years later.

An article in the camp newspaper, the *Granada Pioneer* (1943:5), tells a similar story of Kaneji Domato, who spearheaded the planting of trees in Block 6G. Archaeological research helps to refine our understanding of his contribution to the camp landscape. Intensive pedestrian surveying of nearly half the barracks blocks indicates that many had blockwide tree-planting schemes. Most of them appear to be fairly regimented, using even spacing and rectilinear plantings. However, Kaneji Domato appears to have arranged his trees in more natural groupings (Riggs 2013). Kaneji's father, Kanetaro Domato, ran a very successful nursery prior to the war. Kaneji had parlayed that experience, and university training in architecture, into a spot on the team that designed and built several Japanese-style gardens in the Bay Area, including the World's Fair on Treasure Island (Riggs 2013). His tree-planting scheme likely reflects his training in Japanese garden design, which tends to favor plantings that evoke nature rather than abstract geometry.

Regardless of their designs, both Mr. Shigekuni and Mr. Domato contributed significantly to improving the quality of life at Amache. Trees deterred erosion, brought green into the drab landscape, and provided shade for internees. This was particularly appreciated by the people who had to wait in line for their turn in the mess halls. If a block has only a few trees, we tend to find them shading the area adjacent to the mess hall.

Many, many others contributed to making over Amache anew. Historic photographs confirm what we see in survey; the internees at Amache did not just modify the landscape, they completely transformed it (figure 5.2). A good example is Block 9L, occupied primarily by residents from Los Angeles. As shown in this map derived from our intensive survey, only one pair, two of the twelve barracks, were not fronted with gardens obvious on the surface of the site (figure 5.3). Yet because there are trees planted in front of the other two barracks, it is likely that excavations would reveal they too had gardens. In addition to the barrack entryway gardens, Block 9L is landscaped in public spaces, including a pair of oval garden beds discovered during the original survey of Amache (Carrillo and Killam 2004). Test excavations in one of the beds provide evidence for different forms of investment in gardening.

Whoever designed the Block 9L garden features took great care in their design. Each bed is a precise oval of exactly the same size. Directly on the centerline of the bed, we recovered the remains of a Chinese Elm tree that had been planted there (figure 5.4). Off to one side we discovered a rectangular soil stain and some copper wire. It is very likely these are the result of staking the tree, giving it a fighting chance against the ravages of the local wind. Copper was rationed during the war,

FIGURE 5.2. Panorama of Amache showing common internee modifications to the landscape including tree plantings, gardens, and laundry lines. Image courtesy of the Amache Preservation Society.

so the wire we found was scavenged, or more likely stolen, from stores of camp construction materials. That is probably the same source for the cinderblock out of which the beds were made. Those who built the garden took great pains to hide the material's industrial nature; each block was carefully split into three portions and laid in a way that disguises the defining features of the block, its circular center holes. Without rather close inspection, the pieces appear to be carefully quarried basalt blocks, a material that would have been familiar to any gardener practicing in California.

Despite what appears on the surface to be a very Westernized design, whoever created the 9L garden was still informed by Japanese landscape principles. One of the most influential of these is *shakkei*, a literal translation of which is "borrowed scenery." This can be accomplished at multiple scales but is most clear when garden design accommodates distant views, such as natural woods (Itoh 1973). It was employed at other camp gardens, too. For example, some of the gardens at the California internment camp Manzanar are sited to draw the eye to particular mountain peaks (Helphand 2006:184). On the High Plains, the location of Amache affords fewer such opportunities. Still, the site is on a terrace above the Arkansas River, and in a few locations one sees the trees that line the riverbank. To the northeast also lies the small town of Granada, a view you can see from 9L because the

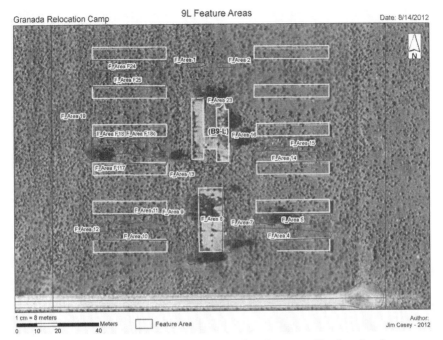

FIGURE 5.3. Block 9L at Amache with building foundations and landscaping features (labeled with feature number) discovered during survey, 2012. Map by Jim Casey.

block juts out east from all the other barracks blocks. Although not as majestic as the Sierra, the borrowed scenery at this Amache garden would have been reassuringly civilian. The importance of places that provided respite from the internment camp landscape is hard to overstate. Jeanne Wakatsuki Houston recalled that in the Manzanar gardens, facing away from the barracks, you could "for a while not be a prisoner at all" (Houston and Houston 1973:72).

The plant remains recovered from the 9L oval bed are likewise intriguing. We recovered high numbers of seed of the *Portulaca*, or purslane. This strongly suggests that a *Portulaca*, a weedy plant found around the world, may have been "deliberately grown as a ground cover for the garden feature, being a drought-tolerant, attractive choice for such a purpose... *Portulaca* does not seem to have tremendous significance in Japanese gardening traditions, but as abundantly evidenced elsewhere, Amache internees were adept at substituting or being inventive with local materials, including plant materials" (Archer 2009:5).

Research in two of the school-area entryway gardens indicates that place making through gardening was not confined to the Issei of the camp. A number of historic

FIGURE 5.4. Oval garden in Block 9L after test excavations, 2008. Remains of the tree planted in the center of the bed visible at the top of the image. Photograph by author.

records document the landscaping of the barracks block that was used as the elementary school. Like the rest of the camp, it had been denuded of all vegetation during construction. As the principal of the Amache school wrote in an education journal, "Passage from room to room, to library, office, or lavatory, could be attained only by stepping out in the periodic fury of dust and sand" (Dumas and Walther 1944:40).

The children of Amache were no doubt either aware of or recruited into the camp landscaping projects of the older generations. Those who landscaped with their families were likely among the children who approached the school administrators with the suggestion that the school also be thus transformed. In fact fifty children submitted landscaping plans for the school (Dumas and Walther 1944). The 2008 intensive survey in the school block suggests a similarity in the size, placement, and boundary hardscaping of the individual beds (Clark 2008). The edges of almost all the beds were delineated by limestone likely quarried from an outcropping within the boundaries of the camp. We excavated units in a pair of beds that flanked a doorway of one of the barracks used as a classroom. These two beds were approximately the same size and both bounded by limestone. However, excavation revealed that the children who designed and built them put into place quite different plans. One of these beds was landscaped with consistently sized gravel that almost certainly came from the banks of the Arkansas River. The adjacent bed had no gravel at all. From one bed we recovered ornamental morning glory seeds (*Ipomoea*) but none from the other. Morning glory is not only a traditionally valued ornamental, but its quickly growing vines would have effectively hidden the military architecture of the camp.

The excavations at the elementary school demonstrate that some Japanese American children had already learned a good deal about transforming the land and were applying that knowledge to the arid setting of the camp in very different ways. They were growing into their own aesthetic understandings of what is appropriate in an entryway garden, a type of landscape that has long precedent in Japan (Helphand 2006).

A final example of commitment to making Amache a better place comes from our studies of the site's soil chemistry. From the onset of our research, we have investigated if and how the internees were amending the nutritionally poor soil of the site. Studies in 2008 suggested higher carbon content in the soil samples from gardens, which could indicate soil amendment. However, the results were not definitive due to the ubiquity of clinker and coal, which was burned throughout the camp. Broadening the nutrient analysis in the 2010 research design allowed for a more fine-grained approach. What we found was that nutrient content was both higher and more spatially concentrated in samples taken from garden features (Marín-Spiotta and Eggleston 2011). Microartifacts recovered from garden contexts—crushed eggshell, fish scales and bones, and even fragments of iron slag—provide evidence of the variety of soil amendments camp gardeners employed. Given the short period of occupation and the "overly drained" (Natural Resources Conservation Service n.d.) nature of the sediments on site, the presence of such a definitive chemical signature seventy years later is an amazing legacy of internee care for the soil.

Collectively the evidence from the gardens suggests significant effort and care expended on what was essentially a prison. The internees had no say in where they lived and plenty of reasons to suspect they would be uprooted again at any time. Their investment of time, energy, and precious monetary resources would seem at the least ironic, if not downright counterintuitive. Such a position, however, is only tenable without a cultural knowledge of the Nikkei (people of Japanese descent) in the United States. Many fit Lawson Inada's description of his farmer uncle: "He lived with the land, on the land, and was *of* the land" (Inada 1997:32, emphasis original). Poet Sankyaku Seki, himself an American immigrant from Japan, links gardening to "Nikkei consciousness" (Seki 2007:38). A site visitor whose parents were confined at Amache interpreted the plethora of gardens there succinctly: "We're Japanese. We grow things. It's what we do."

The anthropology of place provides another avenue to understanding this data. Among the displaced, claiming territory, even if briefly, provides a psychological sense of belonging. This urge has been revealed through the archaeology of the homeless, who use a variety of place-making techniques from caching to graffiti (Zimmerman and Welch 2011). In Hong Kong, Filipino domestic laborers take over a small part of the city on their one day off. Little Manila is primarily a temporary sense-scape, marked by the smells and sounds of their home country (Law 2005). As Law's work suggests, such efforts at claiming territory are even more effective when, as in gardens, multiple senses are engaged. By making Amache look, smell, perhaps even sound more like home, its gardeners reaffirmed their sense of self, while normalizing the surroundings for their entire community. In that way they performed a service perhaps even more satisfying and valuable than keeping the dust down.

CULTIVATING COMMUNITY

Close examination of the gardens also reveals networks and innovative strategies that brought the whole Granada project—the barracks blocks, the service areas, and the associated farms and ranches—together. Although shortages and rationing were experienced widely during wartime, access to materials was even more limited for internees. Many internee families not only had lost their source of income, but their assets had also been seized. These were the families hardest hit economically, and many of them chose to take jobs in camp to support their families. All in camp had been restricted to what they could carry when they left first for the temporary assembly centers and then the more permanent internment camps. It was, to put it very bluntly, a materials-poor environment. As evidenced in the gardens of 9L, the setting gave rise to a thriving underground network of recycled or repurposed items and purloined materials.

One of the entryway gardens we excavated in 2010 provides evidence for a number of the projectwide networks that supported such features. This garden, which is directly in front of the barrack occupied in 1945 by Saiichiro and Bun Hirota, was amended throughout with the judicious use of crumbled eggshell. A former internee who visited us that summer recalled that eggshell, tea leaves, and coffee grounds were all highly prized soil amendments. As she told me, not everyone had access to them: you had to know people who worked in the mess halls. Another source for the eggshell could have been the chicken-raising facilities at the project ranch. Workers with access to chickens would have had access to eggshell as well. We also strongly suspect that ranch workers had access to an even more valued soil amendment: manure.

The Hirota entryway garden also employed broken water pipes. These were ingeniously placed upright and sunk into the ground for use as planters. Because they were certainly broken before the gardeners got them, they likely reflect connection to someone who had access to the camp's trash. Internees employed in the sanitation division made regular rounds of the camp and dumped the trash in an area beyond the guarded boundary fence.

Finally, like almost all of the gardens we have excavated at the camp, the Hirota garden yielded a variety of wire of varying gauges. A seemingly pedestrian material, wire appears to have been very valuable in camp. It exhibits a wide range of uses in gardens, from homemade fencing, to hangers for ornaments, to tree supports. Made of metals required for the war effort, wire was rationed during the war. It was not available through popular mail-order catalogs such as Sears-Roebuck, which oral histories indicate was an important source for items in camp. There was a hardware store in Granada, the town just over one mile away from Amache. However, whatever supply of wire it might have had in stock would have been quickly exhausted by the internee population, which was about ten times that of the town. Once that wire was gone, there would have been no replacing it. Much more likely is that the wire in this garden was among the many items internees "liberated" from the WRA stockpiles.

Whereas the materials of gardens are evidence of projectwide networks, the design of key gardens reveal the image that internees were presenting at the community level. This is perhaps most obvious in the garden that internees built in block 6H. One of the first occupied blocks, the recreation building there served as the office for elected representatives from each barracks block. The block managers' office was also known as Amache City Hall. The public space adjacent to it held one of the most elaborate gardens in camp. The centerpiece of the garden was a small hill and pond garden featuring a kidney-shaped pond with a bridge and islands of plantings adjacent to a hardscaped hill. With its roots in the strolling gardens of the Edo period, hill and pond features are quite typical elements of Japanese-style gardens in the United States. Harmonious, beautiful, and also almost stereotypically "Japanese," this garden was a place where Amache residents presented themselves both to each other and to outsiders. This image making is documented in a wide variety of photographs taken there of community leaders and visiting dignitaries. This garden, which was excavated by a group of local high school students prior to any formal archaeology at the camp, remains to this day a powerful part of the visual iconography of Amache. Not surprisingly, this garden is also an important place for former internees and their relatives. It is among the ten stops on the current iPod tour of the camp. By constructing this locale with such care, Amache's gardeners created a graceful symbol of their community, one that continues to serve that purpose today.

Reclaiming Memory at Amache

The archaeology of Amache has been significantly energized by collaboration with former internees and their families. Our knowledge has been "thickened" by memory and personal photographs. Syntheses such as those elaborated above paint a much more vibrant picture than any specific line of evidence alone could do. This would seem impetus enough to do engaged research there. But the significance of archaeology at Amache, as at other sites with a shadowed history, goes much deeper. An ongoing, place-based research project provides multiple opportunities for community members to reclaim a connection to a difficult past (see also Saitta 2007). In the case of sites of Japanese confinement, what former members confront is a legacy of silence. The choice by most Issei not to discuss their experience has been interpreted as a coping mechanism (Nagata 1993). Yet what this narrative disjuncture caused was an entire community whose shared experience was treated like a family secret (Yee 1995). Silence about internment is not so much a tear in the family narrative as it is a black hole, a force that bends the fields of memory while itself remaining invisible. Yet the site remains, a physical manifestation of this experience.

Promoting our field school to the community of former internees, as well as Japanese American organizations, has been a priority for each one of our three field seasons. We invite people to come visit us throughout our four weeks in the field and especially at our open house day. These popular events allow local residents and tourists a chance to see firsthand the results of our month of research. We make special arrangements for former Amache internees and their families, preparing by researching something of their family history in camp. They are interested in our research as a whole, participating in our field lab and museum activities excitedly. Yet beyond that experience all open house visitors have, almost all the Amacheans want to visit the exact location where they or their families lived in camp.

Many of the ten internment camps have had significant impact to the blocks that housed internee barracks. For example at Heart Mountain in Wyoming, only the administrative area still maintains physical integrity. The barracks blocks are now agricultural fields. Manzanar retains high integrity, but it had only concrete piers for barrack foundations. This makes the exact location of any family barrack both more difficult to ascertain and hard to visualize. At Amache, the barracks had continuous concrete foundations, which are still present and visible on the site surface in most blocks. The three doorways had lowered thresholds, so it is easy to bring people to the exact doorway of their barrack then to direct them right or left to the living unit itself.

This is an invariably powerful moment. Those who were older during their incarceration often walk me or their family members through the room—indicating who slept where, perhaps noting the location of their few homemade furnishings. Others tell stories of events that happened in that room or of family and friends in

FIGURE 5.5. Excavation crew chief and former internee volunteer talk at the site of her family's barrack. Photograph by Wayne Armstrong. Courtesy of the University of Denver.

the nearby barracks (figure 5.5). One man, who was born at Amache and had never before returned, retold one of the few stories about camp his mother shared with him. With his extended family to witness, he spoke of how he had crawled too near the single heat source in each barrack, the potbelly stove. He then lifted his pant leg to show us all the scar that still marked where he had been burned. The scars of internment are many; this one is literal.

This moment of return is typically captured photographically. Indeed, one former internee began our conversation by saying, "I know exactly where I want you to take my picture." She handed me a family photograph from camp of her and her parents at the building next to their barrack, the mess hall where her father had worked. A mess hall garden visible in the photograph was still demarcated on the site surface by a ring of limestone on the ground. We posed her in front of the garden, just as she had been in the original photograph. In these moments, the touristic snapshot that documents presence takes on deeper import. The photograph proves the place is real, the whispered history happened.

Ethnographic studies of disrupted communities help us understand why people seek to physically experience, share, and document such places. Sharing even painful memories in the place where they happened helps individuals establish a sense of continuity with their past, while also reclaiming a part of their identity to which the ties may have frayed. In Medellín, Columbia, many people impacted by drug violence were displaced from their childhood homes. When they retell those stories they often physically reenact the event, much like at Amache, showing how place is an embodied memory (Riaño-Alcalá 2002:286). Indeed, these moments have the flavor of what psychologists call reminiscence therapy. Patients who are encouraged to reflect on past events can better understand and reconcile whom they have become with their life history (Scogin et al. 2005).

One of my first experiences taking someone back to a barrack was a man born after his parents left camp. Like so many of their generation, his parents never spoke of their experience at Amache. I led him to the barrack, making sure that while he stood at the doorway, I walked over to where the wall had been, letting him feel just how small the twenty-by-twenty-foot room they lived in was. I also toured him around other buildings in the block. We discussed the lack of privacy in the shared bathrooms, the trees planted to shade people waiting in line at the mess hall. I pointed out a few of the objects still visible on the site surface. As we completed our tour, he thanked me and said, "I know my parents so much better now." By returning to the camp, the descendants of internees displace the empty memories of internment with something tangible, a physical experience of the place. This echoes Barbara Bender's experience of heritage sites, "where the ancestral past is renewed through the activity of the living" (Bender 2002:S108).

DIGGING FOR THEIR ROOTS

The effect of an embodied experience of a past place is perhaps most salient to better understanding the experience of former Amache internees who don't just visit our field school but participate as crew. When this project was first conceived, it really hadn't occurred to me that the population of former internees would be interested in joining the crew. If you want to get a lively conversation going among former internees of any internment camp, ask them about environmental conditions. Amacheans speak passionately about the hot, dry summers and the punishing, sandy wind that characterize the High Plains' setting of the site. As one survivor told me, "Every time the wind blows I think about camp." Add in that not a one of them is younger than seventy, and it is easy to see why spending significant time at Amache would seem unappealing. And yet, that is exactly what has happened. During a research trip prior to our first field season, I met Gary Ono, a former Amache internee and retired professional photographer and volunteer at the Japanese American National Museum (JANM) in Los Angeles. We were introduced during my visit to the museum. After I told Mr. Ono about our upcoming fieldwork plans, he asked if he could join us as the site photographer. My answer was an enthusiastic "yes," as it was when he later asked if he could bring along his grandson.

Mr. Ono has written a number of online articles for JANM about his family history and about Amache, and several specifically about his experience with the field school. One article documents a moment of discovery when he first arrived. During a tour of a block far from that where his family had lived, I pointed out several signatures in a concrete block. The bottom one was partially eroded away, but Mr. Ono excitedly identified it as his father's. It was a moment when we both, to quote Mr. Ono, "were just awe-struck" (Ono 2009:n.p.). Later Mr. Ono and his grandson pitched a tent on the family barracks and spent the night over the Fourth of July. They chose that night for its significance in their own and the nation's history. Of that night, Ono wrote, "We imagined what it must have felt like to be imprisoned while the rest of America celebrated their independence and freedom" (Ono 2008:n.p.). This vivid evocation echoes Keith Basso's (1996) experience with Apache elders who used spatial clues and place-names to stand in the footsteps of the ancestors.

In 2010 we were joined by two more former internees. Both of them had been toddlers during World War II. Their personal memories of camp are very limited and focused on particular experiences. Like their older counterparts, some of those memories have to do with environmental conditions. Those same conditions combined with the spatial layout of the camp can bring back previously forgotten memories, which come on quite suddenly. One of those volunteers wrote about the experience of returning to her barrack after a seventy-year absence. "Just standing there, for several minutes, I could then remember where the cots were, where the stove was, the single light bulb, the blanket that separated my parents' cot from mine" (personal communication, Tinker, 2015). On returning with former residents of an Irish community abandoned in the 1960s, archaeologists have noted a similar flood of seemingly forgotten memories (Kujit 2013). Cognitive scientists call this "long-term reinstatement," theorizing that reconnecting to the context where memories were encoded allows the revival of memories that would be otherwise inaccessible (Smith 1988). For an individual who grew up in a place their parents never discussed, these reclamations are significant and empowering.

CONCLUSION: PLACE REVEALED AND REMEMBERED

Despair comes easy in a prison. They are places more commonly associated with destruction rather than creation. Once abandoned they can become negative heritage, "a repository of negative memory in the collective imaginary" (Meskell 2002:558). Yet the physical remains at Amache tell a different story, one where hope was literally planted into the soil—hope for a seed to sprout, a tree to shade, a flower to bloom. Gardens were a gift from the internees to themselves and to their community. They were also, it turns out, a gift to the future. The gardens of Amache are repositories of generational knowledge. In them a philosophical stance toward nature is made manifest through horticultural skill. They reveal a hybrid aesthetic with deep roots in the homeland but informed by the front yards of America. Materials employed in the gardens evidence internee networks and ingenuity. In these gardens an uprooted people reclaimed a connection to the land.

That reclamation continues today, as former internees and their families return to Amache. At the site they walk with the ancestors, sometimes armed like detectives with a few clues—a family photograph, a story told in passing. If it's a windy day (which it usually is), they literally get a taste of the place. A drink of cold water will wash the grit out of their mouths, but its texture lingers, informs. At our garden excavations, they see how internees combatted that dust, not with curses but with beauty. Here they learn a different story as read through the land and have one more reason to be proud of their ancestors' legacy. As one of my volunteers wrote in his personal field journal, "By being at the site, I have gained a greater respect for my parents' determination to make the best of a bad situation: to endure with perseverance and dignity, and to thrive."

By combining intensive landscape archaeology with engagement, work at Amache is enabling the site to come alive. We reveal a past community and the strategies of the individuals within it. By working and talking together, we are also creating a new community centered around both the tangible and intangible heritage of this site. Despite our varied backgrounds, we all share an embodied experience of this place that for so long was in the shadows. We also share a commitment to preserving this critical locale. Not just because it is a significant historic resource, which it is, but because we owe it to those who so carefully remade it.

REFERENCES

Archer, Steven N. 2009. "Amache Garden Testing—Archaeobotanical Analysis." Manuscript available through the University of Denver, Department of Anthropology.

Basso, Keith. 1996. *Wisdom Sits in Places: Landscape and Language among the Western Apache*. Albuquerque: University of New Mexico Press.

Bender, Barbara. 2002. "Time and Landscape." *Current Anthropologist* 43 (S4). http://dx .doi.org/10.1086/339561.

Carrillo, Richard F., and David Killam. 2004. *Camp Amache (5PW48): A Class III Intensive Field Survey of the Granada Relocation Center, Prowers County*. Colorado: Prepared for the Town of Granada by RMC Consultants.

Casella, Eleanor Conlin. 2007. *The Archaeology of Institutional Confinement*. Archaeology of American Experience. Gainesville: University Press of Florida.

Clark, Bonnie. 2008. "The Archaeology of Gardening at Amache: A Synthesis of Results from University of Denver Field Investigations." Manuscript available through the University of Denver, Department of Anthropology.

Clark, Bonnie. 2011. *The Archaeology of Gardening at Amache Summary Report-Summer 2010*. Prepared for Dumbarton Oaks. Manuscript on file at the University of Denver, Department of Anthropology.

Clark, Bonnie J., David Garrison, and Paul Swader. 2012. *Archaeological Investigations at the Granada Relocation Center (Amache), National Historic Landmark, Prowers County, Colorado: Report on the 2010 Field Season*. Prepared for the State Historical Fund, History Colorado, by the University of Denver, Department of Anthropology.

The Commission on Wartime Relocation and Internment of Civilians. 1997. *Personal Justice Denied: Report of the Commission on Wartime Relocation and Internment of Civilians*. Seattle: University of Washington Press.

DeWitt, J. L. 1943. *Final Report: Japanese Evacuation from the West Coast*. Washington, DC: Government Printing Office.

Dumas, Enoch, and Margaret Walther. 1944. "Landscaping for Beauty and Health." *School Executive* (May 1944): 40–41.

Granada Pioneer. 1943. *Thumbnail Sketches* (May 15, 1943): 5.

Helphand, Kenneth I. 2006. *Defiant Gardens: Making Gardens in Wartime*. San Antonio: Trinity University Press.

Horiuchi, Lynn. 2005. "Dislocations and the Relocations: The Built Environments of Japanese American Internment." PhD diss., University of California, Santa Barbara.

Houston, Jeanne Wakatsuki, and James D. Houston. 1973. *Farewell to Manzanar*. New York: Houghton Mifflin.

Inada, Lawson. 1997. *Drawing the Line*. Minneapolis: Coffee House Press.

Itoh, Teiji. 1973. *Space and Illusion in the Japanese Garden*. New York: Weatherhill/Tankosha.

Kujit, Ian. 2013. "On a Snail's Back: Ethnoarchaeology, Residential Mobility, and Homemaking in 1950s Inishark, Co. Galway, Ireland." Paper presented at the American Anthropological Association meetings, Chicago, IL.

Law, Lisa. 2005. "Home Cooking: Filipino Women and Topographies of the Senses in Hong Kong." In *Empire of the Senses: The Sensual Culture Reader*, ed. David Howes, 224–41. Oxford: Berg.

Marín-Spiotta, Erika, and Emily Eggleston. 2011. "Camp Amache Soil Chemistry Report." Manuscript available through the University of Denver, Department of Anthropology.

Meskell, Lynn. 2002. "Negative Heritage and Past Mastering in Archaeology." *Anthropological Quarterly* 75 (3): 557–74. http://dx.doi.org/10.1353/anq.2002.0050.

Nagata, Donna K. 1993. *Legacy of Injustice: Exploring the Cross-Generational Impact of the Japanese American Internment*. New York: Plenum. http://dx.doi.org/10.1007/978-1-4899-1118-6.

Natural Resources Conservation Service. n.d. Description for Td—Tivoli Sand. Accessed April 15, 2008. http://websoilsurvey.nrcs.usda.gov/app/WebSoilSurvey.aspx.

Ono, Gary. 2008. "Amache Night." *Discover Nikkei*. Accessed November 1, 2013. http://www.discovernikkei.org/en/journal/2008/8/1/amache-night/.

Ono, Gary. 2009. "Significant Signatures." *Discover Nikkei*. Accessed November 1, 2013. http://www.discovernikkei.org/en/journal/.2009/04/24/significant-signatures/.

Riaño-Alcalá, Pilar. 2002. "Remembering Place: Memory and Violence in Medellín, Columbia." *Journal of Latin American Anthropology* 7 (1): 276–309. http://dx.doi.org/10.1525/jlca.2002.7.1.276.

Riggs, Erin Paige. 2013. "The Domoto Diaspore: An Investigation of One Family's Experience of and Influence within American Landscapes from 1882 through Today." Undergraduate thesis, University of California, Department of Anthropology, Berkeley.

Saitta, Dean. 2007. *The Archaeology of Collective Action*. Gainesville: University Press of Florida.

Scogin, F., D. Welsh, A. Hanson, J. Stump, and A. Coates. 2005. "Evidence-Based Psychotherapies for Depression in Older Adults." *Clinical Psychology: Science and Practice* 12 (3): 222–37. http://dx.doi.org/10.1093/clipsy.bpi033.

Seki, Sankyaku, ed. 2007. *Gardeners' Pioneer Story as Preserved in Senryu Poems Written by Nikkei Gardeners*. Los Angeles: Southern California Gardeners' Federation.

Silliman, Stephen W., ed. 2008. *Collaborating at the Trowel's Edge: Teaching and Learning in Indigenous Archaeology*. Tucson: University of Arizona Press.

Simmons, Thomas H., and R. Laurie Simmons. 1993. *Granada Relocation Center, National Register of Historic Places Nomination Form*. Denver: Front Range Research Associates.

Smith, S. M. 1988. "Environmental Context-Dependent Memory." In *Memory in Context*, ed. G. Davies, 13–31. New York: John Wiley and Sons.

Tsukashima, Ronald T. 2000. "Politics of Maintenance Gardening and the Formation of the Southern California Gardeners' Federation." In *Greenmakers: Japanese American Gardeners in Southern California*, ed. Naomi Hirahara, 67–77. Los Angeles: Southern California Gardeners' Association.

Yee, Barbara. 1995. "What Is the Legacy of Internment for Japanese Americans? Review of Legacy of Injustice: Exploring the Cross-Generational Impact of the Japanese American Internment, by D. K. Nagata." *Contemporary Psychology: APA Review of Books* 40 (3): 274–75.

Zimmerman, Larry J., and Jessica Welch. 2011. "Displaced and Barely Visible: Archaeology and the Material Culture of Homelessness." *Historical Archaeology* 45 (1): 67–85.

6

Indigenous House Plans and Land in Mexico City (Sixteenth Century)

Reflections on the Buying and Selling, Inheritance, and Conflicts Surrounding Houses and Land

KEIKO YONEDA
TRANSLATED BY HANNAH BECKER

This chapter examines a series of sixteenth-century documents that provide valuable insights into the organization of household space and the stewardship of private and familial property among Nahua-speaking people in the Valley of Mexico. It documents how indigenous notions of household organization and uses of space were translated into the idiom of Spanish legalism, laying the foundation for the means through which the descendants of the conquered would assert land title in the colonial and postcolonial eras. This dialog between indigenous and Western notions of property and land tenure created space for cultural continuities whose effects are still evident in contemporary Nahua-speaking communities. Some additional insights that emerge from this research involve questions regarding the role of different forms of property in indigenous society, as well as the complex historical and social relationships that often exist behind the seemingly simple concept of a "house."

Central to this analysis are a series of narrative and pictorial texts derived from the rich corpus of colonial-era Nahua documents. The possession and demarcation of land and territories motivated the creation of different categories of pictographic documents in sixteenth-century New Spain. These include paintings that appear in present-day archive catalogs as large-scale historical maps; large-format site plans that depict large areas such as entire cities or parts of a city; and smaller-format site plans that depict plots of land, buildings, and agricultural fields.[1] This work will analyze the small-format pictographic documents that are attached to files that document lawsuits over the privately owned lands and houses.[2]

DOI: 10.5876/9781607325727.c006

As a compilation that includes many of the texts involved in this study, I will make frequent references to *Documentos nahuas de la ciudad de México del siglo XVI* (Reyes García et al. 1996).[3] From this larger corpus, I focus on a number of pictographic site plans that were originally filed in the branch of Mexico's National Archives (Archivo General de la Nación, AGN) that deals with land tenure (the Ramo Tierras). The study of these site plans, which focuses on the graphic elements of the plans themselves, formed part of an investigation that was carried out in a collective project.[4] The texts of the files from AGN in the current chapter are taken from the book *Documentos nahuas*, which was the result of a separate project that focused on the publication of primary texts in Spanish and Nahuatl that were written in the Latin alphabet. This study was directed by Luis Reyes García. My analysis here will be based on sixteen of the twenty site plans in the original collection, with a close focus on four of particular interest (see, for example, figure 6.1).[5]

In each of these sixteen site plans, I tried to locate the houses (*calli*) and the lands (*tlalli*) in question in four major neighborhoods or territorial divisions of Mexico-Tenochtitlan that surround the thirteen-block district that was designated for Spanish occupation. These peripheral neighborhoods were home to the city's indigenous community and corresponded to the outer portion of the four original indigenous neighborhoods of Santa María Cuepopan (Tlaquechiuhcan), San Sebastián Tzacualco (Atzacualco, Atzacualpa), San Pablo Zoquipan (Teopan, Xochimilco), and San Juan Moyotlan (see Appendix 6.A). Of the sixteen site plans, nine refer to properties in San Juan Moyotlan and three to properties in San Sebastián Atzacualco (three planos), and four planos are not tied specifically to a neighborhood.

As a group, these plans provide priceless insight into the organization of lived space among sixteenth-century Nahua speakers. They contain drawings of houses, diverse plots of land, *chinampas* (raised agricultural fields), and water canals, as well as the measurements of these elements. In some cases these documents include additional glyphs such as human figures that represent couples that currently or formerly owned the property, glyphs that state the price of their estates, or calendrical glyphs that state the years of possession of houses and lands. The houses are depicted with parallel lines, leaving the entryway open. The canals are often represented by curving lines or swirls that recall the rivers in historical-cartographic documents in the indigenous tradition.

A number of additional glyphs are used to document the size of different lands and structures, also providing insight into common units of measurement in colonial Mexico. For example, the measurement known as *maitl* is commonly represented with the hieroglyph for "hand," and translated in *Documentos nahuas* as

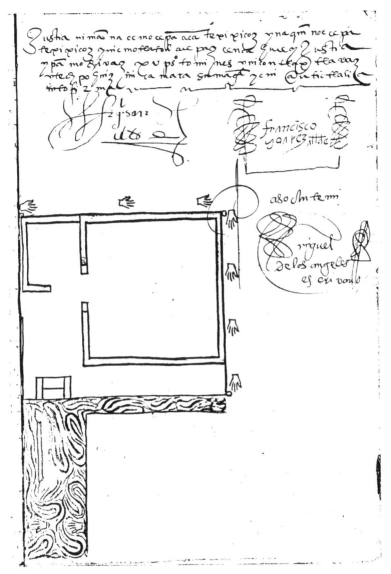

FIGURE 6.1. Plan 9 (AGN, Tierras, vol. 29, exp. 5, f. 14r) [*Documentos nahuas* 123] 1566.

braza (roughly equivalent to an English fathom). *Mitl*, represented with the glyph for "arrow," is translated in paragraphs 403 and 981 as "the span from the elbow to the other hand."[6] *Yolohtli*, represented by the glyph for "heart," is translated as "the span from the chest to the hand." *Omitl*, represented with the glyph for "bone," is translated as "an elbow."[7]

The close association between the written documents in Nahuatl and these site plans hint at the close relationship between the content of these paintings and the larger cultural and linguistic world of Nahuatl speakers from central Mexico. It must be noted, however, that the style of the glyphs such as *maitl* and *yolohtli* have features that remind us of the forms of these elements in Western art.[8] We also find the cross element (three crosses in Plano 16 associated with the lines that unite the pairs in this plano) and posts drawn with white or black circles and in a more naturalistic manner in various planos. The posts are associated with the mediation or the act of possession of lands and houses. But these and other minor traces of Western influence notwithstanding, the terms and concepts of space embodied by these documents show clear continuities with pre-Hispanic forms of land tenure.

Besides tracing these continuities in ideas of lived space, my goal in examining these documents is to learn how the inhabitants of Mexico-Tenochtitlan used the stewardship of private property as a means of physical and cultural survival in the early colonial period. These survival strategies involved both household spaces and abutting properties and hydrological features. Thus, I will demonstrate how the testimonies of individual lives reflected in the plans and documents from the sixteenth century are evidence of how Nahua people responded to their natural surroundings in a specific historic moment and manifested themselves in the form of a sense of identity and continuity. This process is evident in a range of practices with pre-Hispanic roots that successfully incorporated Spanish influences during this period. The long-term ramifications of this process are also observed in the practices of present-day Nahuatl-speaking communities.

I should clarify that the present study is a first attempt that tries to systemize the data on the images found in the indigenous plans that were organized in: (a) a graphic catalog and the preliminary study (Yoneda 1996), and in (b) Nahuatl and Spanish texts written in the Latin alphabet published in *Documentos nahuas*. In this last book, they are edited together in the files of different cases, even though the published files concerning each lawsuit are organized according to their place in the National Archive and aren't presented in chronological order. The presentation of these files in *Documentos nahuas* also stops short of explaining the motives of the production of each document in connection with the development of the lawsuit.

Through this new analysis, I have tried to find the particular conflict or strategies that animated a particular lawsuit, with a special focus on how these were filtered through the kinds of spatial knowledge that is represented visually in site plans. This approach was faced with some problems. Even after finding the connection between a file and a plan, there were often discrepancies between the narrative and visual description of a particular property, which required further analysis and explanation. Still, this particular confluence of narrative and visual descriptions of disputed properties was essential to understanding how particular perceptions of lived space were reproduced within the changing legal regimes of colonial Mexico. Before turning to the documents themselves, I will provide a brief sketch of the history of political geography and different regimes of land tenure in the Valley of Mexico.

HISTORICAL BACKGROUND OF MEXICO-TENOCHTITLAN

Most historical scholarship, drawing on the migration myths recorded in the sixteenth century, state that the ancestors of the Nahuatl-speaking Mexica inhabited the northern part of Mesoamerica. They were nomadic *chichimecas* who practiced a subsistence system of hunting and gathering, trading occasionally with sedentary neighbors. It's possible that some Chichimec groups had known the sedentary lifestyle, practicing agriculture in provisional establishments on the path of longer migrations (Yoneda 2002:12–15). These chichimecas arrived in waves of migrations toward the central and southern parts of Mesoamerica in the twelfth–fourteenth centuries, when climate changes motivated their movement south of the northern agricultural frontier (Rojas Rabiela 1991, tomo 2: 220–21).

The Mexicas' mythological history notes that they departed from Aztlan Chicomoztoc under the guidance of their guardian god Huitzilopochtli. Sometime after 1325, they founded Mexico-Tenochtitlan on the site where they found an eagle devouring a serpent, in the location of *tenochtli* (*tetl*: stone + *nochtli*: edible cactus). Mexico-Tenochtitlan survived for two centuries, from the arrival of the Mexicas in the basin of Mexico to the arrival of the Spanish. López Austin and López Luján (2008:210) describe this 200 years as follows:

From 1325 to 1430, the Mexicas settled on an insular zone of Lake Texcoco and lived under the subordination of groups recognized as *tepanecas*. In 1337, a faction of the Mexica departed from Mexico-Tenochtitlan and moved to the islands immediately to the north and founded the twin and rival statelet of Mexico-Tlatelolco. Both Mexica polities of Mexico-Tenochtitlan and Mexico-Tlatelolco continued to pay tribute to the Tepanecs of Azcapotzalco, who enjoyed customary title over the islands. In the fourteenth century, the Mexicas of Tenochtitlan and Tlatelolco forged marriage alliances with native elite lineages of the Valley of Mexico, and successfully expanded their own territorial base through a series of conquests.[9] By 1430, the basin of Mexico was reorganized in the Triple Alliance ruled by Mexico-Tenochtitlan, Texcoco, and Tlacopan. The Mexican expansion would transform both the political and natural landscape of central Mexico.

Under this alliance, Mexico-Tenochtitlan would construct a levee twelve kilometers long by twenty meters wide to stop the influx of salty water from the east.[10] The regulation of soil and water salination influenced the quality of agricultural and hydrological resources in the valley, a process that was still evident in the different values that were ascribed to some of the sixteenth-century properties that will be discussed later. Of the sixteen site plans that I analyzed, ten have the drawing of water, of which eight site plans represent canals bordering chinampas that form part of the lands referred to in the files. This fact confirms the close relation that the litigants had with the *chinampera* zone.[11] The lacustrine environment of Mexico-Tenochtitlan permitted agriculture in the chinampas or artificial parcels of land constructed in the wetlands and in the riverbanks. The chinampas were plentiful in the lakes of the Valley of Mexico, and probably also in Aztlan, where the Mexicas came from. I will cite what Navarrete Linares (1999:17) explains about the construction of the chinampas and their utility:

> To construct a *chinampa*, one must first place rows of *ahuejotes* or willows and of posts and sticks to form a large square. In between them are placed, one by one, many layers of mud taken from the bottom of the lake. The mud doesn't dissolve in water because the roots of the trees and the sticks enclose it. Once the land rises above the water level, the *chinampa* is ready to be cultivated. A well-kept *chinampa* is very productive due to the fertility of the mud and the abundance of water in the lake.
>
> Thanks to the *chinampas*, the inhabitants of Aztlan and of Mexico could reclaim land from the lake to compliment the abundant food that they extracted from it with agricultural products like corn, beans, pumpkins, chilies, and tomatoes.

This agricultural landscape was overlaid by territorial divisions and diverse property rights that reflected earlier political consolidations and the military expansion that took place from 1469 to 1502. This is the combination of ecological and political features that were reconfigured by Spanish property regimes after the conquest and consolidation of colonial rule. This is the context in which the documents published in the *Documentos nahuas* (Reyes García et al. 1996) were produced, including the plans of Mexico City, that are the focus of this chapter.

POLITICAL AND TERRITORIAL ORGANIZATION AND THE LAND TENURE SYSTEM IN CENTRAL MEXICO

Pre-Hispanic territories in the Valley of Mexico were composed of lands that produced for a more-or-less urbanized nucleus. P. Carrasco (1996:585) characterizes this territorial structure as follows: "The *altepetl* was a political unit ruled by a king, or *tlatoani*. That is, [an *altepetl* is a] *tlatocayotl*, the *tlatoani's* government.

INDIGENOUS HOUSE PLANS AND LAND IN MEXICO CITY (SIXTEENTH CENTURY)   103

Sometimes, the *altepetl* was an independent entity, but in general various *altepeme* [plural of *altepetl*][12] united in superior political entities of varying degrees of complexity, even though each of them maintained their own government."

The cities were the principal seat of the nobility and the specialized artisans (P. Carrasco 1996:585). Each of the three polities that composed the alliance had their corresponding territories for subsistence production. The communities of farmers, organized in *calpicaxgos* led by majordomos, or *calpixque*, supplied the provisions for the palaces or gave other specialized services such as the care of forests and gardens (P. Carrasco 1996:585). Munehiro Kobayashi (1993:53) notes that the specific obligations that the towns had to the *hueytlatoque* (plural of *hueytlatoani* [*huey*: big + *tlatoani*: king, lord, ruler]) varied and could include military service, service work in the royal palace or public works, tribute in kind, work as a bonded agriculturalist, and other form of service.[13] Scholars use the following terms from the colonial sources, whether from the historians or the archival documents, to refer to these territorial units: *altepetl* (town or city), *tlatocayotl, calpulli,*[14] *tlaxila-calli,*[15] for Mexico-Tenochtitlan (P. Carrasco 1996; Gibson 1967; Lockhart 1999); *tlahtocayo* and *tecpan* for Cuauhtinchan and Tepeaca, state of Puebla (Martínez 2000:196n4; Reyes García 1996) and *tecalli,* for Tlaxcala (Rojas Rabiela 1987).[16]

This variation in political autonomy and obligation is also evident in the different forms of land tenure exercised over the territories that were used for subsistence production. Based on the colonial sources, the following types of land can be recognized in the pre-Hispanic era in the Aztec Empire. *Teotlalli,* or land of the temples and the gods; *tecpantlalli,* or land of houses and the community palace (for the latter, Lockhart 1999:224; land of the palace); *tlatocatlalli* (*tlatocamilli*), or land of the *tlatoque* (rulers); *pilalli* and *tecuhtlalli,* or land of the nobles (*pipiltin* and *tetecuhtin*); *milchimalli,* or land of the army; and *calpulalli,* or land of the *calpultin* (Gibson 1967:263n1; Lockhart 1999:224).

Various researchers that address the topic of political and territorial organization in central Mexico and the states of Puebla-Tlaxcala have observed that the territories of different political groups or categories of landholder often overlapped (P. Carrasco 1996:586; Gibson 1967:270; Kirchhoff et al. 1976:224n5; Kobayashi 1993:52; Martínez 1984:53, 88–90, fig. 2; Reyes García 1977:94). In fact, in the *Documentos nahuas* we find this type of information for private properties. Pedro Carrasco (1996:586) explains this characteristic as follows:

> *The intermingling of territories means that all social segments are represented in the many or all territories. [Members of] the principal ethnic factions of the Mesoamerican empires—like colhuas, mexicas, and tepanecas in the tenochca empire—were found in all of the kingdoms. Neighborhoods—also related to distinct ethnic elements and with*

determined professions and cults—were also found in all of the cities. The factions and neighborhoods of a city had lands in their distinct rural dependencies. All of this is a manner of sharing resources of various places and in different environments. But it is also a mechanism of integration, not only economically, but also socially and politically, that acts against the fragmentation of the different segments into independent societies.

The complex tapestry of ethnic groups, factions, and other actors in the Valley of Mexico made certain categories of private or familial landholding particularly important in the reproduction of distinct social segments over time. In "Figure V.3. General perspective of the indigenous categories of land tenure" (Lockhart 1999:231), the following categories are found that relate to the analyzed planos:

5. *calalli* (land of the house): The parcel or parcels closest and associated most permanently with a determined domestic dwelling; they exist among nobles as well as among plebeians; . . .
6. *hueca tlalli, inic oncan tlalli* (distant land, land in another place): Parcels that possessed a domestic dwelling,[17] in addition to *calalli*.[18]
7. *huehuetlalli* (old land, patrimonial land): Land inherited or that was expected to be inherited indefinitely in a domestic dwelling, and that therefore was under the discretion of the possessor; they existed among the nobles as well as among plebeians; in many cases coinciding with the *calalli* and contrasting with the *calpolalli* and *tequitcatlalli*.[19]
8. *tlalcohualli* (purchased land): Often contrasted with *calpolalli* and *tequitcatlalli*; they existed among the nobles; their existence among the plebeians in prehispanic times still hasn't been definitively established, but is probable.

This system of property—intimately linked with the larger webs of ethnic and factional affiliations that defined the political and social life of the Valley of Mexico—entered into dialog with Spanish legal frameworks in the arguments and site plans that are the focus of my work. These plans contain characteristics that suggest that they come from a pre-Hispanic system of records. This raises larger questions regarding the traditional assumption that pre-Hispanic land use had been dominated by different forms of collective tenure. Given the content of these plans and the way in which legal cases were argued in the sixteenth century, there is evidence that purchases of lands also occurred in the pre-Hispanic period and that many of the negotiations over inheritance or sale that took place in the sixteenth century have earlier indigenous precedents. Felipe Castro Gutierrez (2010:121) observes that in the colonial era, the *macehuales* (the commoner *indios*) had private lands that they inherited, bought, and sold: "It must be taken into consideration . . . that not all lands of the towns and neighborhoods of *indios* were communitarian; *patrimoniales* existed as well, assimilated during the colony as private property . . . It would also appear that the common claim that the *macehuales* only had the usufruct of community lands isn't completely true; there are common *indios* that inherited, bought, and sold lands."

James Lockhart (1999:224) notes that there is a clear disparity in period sources between the names of lands that reflect the sociopolitical life of the lords in the pre-Hispanic era, on one hand, and lawsuits regarding lands whose litigants are individuals and not factions, lords, or entire communities on the other hand. This is evident in the texts collected in *Documentos nahuas*, which evidence a distinction between lands belonging to the lordly estates, communities, and the private lands of much smaller scale. Accordingly, the dimensions and characteristics of the pictographic documents differ from one category to the other, just as the corresponding lawsuits involve more or fewer litigants or territories of smaller or larger scale.[20] So, for example, there are cases that air out territorial conflicts between lords or communities that were motivated by the rulers,[21] while others discuss other types of lawsuits initiated between individuals. These questions of scale also seem to be reflected in the gender of the principal litigants. Susan Kellogg (1995) observed that in the suits filed between estates or communities, men are the principal participants. Conversely, in various disputes between individuals, women appear as litigants or as involved in the trials.[22]

It is also important to note that litigation does not appear to have been the purview of a particular social class. Some litigants in the sixteenth century seem to have been relatively well off in the colonial society, given the quantity and quality of lands and items listed in their wills. In other cases it seems that the litigants don't own much of anything but the house and the land in dispute. As Kellogg (1995:64–65) observed: "One social type that appears frequently in the earliest legal texts is the lone woman or widow defending her rights. Another is the noble, descended by kings, surrounded by supporters, and tied politically to Spaniards. Yet another character type is the 'common' man who claimed ownership of modest holdings. Sometimes he appeared before the *audiencia* to make a claim for his own holdings; sometimes he went to defend his wife's ownership of property" (Kellogg 1995:64). Further, she notes, "In case records from the beginning of the colonial period, litigants tended to present themselves in certain stereotypical ways: female litigants constantly referred to themselves as poor; male commoners identified themselves as hardworking and responsible craftsmen or agricultural laborers; communities portrayed themselves as steeped in tradition" (Kellogg 1995:65). These observations from Kellogg suggest that the descriptions that the litigants make about themselves may have common standards that follow the ideology or the customs of this era.[23] Next, I closely analyze how these different categories of landscape, property, and landholder are articulated in site plans.

SITE PLAN 9 (AGN, TIERRAS, VOL. 29, EXP. 5, F. 14R) AND
SITE PLAN 9B (AGN, TIERRAS, VOL. 29, EXP. 5, FF. 23V–24R) 1563–1566

It was already mentioned above that the rulers of Mexico-Tenochtitlan constructed a levee twelve kilometers long by twenty meters wide to stop the influx of saltwater from the east of Lake Texcoco. The management of drinkable water resources continued to figure in land use and property rights in the decades that followed the conquest. I found a site plan that depicts a house called *acalli*, or "water house," which a couple owned and operated after the death of an individual named Ezhuahuacatzintli. It appears that Ezhuahuacatzintli started with this occupation when saltwater flooded the canals, surely because it was necessary to supply freshwater for human consumption. Details about the history of the water house and its place in postconquest society are detailed in the documents referred to as Site Plans 9 and 9b.

Site Plans 9 and 9b (figures 6.1 and 6.2) are enclosed in the file published with the title of "Diego Yaotl against Gabriel Yaotl and María Teuchon,[24] *indios*, regarding a piece of land called Amanalco. Year 1570" (*Documentos nahuas* 118). According to this lawsuit, Diego Yaotl and his wife, Ysabel Tlaco, bought a house and three *chinamitl* (enclosures) from Baltazar Mocnoteca and his wife, María Papan, with the former receiving formal title on December 29, 1563 (document 2). Diego Yaotl and Ysabel Tlaco sued Gabriel Yaotl and his wife, María Teuchon, because the latter sold their water in an acalli that is located in the former's property. On this occasion, in accordance with the verdict, the court imposed a fine of 10 *tomines* to the Cámara de su Majestad on those who sell the water (December 10, 1563) (document 1).

The three chinamitl and plot of land of seven brazas in width that is drawn in Plano 9b coincide with what is mentioned (document 1, paragraph 176) in the file.[25] However, the length of eleven brazas doesn't coincide with Site Plan 9b because they appear drawn about 20–22 brazas. This may be because this measurement includes the length of chinamitl.[26] In the site plan, apart from the three chinamitl and four canals, there are three houses located within the walls that enclose the group. There is a small house beside the canal that is located on the extreme lower left. This could be the acalli or "water house" that is drawn in detail in Plano 9.

Other documents detailing subsequent parts of the case are included in the file, and dated March 5 and 14, 1566. The March 14 document lists three witnesses—a seventy-year-old man, an eighty-five-year-old man, and a sixty-year-old woman—all of whom affirm that the land with a water house that they call acalli, the place where they sell water, two *camellones* of water (even though it's not clear which are the camellones mentioned here), and their canoes were bought by Gabriel Yaotl and María Teuchon from Ana Tlaco *cihuatl* (woman) for 5 *pesos* approximately three years earlier [1563]. But they also note that those properties had already been occupied for forty-four years (paragraph 199–200).

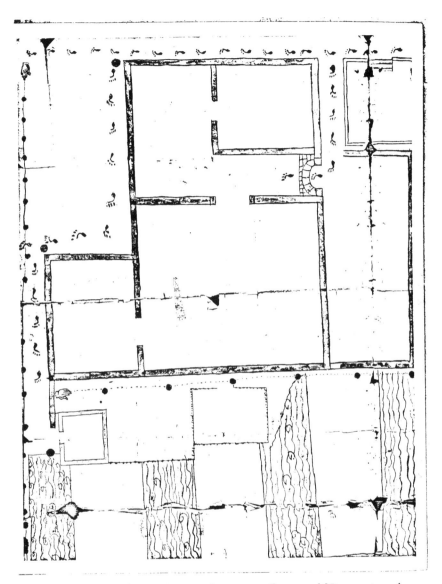

FIGURE 6.2. Plan 9 bis (AGN, Tierras, vol. 29, exp. 5, ff. 23v–24r) [*Documentos nahuas* 126] 1563.

Concerning the origin of this water house, the seventy-year-old male witness notes: "[f. 17r] He said that what this witness knows is where Graviel Yaotl and María his wife sell water, first belonged to an *yndio* named Ezhuahuacatzintli in the time when the salt-water lake was growing and when Motelchiuhtzin was becoming lord (*tlahtoani*) and later he died and said Gabriel Yaotl and his wife took it" (paragraph 202). The fourth document, dated July 5, 1566, mentions that

> Appearing in front of us, Graviel Yaotl and María Teuchon his wife, residents (of the neighborhood) of San Juan Amanaldo and they said that they demand justice on their ownership of a house where they sell water that they call *acalli*[,][27] that has in back (measurements of said house) three *brazas* and of length it has four *brazes*. (paragraph 191)
>
> That which they have and own for forty years this part, and now Diego Yaotl and Ysabel [Tlaco] his wife (they are worried and they want to leave said house) and that at forty years that they bring in cases on the said water house. (paragraph 192)

Paragraph 193 notes that the witnesses confirmed that Gabriel Yaotl and María Teuchon, his wife, had the water house in their possession for forty years. Furthermore, in paragraph 194 it mentions that Diego Yaotl and Ysabel Tlaco bought the house and the land, but didn't buy the "house to sell water" that was still legal property of Gabriel Yaotl and María Teuchon.

Plano 9 contains only the house known as acalli (water house) and the surrounding plots of land with measurements.[28] There is also a structure that seems as if it were made of boards and that perhaps represents steps to descend to the water, either to collect the water for sale or to board a canoe that is in the water.[29] The water from the canals, depicted in the form of an inverted L, is drawn in light and dark blue with black lines that signal the movement of the water, in which there is a canoe drawn in brown.[30]

As represented in the site plan and in the narrative descriptions of the case, it is evident that when the brackish water rose, an indio named Ezhuahuacatzintli started to sell the freshwater that comes from this part of the canal drawn in Plano 9, and Gabriel Yaotl and his wife continued selling it for more than forty years. The acalli appears embedded in the land with a house bought by another couple, about seven by eight brazas and three chinamitl (paragraph 176).

Although the case began on December 10, 1563, in terms that seemed less advantageous to the water sellers, they received a favorable ruling on July 5, 1566. Great weight seems to have been given to litigants' presentation of three elderly witnesses who could testify to the sale of water by this couple some forty-four years prior. The case is interesting in that it shows how the sale of freshwater (probably from a source in this canal) existed in the chinampa zone from the time when the brackish water rose, and that its sale lasted over forty years until this conflict was brought forth and dealt with. Furthermore, it hints at a range of different usufruct or customary rights to occupy different sites and use different resources that existed alongside the simple sale and purchase of plots of land. The next case study provides further detail on the complex ways in which families and other groups occupied sites, and the diverse meanings of the concept of "house" that emerge in these texts.

CALLI GLYPHS

When I started to analyze the small-formal site plans, I was drawn to the following aspects of the pre-Hispanic glyph *calli*. One of them is the similarity to an occurrence of this glyph in the plans to conventions in the *Mapa de Cuauhtinchan No. 2* (MC2), which uses parallel lines with raised entrances for representing the walls of buildings or of an enclosure. An example of these drawing conventions appears in the toponymic glyph that combines an eagle (*cuauhtli*) and a shield (*chimalli*), and two enclosed areas with walls drawn with two parallel lines with an opening or entrance (glyph P19) (figure 6.3). Another example of walls drawn with two parallel lines and openings for the entrances is the depiction of the enclosures of the architectural complex of Cholollan (Cholula) (glyphs D17–D28) (figure 6.4).[31]

The fact that the same conventions were used to depict a range of different buildings and architectural arrangements reflects the tendency of the same word, *calli*, to be translated as "bedroom" or "room" and not simply as "house" in the Spanish glosses and translations of the Nahuatl texts published in *Documentos nahuas*. The analyses of Site Plans 7 and 18 presented below try to further investigate the meaning of the glyph calli. First, I will explain the general observation about the glyph calli in the sixteen site plans as a whole, and later I will present the analyses of Planos 7 and 18.

As I already said above, this corpus of site plans uses two parallel lines to delimit the glyph calli, depicting structures as if they were seen from a certain height and with the different entrances and exits clearly visible. In many cases, these documents depict supports that hold up the walls by the entrance of the building, with small rectangles drawn from the same perspective. Only in the case of Site Plan 16 do we see the frontal part of the house with the entrance of the calli marked by doorposts and lintel like those in the glyphs that represent a *tecpan*, or residence of a ruler in the colonial codices. Site Plan 9b marks the entrance from the exterior to the group of *calli* (houses) and *tlalli* (land) with an arch made of bricks seen from the front. Probably, the element of the arch in the site plan is due to colonial influence. Plano 14 also has an element in the form of an arch as part of the construction of the house.

Aside from the glyphs of calli, these two parallel lines are also used to depict the boundaries of a tlalli, or plot of land, probably indicating the constructed walls. The fact that this convention is used to represent constructed walls seems

FIGURE 6.3. Toponymic glyph *cuauhtli* (eagle), *chimalli* (shield) and two areas that are enclosed by walls with an opening or entrance (glyph P19). [The identification codes are based on Yoneda 2002 (thesis) and Yoneda 2005, and are also used in Carrasco and Sessions 2007, 2010]. [The drawing is based on the digital restoration of the *Mapa de Cuauhtinchan núm. 2* by Castro Mainou, in Marina Straulino (2010:74, fig. 2.38)].

more likely given that other documents use simple dotted lines to depict similar boundaries.[32] Access points to plots of land or structures are also often depicted with human footprints, which are also drawn to depict paths.[33] To note the orientations of the entrances of the houses and of the bedrooms and of the location of the same with respect to the terrain where they are constructed, they use expressions such as *Tonatiuh iquizayampa* (where the sun rises), *Tonatiuh icalaquiyampa* (where the sun sets), or references to Xochimilco,[34] Coyohuacan, and Tenayocan, among locations.

In the documents of wills and lawsuits, these different ways of depicting the physical forms of structures and plots of land that were purchased or inherited

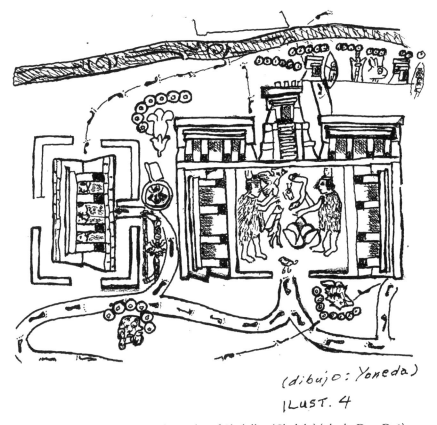

(dibujo: Yoneda)
ILUST. 4

FIGURE 6.4. The archaeological complex of Cholollan (Cholula) (glyphs D17–D28). [The identification codes are based on Yoneda 2002 (thesis) and Yoneda 2005, and are also used in D. Carrasco and Sessions (2007, 2010)]. [The drawing is based on the digital restoration of the *Mapa de Cuauhtinchan núm. 2* by Castro Mainou, in Marina Straulino (2010:74, fig. 2.38)].

were complemented by descriptions of different rituals of ownership or possession. These include entering the house or the bedroom, throwing stones from one side to the other, measuring the lands by placing stakes or digging up land with an agricultural tool next to the houses or bedrooms and scattering the dirt on the houses and land.[35] Perhaps, as Lockhart (1999:243) notes, part of these rituals come from the Spanish tradition. However, rituals such as throwing stones are reminiscent of the act of shooting arrows in the four cardinal directions that the Chichimecs performed when taking possession a land or territory (*Anales de Cuauhtitlan* 1975:6).

Certain elements of the domestic spaces described in these documents remain somewhat obscure. This is the case with the terms *cihuacalli* and *miccacalli*.[36] In the case of the plans reviewed for the present study, it seems that cihuacalli corresponds to a bedroom larger than the other bedrooms in a house. The structures referred to as miccacalli may have played a role similar to a present-day structure referred to as a *santohcalli* in Zongolica, state of Veracruz. Today, this is a room where members of a household put the body of the deceased to hold vigil:

> During the funeral rites, they put the body of the deceased in the *santohcalli*, space in the indigenous house where they place the domestic altar, with the images of saints, candles, incense, flowers, and other ritual paraphernalia . . .
>
> It is in the *santohcalli*, facing the altar, where they perform the vigil. On a bed of tables covered with a mat and white sheets, the body, barren and lifeless, [lies] surrounded by flowers and lit candles. (Rodríguez 2012:100)

Next, I present the analyses of different functions of *calli* in Site Plans 7 and 18.

PLANO 7 (AGN, TIERRAS, VOL. 22, 1A. PARTE, FILE 5, F. 122V) 1564

This site plan (figure 6.5) is included in a file that was published with the title "The case of Juan Quauhtli, *indio*, and Juana, *india*, about a house and *chinampas* (*camellones*) [1564]." Also appearing in the document are Doña María, wife of Don Diego, and Don Pedro Dionisio, residents of San Pablo Teocaltitlan, who are the sellers of a house (*centetl tocal*) and three chinampas of land (*yetetl in chinamitl*). The buyers are Juan Quauhtli, his son Miguel Popoyotl, his wife, María Tiacapan, and his daughter-in-law, Ysabel Jacobia. The property was purchased for twenty-five pesos. A second seller named Anton Tlahui sold a house and a chinampa for the price of six pesos of gold to the same buyers. Doña María and Don Pedro Dionisio clarify that they also have two separate houses that are in the west side of the property, though they appear as two houses with their entrances facing west.[37] These were built by the indios Simón and María, of Tlatilco. They request that the sellers demolish those two houses and that they sell them with the remainder of the property; that is, the house, the dry land, and the chinampa.

On a first glance at the site plan, it would seem that the houses and the chinampas on the property belong to a family, being that the houses share the same patio and the chinampas are together. But, as I discussed above, the text of the file notes that they correspond to two different owners who sold properties to the same buyers, as well as two houses that were built by the couple from Tlatilco.

Site Plan 7 is significant because it illustrates the more complex social histories that can contribute to the origins of a household complex. Despite its initial

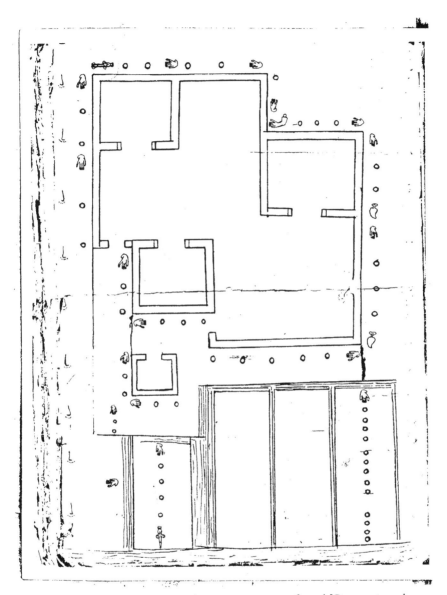

FIGURE 6.5. Plan 7 (AGN, tierras, vol. 22, 1a. parte, exp. 5, f. 122r) [*Documentos nahuas*: 112] 1564.

appearance, the combination of land, houses, and chinampas that are drawn in this plan don't belong to just one family. In the case of this site plan and the accompanying documents, *calli* is translated as "house," reflecting the fact that they are from different families. This instance is in marked contrast to many of the other site plans that I reviewed, in which *calli* is frequently translated as "bedroom" or as "room," being a component of a larger structure that belongs to a single family.

PLANO 18 (AGN, TIERRAS, VOL. 48, FILE 4, F. 16R) 1566, 1576, 1582

Plano 18 (figure 6.6) is connected to a file that is composed of three documents that can be presented in the following chronological order (*Documentos nahuas* 17):[38]

Document 3, dated to 1566, is the Will of Diego Tlacochcalcatl, which mentions his wife, María Tiacapan and his daughter, Ana Tepi.[39] Document 1, which is dated 1576, is the will of Juana Francisca, resident of San Sebastián Tzaqualco. Finally, Document 2, which is dated 1582, provides information about the ownership of houses and lands that Balthasar Pedro and Marta Tepi inherited from Juana Francisca.

In this file, it is evident that the houses and bedrooms (*calli*) underwent different processes of construction and modifications throughout the years. House Plan 18 appears to be most closely associated with Document 2 (year, 1582), both due to the number of pages that make up the file and to its contents.[40] This document mentions that "now only Ana Tepi remains" (paragraph 432), suggesting that the women who had inherited different calli the years before are already dead.[41] It is also evident that Martha Tepi (the older sister of Juana Francisca) and Balthasar Pedro were in charge of the houses while Ana Tepi came to the "age of understanding" (paragraph 432). The site plan depicts a house that is labeled as "the large chamber that they call reception place for women, or *ciucalli*" (paragraph 439).[42] The image of that structure is accompanied with the text of "*yzcatqui ynical* Ana Tepi (here is the house of Ana Tepi)." This document also includes two separately drawn *calli*. One is mentioned as *caltepiton,* or "small bedroom" (paragraph 439), and the other as "*icalnemac* Martha, or "house and bedroom given to said Martha" (paragraph 440). Document 3 (1566) refers to a *miccacalli,* which is translated as "the house of a deceased person."

REFLECTIONS ON THE ANALYSIS OF PLANOS 7 AND 18

In the two examples I analyzed, only Site Plan 18 deals with a group of houses or rooms that all belong to members of the same family and have their entrances to the same patio. At first glance, Site Plan 7 seems like a group of houses or rooms of one family that share the same patio with their chinampas, but further review of the file makes us realize that it isn't so.[43] Site Plan 18 contains information on the houses and lands of which Ana Tepi took possession in 1582. This property was inherited from generation to generation, starting with Diego Tlacochcalcatl and

INDIGENOUS HOUSE PLANS AND LAND IN MEXICO CITY (SIXTEENTH CENTURY) 115

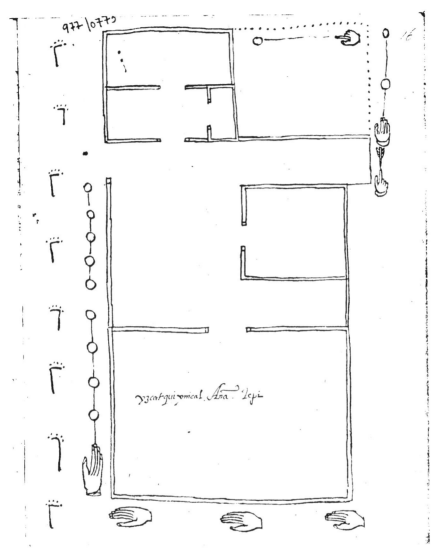

FIGURE 6.6. Plan 18 (AGN, tierras, vol. 48, exp. 4, f. 16r). [*Documentos nahuas*: 179] 1582.

María Tiacapan, his wife. They seem to have built and modified the houses (which function as bedrooms) over time until they reached the hands of Ana Tepi in 1582. The houses, the patio, and the contiguous land were used by a single family until 1582, when Ana Tepi took possession of all of the property as the sole survivor of the family that had the rights to the houses and land. In summation, Site Plan 18 represents the patio around the houses (or bedrooms) and were occupied by the members of different generations of a single family, not by members of different families like in Site Plan 7.

As observed by means of analysis of Site Plans 7 and 18, the drawing of the group of calli that surrounds a patio—together with the canals, chinampas, and lands—doesn't necessarily represent the groups of houses where members of the same family lived. To continue the discussion of this topic, I will turn to ethnographic research on the houses built and modified by the present-day Nahua people of Zongolica. Contemporary practices offer important insights into the larger linguistic and cultural context of household space among Nahua-speaking people. In particular, these ethnographic analogies are useful for understanding why *calli* is a polysemic term, which can refer to both (a) a single-family house composed of various structures, and (b) rooms that form part of a household unit.[44] These analogies also offer insight into the different functional roles that these structures play in the everyday life of Nahua communities.

ETHNOGRAPHIC REFLECTIONS: HOUSEHOLDS IN ZONGOLICA, STATE OF VERACRUZ (END OF THE TWENTIETH CENTURY)

In her work *Ritual, identidad y procesos étnicos en la sierra de Zongolica, Veracruz*, Rodríguez (2003:58) describes the evolution of households in the Nahua-speaking municipality of Atlahuilco. The tendency in this community is for parents, their children, and their children's spouses to share a house until the younger couples become independent. This act of becoming independent is often referred to with the metaphor of "light separate cook fires," referring to the creation of a separate kitchen. Referring to the physical structure of houses, Rodríguez (2003:57) observes that

> the majority of indigenous dwellings are wooden constructions, with a packed earth floor and a peaked roof of hay, shingles,[45] tin sheets, or tiles of baked clay. Even though the mestizo families of the community have gas stoves, the whole population uses open kitchens with wood-burning hearths. The latter are placed on earthen floor at the farthest point from the center of the room in an earth-filled square brazier of about a meter in height. These houses almost always have also another, larger room that they call *santohkalli* (house of the saints), which is used as a bedroom, shrine, and storehouse for harvested corn.
>
> The poorest homes in the community have only one room, in which they cook and sleep. [Even in these poorer homes] it is considered desirable to have a *santohkalli*, a space designated also for the reception of guests during ceremonial commitments.

Although a shrine that is built expressly for ceremonial activities doesn't need to exist, every home has an altar where they place images of saints, candles, grains of corn, medicinal herbs, eggs, incense, and other equipment for ceremonial use.

These ethnographic examples provide insight into the various uses of *calli* in sixteenth-century texts. Probably, various "houses" or rooms that appear drawn in the site plans of Mexico City have been used as a bedroom, storehouse, shrine, or kitchen. Given their location in the lagoon district of Tenochtitlan, and the fact that chinampas are depicted in a number of the site plans, it is also likely that corn for household consumption was stored in some of these structures, even if a broader range of produce was grown on the chinampas or if grain was purchased in the market.

Ethnographic analogy also suggests that households began to evolve when a nuclear family composed of a single married couple built one room. The construction of santohkalli occurs sometime after the initiation of the nuclear family in the house of the parents of the young husband.[46] Its construction implied that the couple is more autonomous than in their initial phase. Rodríguez (2003:57) notes: "The construction of the *santohkalli* generally occurs after some years that accomplish the process of fission of the extended family, that is to say, that they make their 'own cook fire.'"

The construction of a santohkalli thus represents the conclusion of a period in the cycle of development of a domestic group. It is the moment in which the social status of a new couple starts to be recognized. It is likely that a similar process was at work in the sixteenth century, accounting for the emergence of the different calli elements that are depicted in the various site plans. This construction also provides evidence of the multigenerational kinship relationships that existed between the inhabitants of different calli units depicted on the plans.

From this perspective, we can infer that the calli elements in the site plans can have the following meanings: *a house of a family* extended or nuclear, or *a first room* built by newlyweds that is *a house of a nuclear family within the house of an extended family* of two (or more) generations, which represents *the house of the newlyweds*. We can conjecture, also, that the element *calli* in the site plans can be interpreted in different ways for each file. In essence, this term could have had different connotations for each family, be it as a house or as a room with various functions depending on each group of the inhabitants.[47]

In this context of discussion, it is interesting to introduce the following reflection of P. Carrasco (1971:368, in Kellogg 1995:169): "Nahuatl words for family are mostly descriptive terms that refer to common residence and thus correspond more exactly to the English 'household': *cencalli* ('one house'), *cemithualtim* ('those in one yard'), *techan tlaca* ('people in someone's dwelling'), and *cenyeliztli (literally* 'one stay')."

Lockhart (1999:89) mentions that for Molina, *cenyeliztli* means "to be together" and corresponds with the idea of "people whole live in one house." He observes that all of the words that have to do with the notion of "family" emphasize the place where life together happens.

Finally, we can't forget that the residents of a calli are not only relatively young, recently married couples, but an extended family. In the lawsuits, some cases appear in which in these calli lived an unmarried sister of the husband, or a widow or widower of the first generation. Single people, widows, or widowers of both sexes could live in these calli. We have seen, as well, that the site plan and its components—calli, patio, land, and chinampas—apparently of one family, could pertain, in fact, to various families, as is the case of Plano 7.

CONCLUSIONS

In summary, this chapter has focused on investigating the Nahuatl-language documents and house plans drawn according to indigenous pictorial traditions, which can be found the Archivo General of Mexico City. The documents reflect disputes that were aired within the indigenous *barrios* of Mexico-Tenochtitlan, which I have sought to place in their larger social and historical context. To do this, I explained the pictorial system used to represent houses, land, canals, and raised fields, as well as various units of measure that establish their dimension. From there, I turned to the domestic organization of the units of property that were referred to as *calli*, (a term that can be translated alternately as "house" or "room") as well as the different lands and water resources. In order to further contextualize the history of the particular properties described in these disputes, I outlined the broader trends within the politico-territorial organization of pre-Hispanic Mexico, as well as questions regarding the nature of land tenure.

Sixteenth-century documents are especially valuable for understanding this confluence of family and household structure, political geography, and land tenure, as they reflect the heritage of privately and collectively held lands that could be sold, purchased, and inherited through processes for which there are few available data from pre-Hispanic sources. From these early colonial documents, we can surmise that different practices of inheriting, buying, and selling houses and land among indigenous commoners in Mexico probably have pre-Hispanic roots. Through an analysis of house plans 9 and 9b, we see the dispute regarding an *acalli* or "water house" which was used to sell freshwater for over forty years after the salination of water in the lake. In plans 7 and 19, we can observe how houses and lands that bear the superficial appearance of single domestic units have more complicated histories and social compositions. For example, Plan 7 demonstrates a single plot of land with homes belonging to different families, while plan 18 shows a property whose use and form evolved as it was inherited by a single family over numerous generations.

Finally, the analysis of these two house plans alongside ethnographic data from the Nahua community of Zongolica, Veracruz, suggests some of the ways in which we can understand the different permutations of the concept of *calli* and the change of properties and domestic units over time. In particular, these data help us understand how the complexity of these different house sites reflects the changes, additions, and subdivisions that were created as families grew and split.

As a group, these site plans demonstrate elements of household structure and ownership in pre-Hispanic and early colonial Mexico that complicate both our ideas about the nature of domestic spaces and of traditional indigenous land tenure. Just as ethnographic analogies provide insight into the family histories that contributed to the development of different households, the process through which the site plans and legal cases translated indigenous land tenure into the idiom of colonial legalism hints at the mechanisms through which some of these cultural forms survived into the present. Together, ethnographic and historical materials provide a vivid record of the history of quotidian spatial practices and cultural adaptations that are the historical legacy of people like the Nahuatl speakers of Atlahuilco.

Appendix 6.A

SITE PLANS FROM MEXICO CITY (SIXTEENTH CENTURY)
ORGANIZATION OF DATA:

Number: This is the number that was assigned to each site plan during the project.

(Vol., exp., f.): Location of the plan in the Archivo General de la Nación (AGN), Ramo Tierras: volumen, expediente, and folio.

[ ]: The page by number on which the plan is found in the compilation

Year of the case: Year as it appears in the files themselves.

(Name of the major or minor barrio discussed in the case): Some of the cases in *Documentos nahuas* do not include the name of the barrio containing the lands or houses being sued over, but they do always name the barrio of the litigants, witnesses, or person who signs a testimony. In these cases, I took the barrio of the litigants to refer to the barrio that included the properties in question, as these were likely omitted by scribes to avoid redundancy.

....

Plan 4
> Vol. 20, 1a. parte, exp. 3, f. 11v [90] 1567
> (San Juan Moyotlan) San Juan Moyotlan

Plan 7
> Vol. 22, 1a. parte, exp. 5, f. 122v [112] 1564
> (San Pablo Teocaltitlan) San Juan Moyotlan

Plan 9
> Vol. 29, exp. 5, f. 14r [123]1566
> (San Juan Amanalco) San Juan Moyotlan

Plan 9bis
> Vol. 29, exp. 5, ff. 23v–24r [126] 1563
> (San Juan Amanalco) San Juan Moyotlan

Plan 14
> Vol. 38, exp. 2, f. 25v [145] 1553
> (San Juan Xihuitonco) The main barrio is not identified.

INDIGENOUS HOUSE PLANS AND LAND IN MEXICO CITY (SIXTEENTH CENTURY) 121

Plano 15
Vol. 39, 1a. parte, exp. 2, f. 13r [163] s/f?
(San Juan Yopico) San Juan Moyotlan

Plan 16
Vol. 39, 2a. parte, exp. 1, f. 2r [166] 1577
(Santa María Cuepopan) San Juan Moyotlan

Plan 17
Vol. 45, exp. 3, f. 8v [174] 1557
(Pochtlan [Amanalco]) San Juan Moyotlan

Plan 18
Vol. 48, exp. 4, f. 16r [179] 1582
(San Sebastian Tzacualco) San Sebastián Tzacualco

Plan 20
Vol. 54, exp. 5, f. 6r [206] 1587
(San Juan Tlatilco) The main barrio is not identified.

Plan 23a
Vol. 55, exp. 5, f. 16r [249] 1564[48]
(Tlachcuiltitlan) The main barrio is not identified.

Plan 23c
Vol. 55, exp. 5, f. 15v [249] 1564
(Tlachcuiltitlan) The main barrio is not identified.

Plan 25
Vol. 59, exp. 3, f. 16r [267] 1586
(San Juan Necaltitlan) San Juan Moyotlan

Plano 27
Vol. 1810, exp. 1, f. 5r [280] 1585
(Ueuecalco) San Juan Moyotlan

Plano 29b
Vol. 2789, exp. 1, f. 8v [revisar] [286] 1572
(San Sebastián Ahuatonco) San Sebastián Tzacualco

122 YONEDA

Plano 29d
> Vol. 2789, exp. 1, f. 6r [290] 1584
> (San Sebastián Zacatla) San Sebastian Tzacualco

NOTES

1. The registration system used in pictographic documents catalogued as cartographic or historical-cartographic from the early colonial era (Glass 1975) probably has its origin in the pre-Hispanic era. The historical-cartographic documents often, on the one hand, mark the trajectory and route of migrations and conquests; and on the other hand, record lands and borders of the lords who produced the paintings. The principal objective of the production of these maps and canvases is, almost always, political and territorial to justify the reasons for which they claim to defend certain lands, including the involved lords or estates. For better information on the cartographic and historical cartographic documents of different owners and their registration systems, see Boone (2000), Caso (1949), Dibble (1951), Douglas (2010), Glass (1975), Leibsohn (2009), Melgarejo Vivanco (1970, 2015), Smith (1973), Mundy (1996), Williams and Hicks (2011), and Yoneda (1981, 1991, 1994, 1996, 2002, 2005, 2007, 2010).

2. The sixteen planos reviewed for the present chapter, which share general characteristics that are explained soon, in general measure approximately 21.5 cm × 31.5 cm, with the exception of Plano 9b (28 cm × 34.5 cm), Plano 16 (39 cm × 43 cm), and Plano 29b (24 cm × 31 cm).

3. From here on, I will cite this work as *Documentos nahuas* or with the complete title.

4. The collective project I-8a was ascribed to the institution in the period of transition from CISINAH to CIESAS in 1979–1980 and was coordinated by Joaquín Galarza and Keiko Yoneda. The manuscript is dated 1981. This investigation did, however, remain inconclusive, leaving two volumes of preliminary, unfinished manuscripts (Yoneda et al. 1981, Ms.): (vol. 1) typological classification of the component elements of the planos (graphic repertoire); and (vol. 2) preliminary analysis of the elements that contain the planos, by means of the comparison between the planos and the texts in Nahuatl and in Spanish of the reunited files in *Documentos nahuas*.

5. In Appendix 6.A (end of this chapter), I present the data on these sixteen planos as the number of the plano assigned in the study, the location and year of the document, and the names of the major and minor neighborhoods. Through this study, I refer to each plano with the number used in Yoneda et al. (1981, Ms.) noted in this figure.

6. For now, it is not known why the measurement mitl is the only unit of longitudinal measure used to measure houses and lands that doesn't have an apparent relation with the human body (see Matías Alonso 1984). I think, in that regard, that the measurement mitl, which is translated as "the span from the elbow to the other hand" in paragraphs 403 and 981 in the *Documentos nahuas*, originates from the position of the arms and hands when they

INDIGENOUS HOUSE PLANS AND LAND IN MEXICO CITY (SIXTEENTH CENTURY) **123**

place an arrow in a bow in preparation for shooting an arrow. In this manner, it is explained that the measurement mitl in reality has a close relationship with the human body when the body is preparing to shoot and, it is probable, a close relationship to the indigenous concept of using the bow and arrow with dexterity, with these instruments conceived as an extension of their own bodies.

7. The translation of these measurements can vary. See Matías Alonso (1984), Lockhart (1999:209, fig. V. 1.)

8. In the forms of the glyph of maitl there is a great variety, and in many of the forms there is a noticeable occidental influence in how they are stylized. Some glyphs of yolohtli look like hearts of metallic votive offerings or of paintings from the Catholic religion.

9. Thus, the people of Tenochtitlan obtained their first *tlatoani* (ruler) from the Culhuacan lineage, while those of Tlatelolco received theirs from Azcapotzalco. By means of these matrimonial and military alliances, the Mexicas succeed in improving their political position and became allies of the tepanecas from Azcapotzalco. When Huitzilihuitl ruled Mexico-Tenochtitlan, the Mexicas conquered the *colhuas*, the people from the town where their ruling lineage came from. Upon the death of Tezozomoc, lord of Azcapotzalco and ally-protector of the Mexicas, Maxtla, the successor to Tezozomoc, assumed the throne. Given that there was no alliance between the Mexicas and Maxtla, this time the Mexicas allied themselves with the *acolhuas* from Texcoco and defeated the tepanecas in 1430.

10. I refer to the construction of the wall/cistern because planos 9 and 9b, analyzed later, have to do with the sale of freshwater.

11. Ten of the sixteen planos have the element of water as chinampas and canals, only canals, or a dike. It is observed as a rule to draw the chinampas and canals in the lower part, or on the right side of the planos, since five of the ten planos have canals and chinampas or another type of water (only canals, dike) in the lower part, four plans draw them in the right side, and one plan puts the element in the upper part.

12. Yoneda's clarification.

13. Kobayashi (1993:54) explains as follows the hierarchical relationship between a tlatoani and a hueytlatoani: "The estates of the basin of Mexico varied greatly in their population and territorial extension. Consequently, some were under the intervention of the other, more powerful *tlatoani*. For example, the *hueytlatoani* of Tenochtitlan imposed his *calpixque* on the estates of the Basin of Mexico and its environs."

14. The definition of *calpulli* was a topic of discussion between academics since the work presented by Bandelier (1966). Gibson (1967:263) in note 1 comments on the studies that correct Bandelier's idea. L. Reyes García (1996) and H. Martínez (2000) present other reflections to specify the definition in the sense that *calpulli* doesn't represent a self-sufficient community of the *macehualli* that existed in the prehispanic era, and should be better recognized as a synonym of *tlaxilacalli*, *tecalli*, *tecpan*, or *tlahtocayo*. In spite of the fact that many

decades have already passed since scholars started to correct the proposal made by Bandelier (1966), to date, researchers exist that repeat his same proposal.

15. *Tlaxilacalli* was translated as neighborhood or *señorío* in the documents in Spanish (Gibson 1967:37).

16. It seems there are terms that include concepts associated with the land or the locality where the seats of political and territorial units are established, connected to the supernatural entity attributed to the place and the ritual that was practiced in the entity's honor, such as *altepetl, calpulli*, and *tlaxilacalli*. Other terms underline more, rather, the authority and political territory of the aforementioned entity (Reyes García 1996; P. Carrasco 1996:146; Lockhart 1999:235).

17. I consider that rather a family or a "domestic unit" possessed *hueca tlalli* or *inic oncan tlalli*.

18. In Plano 4 reviewed for the present study, the lands are drawn in Tola that aren't found next to the *calli* (house, accommodation) wherein lived the owners of the calli. In some records written in Latin, characters published in the *Documentos nahuas* also refer to the lands located far from the place where the owners lived.

19. (2. *Calpolalli*) lands of the *calpulli*. The right of corporation was strong, and these lands were subject to allocation. (3. *Tequitcatlalli. Tequitlalli.*) land with obligations of tribute. Essentially, they are the same lands as calpolalli (Lockhart 1999:231, fig. V.3.).

20. As already mentioned above, the majority of the measurements of the pages of the 16 planos consulted for the present study are about 21.5 cm × 31.5 cm, with the exception of Plano 9b (28 cm × 34.5 cm), Plano 16 (38 cm × 43 cm), and Plano 29b (24 cm × 31 cm).

21. See Yoneda (1996:ch. IV; 2007, 2010).

22. In some of these suits, women don't only participate in the disputes as litigants but are the *ones* who "talk" when their husbands silently file the complaint (Gibson 1967:154n75).

23. Kellogg notes that these characterizations of the indios and other characteristics of the Spanish start to disappear through the sixteenth–seventeenth centuries.

24. María Teuchon appears as María Tiacapan (paragraph 177) and María Papan (paragraphs 179 and 180). The motive for these variations is unknown for now. Besides, in the title of the third document it says María Teuhcho, and in paragraph 198 of the same document, María Teucchon. She is mentioned, also, as María Tecuicchon in the title of the fourth document. Gabriel Yaotl appears referred to, as well, as Graviel or Grabiel (paragraphs 202 and 191).

25. In accordance with Yoneda et al. (1981, Ms. Vol. 1), the separated "Position of the *planos*" mentions that Plano 9b seems to be missing after it was photographed in 1978. Based on the upper/lower relationship of the text in the following page, I determined the position of the plano in such a way that the chinampas are located in the lower part of the page. It should be noted that the position in which Plano 9b is published in the book *Documentos nahuas* is turned 180 degrees, leaving the upper and lower parts inverted.

INDIGENOUS HOUSE PLANS AND LAND IN MEXICO CITY (SIXTEENTH CENTURY)   **125**

26. "... and the land on which the house is located measures seven *brazas* in width, and eleven [*brazas*] in length with three *chinamitl*" (*Documentos nahuas*: paragraph 176).

27. As Fray Alonso de Molina (1977) mentions, *acalli* means canoe, and in fact there is a glyph of a canoe in the water, but in the case of this file, I mention that the "casilla de agua (little house of water)" or the house where they sold water is what they called *acalli*. Lockhart (1999: 383n5) observes that *acalli* literally means "water house." Based on this information, I think that the glyph *acalli* (canoe) drawn in the water (in Plano 9) represents the name of the house where they sold water and doesn't indicate precisely the existence of a canoe in itself.

28. The walls of the house are drawn in red.

29. The structure is drawn in yellow.

30. It's important to mention that the form in which the water is drawn with movement (by way of curved lines) using the colors light blue, dark blue, and black lines, adds information about the characteristics of the water. It should be remembered that the water in the canals in other planos are drawn with simple lines, without color, representing the lack of movement. Probably, the water in Plano 9 is a source, and for this reason served for sale when the brackish water rose.

31. The identification codes are based on: Yoneda 2002 [thesis] and Yoneda 2005, used also in D. Carrasco and Sessions (2007, 2010).

32. As already mentioned in previous pages, in these plans the chinampas are separated by the water from the canals. These canals are generally located in the lower or right side, and are drawn with wavy or straight lines, occasionally combined with swirls. Some terms in Nahuatl relative to the parts of the house or architectural characteristics of calli are saved in the work of Marcos Matías Alonso (1984:95–97), and the names of the longitudinal measurements of calli and tlalli are found in Matías Alonso (1984) and in Lockhart (1999:209, fig. V. 1.).

33. The human footprints are one of the most versatile glyphs that are found in the pictographic documents of the indigenous tradition in central Mexico. Aside from marking the entrance/exit and paths, they indicate routes of migration, routes to note boundaries, military expeditions, and transfers of various meanings. The human footprints indicate, also, longitudinal measurements, and they form part of the anthroponymic and toponymic glyphs.

34. Perhaps this refers to the larger neighborhood of this name: San Pablo Zoquipan (Teopan, Xochimilco).

35. "And as a sign that the buyers took ownership (with a *coa* they dug up land next to said houses) and they took from it and scattered it over all that they had bought [so that those who sold it don't say something again]" (paragraph 168 of *Documentos nahuas*, referring to the file that contains Plano 7).

36. Concerning *cihuacalli*, Lockhart (1999:88–89, 201) presents some reflections.

37. We consider that the tlacuilo described in Nahuatl information on these houses is incorrect, because the only houses that could correspond to these two houses in Plano 7 have their doors facing west.

38. In the book, the order of publication of the documents is 1, 2, and 3.

39. This Ana Tepi isn't the Ana Tepi that appears in documents 1 (1576) and 2 (1582), since in the latter, Ana Tepi is mentioned as the daughter of Juana Francisca. Probably, the names of family members repeat in different generations of the same family.

40. Document 2 is composed of pages 15r, 15v, 16r, and 17r, with the plan being page 16r. We can connect, without equivocation, Plano 18 to this document.

41. These are María Tlaco (the sister of Ana Tepi and daughter of Juana Francisca) (paragraph 430) and Marta and Magdalena (who "were born together") (paragraph 431).

42. As I already mentioned above, the function of *cihuacalli* isn't clear (see Lockhart 1999:88–99, 201). In the files and *planos* that I consulted, it seems that, in general, they are *calli* of a larger size than the rest of the bedrooms.

43. It is still not clear if the two houses toward the top of the plano correspond effectively to these houses that they thought of demolishing because, as I noted above, the orientation of the doors doesn't correspond to the orientation mentioned in the text.

44. On this and other topics connected to calli, see "Chapter III: The domestic dwelling" by Lockhart (1999:89).

45. *Tejamaní, tejamanil, tajamanil* (s.m. Cuba, Mexico, and Puerto Rico): thick panel placed like a tile on the roof or ceiling of a house (*El pequeño Larousse ilustrado 2004* 2003).

46. The community of Zongolica, Ver. The term patrilocal (however, for the moment, I don't know if it is patrilineal or not). "*Patrilineal*: adj. ANTROP. Said of a form of filiation that only has kinship through the paternal line" (*El pequeño Larousse ilustrado 2004* 2003). "*Patrilocal*: adj. ANTROP. Said of a form of residency of newlyweds, who must live with the family of the husband" (*El pequeño Larousse ilustrado 2004* 2003).

47. It should be mentioned that the works referenced in the chapters of the book *About the House: Levi-Strauss and Beyond* (Carsten and Hugh-Jones 1995) offer many possibilities for deepening the study of the concept of *calli* by means of focusing attention on the house as an object of study through different perspectives. It would be interesting to contrast the results of the chapters of the book *About the House* with the data contained in the planos and the files material of the present study, in future research.

48. For plans 23a and 23c I retained the labels that were used in the original project (Yoneda et al. 1981). I should add that despite the ordering of the individual pages in plan 23c, (found in file 15v), this one is placed before plan 23a (located in file 16r). Also, the file indicates that 23a was first used as a reference during the trial and 23c after the resolution.

REFERENCES

Anales de Cuauhtitlan. 1975. *"Véase Códice Chimalpopoca." Anales de Cuauhtitlan y Leyenda de los soles* (1975).

Bandelier, Adolfo. [1878] 1966. "Sobre la distribución y tenencia de tierras y costumbres sobre herencia de los antiguos mexicanos." In *El desarrollo de la sociedad mexicana*, ed. Mauro Olmeda, 1:231–57. Mexico City.

Boone, Elizabeth Hill. 2000. *Stories in Red and Black: Pictorial Histories of the Aztecs and Mixtecs*. Austin: University of Texas Press.

Carrasco, David, and Scott Sessions. 2007. *Cave, City and Eagle's Nest: An Interpretive Journey of Mapa de Cuauhtinchan No. 2*, ed. David Carrasco and Scott Sessions, 161–203. Albuquerque: University of New Mexico Press.

Carrasco, David, and Scott Sessions. 2010. *Cueva, ciudad y nido de águila: Una travesía interpretativa por el mapa de Cuauhtinchan Núm. 2*, ed. David Carrasco and Scott Sessions, 161–203. Albuquerque: University of New Mexico Press.

Carrasco, Pedro. 1971. "Social Organization of Ancient Mexico." In *Archaeology of Northern Mesoamérica, part 1*, ed. Gordon F. Ekholm and Ignacio Bernal, 349–75. Vol. 10 of *Handbook of Middle American Indians*, Robert Wauchope, general editor. Austin: University of Texas Press.

Carrasco, Pedro. 1996. *Estructura político-territorial del Imperio tenochca: La Triple Alianza de Tenochtitlán, Tetzcoco y Tlacopán*. Mexico City: FCE / El Colegio de México.

Carsten, Janet, and Stephen Hugh-Jones, eds. 1995. *About the House: Levi-Strauss and Beyond*. Cambridge: Cambridge University Press.

Caso, Alfonso. 1949. *El mapa de Teozacoalco*. México: Editorial Cultura.

Caso, Alfonso. 1965. "Los barrios antiguos de Tenochtitlan y Tlatelolco." In *Memorias de la Academia Mexicana de la Historia* 15 (1965): 7–63.

Castro Gutierrez, Felipe. 2010. "El origen y conformación de los Barrios de Indios." In *Las Indias y las ciudades en Nucun España*, ed. Felipe Castro Gutierrez, 105–30. Mexico City: UNAM.

Códice Chimalpopoca: Anales de Cuauhtitlan y Leyenda de los soles. 1975. Traducción del nahuatl al español: Primo Feliciano Velázquez. México: UNAM.

Dibble, Charles, ed. 1951. *Códice Xolotl*. México: Universidad Nacional de México.

Douglas, Eduardo de J. 2010. *In the Palace of Nezahualcoyotl: Painting Manuscripts, Writing the Pre-Hispanic Past in Early Colonial Period Tetzcoco, Mexico*. William and Bettye Nowlin Series in Art, History, and Culture. Austin: University of Texas Press.

[El] pequeño Larousse ilustrado 2004. 2003. Mexico City: Ediciones Larousse, S. A. de C. V.

Gibson, Charles. 1967. *Los aztecas bajo el dominio español (1519–1810)*. Mexico City: Siglo XXI Editores, S. A.

Glass, John B. 1975. "A Survey of Native Middle American Pictorial Manuscripts." In *Handbook of Middle American Indians*, vol. 14, 81–252. Austin: University of Texas.

Kellogg, Susan. 1995. *Law and the Transformation of Aztec Culture, 1500–1700*. Norman: University of Oklahoma Press.

Kirchhoff, Paul, Lina Odena Güemes, and Luis Reyes García. 1976. *Historia tolteca chichimeca*. Mexico City: INAH-SEP-CISINAH.

Kobayashi, Munehiro. 1993. *Tres estudios sobre el sistema tributario de los mexicas*. Mexico City: CIESAS–Kobe City University of Foreign Studies.

Liebsohn, Dana. 2009. *Script and Glyph: Pre-Hispanic History, Colonial Bookmaking and the Historia Tolteca-Chichimeca*. Washington, DC: Dumbarton Oaks Research Library and Collection.

Lockhart, James. 1999. *Los nahuas después de la conquista: Historia social y cultural de los indios de México central, del siglo XVI al XVIII*. Mexico City: FCE.

López Austin, Alfredo, and Leonardo López Luján. 2008. *El pasado indígena*. Mexico City: FCE–El colegio de México, Fideicomiso Historia de las Américas.

Mapa de Cuauhtinchan No. 2 [MC2]. Documento pictográfico (histórico-cartográfico) producido en Cuauhtinchan, estado de Puebla en el siglo XVI. Al parecer entre los años 1918 y 1920 el MC2 fue sacado del pueblo de Cuauhtinchan. Desde 1946 (o aún antes) hasta 2001, el MC2 formaba parte de la colección particular del arquitecto Carlos Obregón Santacilia y de sus descendientes. El día 24 de junio de 1963, el MC2 fue declarado "monumento histórico" por el INAH. El día 13 de noviembre de 2001, el documento pasó a manos de la señora Ángeles Espinosa Yglesias, entonces directora del Museo Amparo en Puebla, y actualmente se encuentra bajo la custodia de sus descendientes [Pictographic (historic-cartographic) document produced in Cuauhtinchan in the state of Puebla in the sixteenth century. It appears that between 1918 and 1920, the MC2 was taken from the pueblo of Cuauhtinchan. From 1946 (or even before) until 2001, the MC2 was part of the personal collection of Carlos Obregón Santacilia and his descendants. On June 24, 1963, the MC2 was declared a "historical monument" by the INAH. On November 13, 2001, the document came into possession of Señora Ángeles Espinosa Yglesias, then director of the Museo Amparo in Puebla, and currently it is under the custodianship of her descendants.].

Mapa de Cuauhtinchan No. 3 [MC3]. Documento pictográfico (histórico-cartográfico) producido en Cuauhtinchan, estado de Puebla en el siglo XVI. El MC3, que se encontraba en manos de Arístides Martel, al parecer fue expropiado por la Inspección General de Monumentos Artísticos e Históricos por el año de 1919. En 1939 el MC3 apareció en los inventarios de la colección de códices del Museo Nacional de Antropología y, en la actualidad, sigue custodiado en el Fondo de códices de la Biblioteca del Museo Nacional de Antropología [Pictographic (historic-cartographic) document produced in Cuauhtinchan, state of Puebla in the sixteenth century. The MC3, which was found in the possession of Arístides Martel, appears to be have been expropriated by the Inspección General de Monumentos Artísticos e Históricos for the year 1919. In 1939 the MC3 appeared in the inventories of the collection of the codes of the Museo Nacional de Antropología and, in the present time, continues to be under the custodianship of the Fondo de códices of the Biblioteca del Museo Nacional de Antropología].

Martínez, Hildeberto. 1984. *Tepeaca en el siglo XVI: Tenencia de la tierra y organización de un señorío, 21.* Mexico City: CIESAS, Ediciones de la Casa Chata.

Martínez, Hildeberto. 2000. "El calpulli: ¿Otra acepción de teccalli?" In *Journal of Intercultural Studies*, (27): 194–208. Osaka: Kansai Gaidai University Publication.

Matías Alonso, Marcos. 1984. *Medidas indígenas de longitud. (En documentos de la Ciudad de México del siglo XVI).* Mexico City: Cuadernos de la Casa Chata 94, CIESAS.

Melgarejo Vivanco, José Luis. 1970. *Códices Tuxpan: Los lienzos de Tuxpan.* México: Editorial La Estampa Mexicana.

Melgarejo Vivanco, José Luis. 2015. *Códices de tierras: Los lienzos de Tuxpan.* Xalapa, Veracruz, Mexico: Universidad Veracruzana.

Molina, Fray Alonso de. 1977. *Vocabulario en lengua castellana y mexicana y mexicana y castellana.* Mexico City: Porrúa.

Mundy, Barbara E. 1996. *The Mapping of New Spain: Indigenous Cartography and the Maps of the Relaciones Geográficas.* Chicago: University of Chicago Press.

Navarrete Linares, Federico. 1999. *La migración de los mexicas.* Mexico City: CONACULTA.

Reyes García, Luis. 1977. *Cuauhtinchan del siglo XII al XVI: Formación y desarrollo histórico de un señorío prehispánico.* Wiesbaden: Franz Steiner Verlag GmbH.

Reyes García, Luis. 1996. "El término calpulli en documentos del siglo XVI." In *Documentos nahuas de la ciudad de México del siglo XVI*, ed. Luis Reyes García et al., 21–68. Mexico City: CIESAS-AGN.

Reyes García, Luis, Eustaquio Celestino Solís, Armando Valencia Ríos, Constantino Medina Lima, and Gregorio Guerrero. 1996. *Documentos nahuas de la ciudad de México del siglo XVI.* Mexico City: CIESAS-AGN.

Rodríguez, María Teresa. 2003. *Ritual, identidad y procesos étnicos en la sierra de Zongolica, Veracruz.* Mexico City: CIESAS.

Rodríguez, María Teresa. 2012. "Rituales de muerte y parentesco en la tradición nahua de la sierra de Zongolica." In *Diálogo andino* (no. 40, December 2012): 97–110, Arica, Chile.

Rojas Rabiela, Teresa. 1987. *Padrones de Tlaxcala del siglo XVI y Padrón de nobles de Ocotelolco.* Colección Documentos 1. Mexico City: CIESAS, Ediciones de la Casa Chata.

Rojas Rabiela, Teresa. 1991. *Pedro Armillas: Vida y obra*, 2 vols. Mexico City: CIESAS-INAH.

Smith, Mary E. 1973. *Picture Writing from Ancient Southern Mexico*. Norman: University of Oklahoma Press.

Straulino, Marina. 2010. "Capítulo Dos. Una nueva visión. La conservación y restauración digital del Mapa de Cuauhtinchan núm. 2." In *Cueva, ciudad y nido de águila: Una travesía interpretativa por el Mapa de Cuauhtinchan núm. 2*, ed. David Carrasco and Scott Sessions, 49–79. Albuquerque: University of New Mexico Press.

Williams, Barbara J., and Frederic Hicks, eds. 2011. *Códice Vergara*. Mexico City: UNAM.

Yoneda, Keiko. 1981. *Los mapas de Cuauhtinchan y la historia cartográfica prehispánica*, 1st ed. México, DF: Dirección de Difusión y Publicaciones del Archivo General de la Nación.

Yoneda, Keiko. 1991. *Los mapas de Cuauhtinchan y la historia cartográfica prehispánica*, 2nd ed. México, DF: CIESAS; Puebla: Estado de Puebla ; México DF: Fondo de Cultura Económica.

Yoneda, Keiko. 1994. *Cartografía y linderos en el Mapa de Cuauhtinchan No. 4*. México: INAH-BUAP.

Yoneda, Keiko. 1996. *Migraciones y conquistas: Descifre global del Mapa de Cuauhtinchan núm. 3. Colección Científica 289*. Mexico City: INAH.

Yoneda, Keiko. 2002. *Cultura y cosmovisión chichimecas en el Mapa de Cuauhtinchan No. 2. Tesis doctoral en Antropología*. Mexico City: UNAM.

Yoneda, Keiko. 2005. *Mapa de Cuauhtinchan núm. 2*. México: Porrúa, CIESAS.

Yoneda, Keiko. 2007. "Chapter Seven Glyphs and Messages in the Mapa de Cuauhtinchan No. 2. Chicomoztoc, Itzpapalotl, and 13 Flint." In *Cave, City and Eagle's Nest: An Interpretive Journey of Mapa de Cuauhtinchan No. 2*, ed. David Carrasco and Scott Sessions, 161–203. Albuquerque: University of New Mexico Press.

Yoneda, Keiko. 2010. "Capítulo Siete: Glifos y mensajes en el Mapa de Cuauhtinchan Núm. 2. Chicomoztoc, Itzpapalotl y 13 tecpatl." In *Cueva, ciudad y nido de águila: Una travesía interpretativa por el mapa de Cuauhtinchan Núm. 2*, ed. David Carrasco and Scott Sessions, 161–203. Albuquerque: University of New Mexico Press.

Yoneda, Keiko, Joaquín Galarza, Jesús Manuel Macías, Marcos Matías, Jorge Pedraza, and Lilianne Taboada. 1981. *Veinte planos indígenas de la ciudad de México. Siglo XVI (vol. 1: texto) (vol. 2: catálogo gráfico analítico)*. Mexico City: CIESAS.

7

The Archaeology of Place in Ebtún, Yucatán, Mexico

RANI T. ALEXANDER

In his 1996 address to the American Society of Ethnohistory entitled *Mesoamerica's Ethnographic Past*, John Chance advocated a more skeptical stance toward cultural continuity lest anthropologists risk inventing their own historical traditions. He remarked that because "an ethnographic past had been fashioned to meet the needs of an ethnographic present" (Chance 1996:385), many of Mesoamerican ethnography's most cherished concepts have not received the historical attention that they deserve. In this chapter I examine one of those concepts—the assumed continuity of relations between place, community, and patronym group on Mexico's Yucatán Peninsula among Maya-speaking descendant communities of Chichén Itzá. Using nineteenth-century censuses and *padrones* from the Archivo General del Estado de Yucatán (AGEY) for the town of Ebtún and related communities located southwest of the city of Valladolid,[1] I examine evidence of the connections between people and place for an era where there should not be any continuity—before and after Yucatán's Caste War, a violent indigenous revitalization movement that unfolded between 1847 and 1901 (Bricker 1981; Dumond 1997; Reed 2001; Rugeley 1997, 2009; Sullivan 1989).

My goal is to examine "who lived where" and to uncover the foundations on which historical memories were reproduced in Ebtún and related communities in the post–Caste War era. Were the same connections between people and place evident after the violence of the rebellion abated? My analysis draws on the notion that landscape change is a historically contingent process (Lightfoot 2004). Landscapes

DOI: 10.5876/9781607325727.c007

are produced as the "spaces" that delimit physical experience and are bound to "places" that are imbued with meanings derived from experience, which create cartographic representations of the world (Ingold 1993; Smith 2003:11). Chief among the practices that ascribe meaning to locations is the act of dwelling (Ingold 1993), which in turn is bounded by residents' decisions of where to live, how long to stay, and when to leave. These processes inscribe the archaeological record and create variation in the life histories of sites and their associated material systems—an *archaeology of place* (Alexander 2012a; e.g., Basso 1996; Binford 1982; McAnany 1995; Rubertone 2008).

POPULATION CIRCULATION AND RESILIENCE

In the nineteenth and twentieth centuries, place making among the descendant communities of Chichén Itzá was inextricably tied to the process of population circulation (see Schachner 2012 for the American Southwest)—the intraregional and multiscalar movements of households and individuals across the landscape, known in Yucatán as dispersal, drift, and flight (Alexander 2006; Farriss 1978, 1984). Changes in an individual's or a group's residence underwrote access to land, resources, and redefined kin and community obligations (Quezada 2014; Redfield and Villa Rojas 1934; Roys 1939). Population circulation typically transforms the relationship between people and space, resulting in subtle shifts in the composition of social groups, interactions, leadership, and the reproduction of social memory. By using written evidence to map out who lived where in space and time, it is possible to understand how past shifts in social configurations underpin representations of both tangible and intangible heritage for contemporary stakeholder communities.

Questions about the cultural changes produced by population movements in the wake of Yucatán's Caste War challenge established explanations for cultural continuity developed for traditional Maya-speaking peasant communities in my study area. Today the narrative of Maya cultural continuity in the face of overwhelming global pressure has a new name—smallholder resilience (Alexander 2012b). Smallholders are autonomous agriculturalists who practice intensive and sustainable cultivation on their own land for their own subsistence and for sale in local or regional markets (Netting 1993). Smallholding agricultural systems are resilient because they have the capacity to cope with political uncertainty and environmental change in ways that are sustainable over the longue durée (Holling and Gunderson 2002; Scarborough and Burnside 2010). Yet, this does not mean they are unchanging and immutable. Over time smallholders create distinctive landscapes recognizable across the globe, which are characterized by high levels of biodiversity and are maintained through careful micromanagement of the environment. Smallholding landscapes owe their longevity to sustained transmission of traditional ecological knowledge that integrates both social and environmental learning (Netting 1993; Stone 1996, 2007; Wilk 1991). Moreover, continuities in the transmission of ecological knowledge clearly depend on the ways that population movement reconfigures residence, place, and the composition of social groups.

Two things especially underwrite resilience among smallholders—stability of land ownership and autonomy of local leadership (Netting 1993). The corpus of Maya-language documents known as the *Titles of Ebtun* (Roys 1939), which basically defines this study, attests to constancy of native leadership and landholding throughout the colonial period for Ebtún and the related communities of Cuncunul, Kaua, Tekom, and Tixcacalcupul (figure 7.1). It is important to note that notions of land ownership do not follow European norms (Quezada 2014). Rather, security of usufruct depended on the historically contingent interplay among patronym groups, residence, kin and community obligations, and place, which were expressed in oral tradition, in Maya- and Spanish-language documents, and in the material record. An important accomplishment of Roys's research was to document long-term continuities in land use that linked patronym groups (*chibal*) to new colonial settlements (*cah*) and to places and locations mentioned in the documents (*cenote*[2] [natural water source], *kax* [forest], *chen* [well], *labcah* [abandoned or rotted town]) from 1600 to 1833. Yet, for the era following Mexico's independence from Spain in 1821, historians point to instability of both native leadership and landholding as causes of the Caste War (Cline 1947; Dumond 1997; Reed 2001; Rugeley 1997). In the area around Ebtún, the violence of the revolt resulted in drastic population decline, settlement aggregation, population movement, and political-economic reorganization.

It is possible to ascertain how the relationships between people and place shifted over time by reading the evidence gleaned from Yucatán's detailed nineteenth-century censuses against the archaeological record. Below, I scrutinize the written evidence from the AGEY censuses for stability in landholding and leadership before and after the 1847 revolt. I begin with an outline of the social and spatial transformations that occurred after the Spanish invasion. Next, I analyze changes in population, settlement, and household size to reveal variation in their composition over time. I compare the distribution of surnames among settlements before and after the Caste War to reveal changes in the stability of leadership. My results show how population movement created different trajectories in the ways communities were tied to place, which are manifest in both tangible and intangible expressions of historical memory (Alexander 2012a). Finally I consider how nineteenth-century population movements and Caste War experiences are reflected in the material record. A discussion of the occupation history of two land parcels, the cenotes

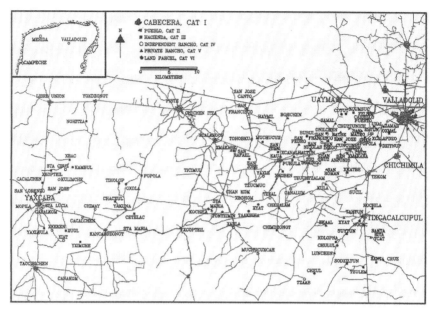

FIGURE 7.1. Locations of sites in the study area in Eastern Yucatán.

of Tzaab and Bubul, in comparison to Chan Kom illuminates the connections between the past and the present. Place making at both Tzaab and Bubul stand in stark contrast to the migration narrative of the founding of Chan Kom (Redfield and Villa Rojas 1934)—an "ethnographic past" (Chance 1996) that has long been considered the archetypical model for intraregional population movement in this region (see Alexander 2006, 2012a).

MAYA SOCIAL ORGANIZATION

In Yucatán, as in other Mesoamerican regions, place—rather than language, class or ethnicity—is the idiom for expressing sociocultural identity (Berdan et al. 2008). The *Titles of Ebtun* (Roys 1939) and other Maya-language colonial documents describe a range of social units that also have spatial referents (Hanks 2010; Okoshi Harada 2006, 2009, 2011; Quezada 1993, 2014; Thompson 1999) (table 7.1). In AD 1450 Yucatán's farming communities were organized under numerous, autonomous political jurisdictions or city-states. Some were politically centralized and ruled by a *halach uinic* (great lord, king); others were collections of towns ruled by *batabs* (governors) (Okoshi Harada 2006; Quezada 1993, 2014; Roys 1943, 1957,). The towns united under the Cupul polity—which later included Ebtún, Cuncunul,

Kaua, Tekom, and Tixcacalcupul—were governed by batabs who were consanguineally related (Quezada 1993, 2014; Roys 1957). The batab was a political leader and member of a noble house who administered various *cuchteel*, a social unit composed of extended or multifamily households, including consanguineous and affinal kin, who recognized a local leader and who often lived contiguously in the same residential unit or ward. The cuchteel also functioned as a corporate unit, providing for cooperative labor arrangements and mutual aid. Households known as *otochnalob* (householders; the suffix *–ob* is plural in Yukatek/Yucatec) also belonged to a patronym group (*chibal*). In addition, householders were identified as native to specific towns (Okoshi Harada 2009; Quezada and Okoshi Harada 2001; Roys 1939; Thompson 1999). Families were identified with particular places, often described as *kax* (forest), *dzonot* (cenote), *chen* (well), labcah (abandoned town), and *col* (milpa), which became the basis for claims of usufruct, community rights, and land tenure in the late sixteenth century.

Since these and other Maya-language terms have come down to us from sixteenth-century and later documentary sources, debates center on how social organization was altered after the Spanish invasion (e.g., Farriss 1984; Okoshi Harada et al. 2006; Quezada 1985, 1993, 2014). In the wake of demographic decline wrought by the disastrous introduction of European pathogens, the Spaniards implemented a forcible resettlement policy known as *congregación*, whereby people living in small, dispersed settlements were relocated to planned towns. The inhabitants of the city-state of Cupul who moved to the new communities of Ebtún, Cuncunul, Kaua, Tekom, and Tixcacalcupul retained the right to cultivate lands near their previous residences (*labcah*—abandoned towns) (Roys 1939:10). In addition, they recorded which families had previously resided in specific places and to which of the congregación towns they had moved. Specific cuchteels became established in named barrios or wards of congregación towns, often maintaining a degree of political autonomy as a *parcialidad* (ward, barrio). For example, in Tixcacalcupul, the parcialidad of Tahtun is still recognized as a separate barrio surrounding the cenote of Tahtun today. Thereafter, the *cah* (community), the chibal (patronym group), and the household (otochnal) became the principal units of social organization (Farriss 1984; Restall 1998).

Demographic information from the early colonial period suggests that households may have ranged in size from two to eleven persons who resided in two–three structures grouped around a patio within a solar or house lot (Restall 1998:3).[3] Spanish authorities also tried to split up large extended and multifamily households and resettle them as nuclear family units, though some evidence suggests that extended family organization persisted, particularly in areas of lax ecclesiastical supervision (Roys et al. 1959; Roys et al. 1940; Scholes and Roys 1948;

TABLE 7.1. Maya social organization

Maya term	Description
Cuchcabal	A politically centralized city-state or kingdom ruled by a *halach uinic* who resided in the capital, and consisting of several dependencies (*batabils*); political jurisdiction composed of noncontiguous places (not territory) containing settlements and resources.
Batabil	Chiefship, a politically decentralized jurisdiction consisting of towns and places under the authority of a *batab* (governor, cacique) and consisting of subunits called *cuchteels*.
Cah	Community, town; labcah—old, abandoned, rotted town.
Cuchteel	a group of patrilineally related extended families, including consanguineous and affinal kin, forming a social and corporate unit who recognized a local leader (*ahcuchcab, ah kul*) and lived contiguously in the same ward. Before *congregación* (explained below), this group gave its patronymic to the location its members inhabited.
Chibal	Patronym group, a shallow patrilineage; patronyms are widely distributed among towns in any given region, but some patronyms are clustered in specific towns.*
Otochnal	Household, homeowner, native of a particular town; usually residing in two– three dwellings grouped around a patio within a house lot or solar.

Sources: Hanks 2010; Okoshi Harada 2006, 2009, 2011; Quezada 1993, 2014; Quezada and Okoshi Harada 2001; Restall 1997; Roys 1939, 1943, 1957; Thompson 1999:35–36.

* The chibal should not be equated with distinct sociopolitical or ethnic groups. Thompson (1999:77) mentions that in the early colonial period, chibals were grouped into patriclans known as *kilacabil*, and some evidence from Tekanto and Sotuta (located south of the area depicted in figure 7.1) suggests that patriclans were viable into the eighteenth century.

Weeks 1988). The fate of the chibal (patronym group) is particularly murky. In the early colonial period, patronym groups held land; marriage was exogamous; and people of the same *chibal* living in different villages recognized a social connection (Farriss 1984; Okoshi Harada 2011; Restall 1998; Roys 1943; Thompson 1999). Yet, by the eighteenth century the chibal had become shallower (Thompson 1999:77). Among some patronym groups, there was a tendency for community endogamy, but it is a common misconception that patronyms are exclusive to specific towns or regions in Yucatán. Some patronym groups dominated the leadership of specific towns over long time periods (Okoshi Harada 2009, 2011; Roys 1939). For example, many batabs of Ebtún were drawn from the Camal patronym group from the sixteenth century to the present (Roys 1939:48–49). Today, we know that people construct identities around place, especially the *cah* (town) and the household, but patronym groups are still pivotal to understanding shifts in political authority and place making.

It is important to point out that the colonial congregación orders entailed much more than the movement of people from one place to another. According to William Hanks (2010:xiv, 7), congregación was a means of coordinating the transformation of space, but the total project of *reducción* (forced resettlement) purposefully reformed conduct and language as well as space and place. Settlement aggregation and changes in town layout went hand in hand with the Franciscan missionaries' efforts to instill Christian civility, correct behavior, and governance among the native population, which in turn were shaped by the transformation of Maya language, grammar, and notions of proper speech (Hanks 2010:4; 2012). Resettlement was coordinated with systematic attempts to alter meanings and usages in the Mayan language, but the consequent landscape transformations did not simply replace older meanings with contemporary ones. Instead, reducción added new semantic values to places, "layering perspectives" in the community's collective memory (Hanks 2010:306).

I suggest that this layering of geopolitics, kin politics, and household organization provided the basis for negotiating leadership and landholding before and after the Caste War. My evidence for who lived where comes from a remarkable series of censuses in the Archivo General del Estado de Yucatán,[4] which list all towns and affiliated outlying communities in my study area and the names of residents with their sex, age, and marital status, grouped into household units for the years 1841, 1883, and 1890 (figure 7.2).[5] The analysis is informed by the results of my 2006 archaeological survey, which relocated many of the places described in the *Titles of Ebtun* and on the censuses (Alexander 2012a; Alexander et al. 2008; Roys 1939) (see figure 7.1).

POPULATION AND HOUSEHOLD ORGANIZATION

The analysis of nineteenth-century censuses indicates that household size and composition shifted markedly during the Caste War. Unlike most regions in Mexico, native people in Yucatán retained Maya surnames. Every resident listed on the nineteenth-century censuses had a single patronym, and women did not take their husbands' names upon marriage. Kinship was bilateral with a strong preference for patrilocal residence after marriage. At least, that is how the census takers saw things; we do not know how many individuals, households, or communities may have resisted inventory.

In the *Titles of Ebtun*, households and families are associated with specific places, but the documents provide no information about their composition and size. Otochnalob (literally, homeowners) is most often translated as "natives of / *natural de*" a specific congregación town, whereas places from which people were

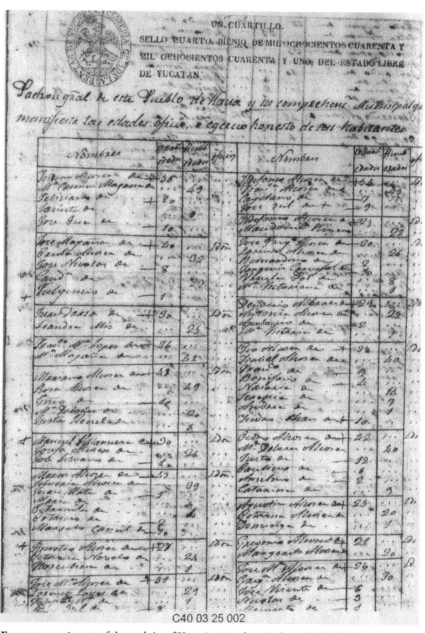

FIGURE 7.2. A page of the padrón of Kaua in 1841 showing household divisions.

resettled (e.g., *lab cah* Panba / the old town of Panba) are associated with a pluralized patronymic (e.g., *Tunob*), translated as belonging to the Tun family (*chibal*) and their ancestors (*kilicabil*, patriclan) (Roys 1939:121–25, see also Quezada and Okoshi Harada 2001).[6] Clearly, this is an example of the layering of perspectives about the associations between domestic groups and places. The form and size of coresidential units, however, are variable in time and space; they are sensitive indicators of how families organize day-to-day activities, as well as how family cycles unfold over time (see Fortes 1958; Netting et al. 1984; R. Wilk 1991). Because most of the nineteenth-century censuses from the study area are organized by household, it is possible to discern variation in household form and size during a period of drastic population decline and among different kinds of settlements.

The 1841 censuses reveal that before the onset of the Caste War, rural populations were large, and settlement was dispersed among *cabeceras* (administrative seats), towns (pueblos), *ranchos* (small communities of maize farmers, or small private parcels used for apiculture and raising pigs and goats), small haciendas (cattle estates with resident workers owned by Spanish creoles), and *sitios* (agricultural parcels). By contrast, the 1883 censuses indicate that in the Caste War's aftermath, settlement was aggregated and overall rural populations had declined by 72 percent (table 7.2).

The 1890 census suggests that redispersal occurred quickly.[7] Most haciendas had been abandoned, and smallholders developed new sites as ranchos and sitios. Generally, the households and patronym groups that resided in specific ranchos in 1841 were not the same patronym groups or descendants who reoccupied them in 1883.

Household size and form are also variable before and after the revolt. Among all households in the study area, household size, mean age, the number of generations, and the ratio of dependents are significantly different before and after the Caste War (table 7.3). Household size and the number of generations increased as the revolt subsided. Mean age increased temporarily, falling back to twenty-two years by 1890, while the ratio of dependents (measured here as the percentage of adults) decreased. The statistical patterns suggest that in 1883, households were composed of older adults with more children, and population recovery resulted in a decrease in mean age by 1890.

Further, if one examines household variation among different kinds of settlements (pueblos, ranchos, and haciendas), the 1841 census clearly shows that before the Caste War, settlements of all sorts were composed of nuclear families (table 7.4). There are no significant differences in household size, mean age, the number of generations, or the ratio of dependents among towns, ranchos, and haciendas in 1841. In 1890, however, the censuses show that household size among all settlement types is significantly larger. Yet, among the few surviving haciendas listed in 1890, household size and the number of generations is significantly smaller than in

140 ALEXANDER

TABLE 7.2 Population distribution in the study area

Year	Settlement class	n	Pop. mean	Pop. sum	%pop	Decline 1841–83
1841	Cabecera	2	1211.5	2,423	14.2%	
	Pueblo	8	1302	10,419	61%	
	Rancho	21	64	1,360	8.0%	
	Hacienda	29	94	2,734	16%	
	Sitio	8	15	122	0.7%	
	Total	**68**	**251**	**17,058**		
1883	Cabecera	2	678	1,356	28.6%	44%
	Pueblo	8	342	2,742	57.8%	74%
	Rancho	20	11	229	4.8%	83%
	Hacienda	10	39.5	395	8.3%	86%
	Sitio	3	7.3	22	0.46%	82%
	Total	**43**	**110**	**4,744**		**72%**

pueblos and ranchos, and mean age is higher. Hacienda laborers did not own their land (i.e., they were not smallholders), and this pattern may suggest that the estates were hiring more single and able-bodied adults with nuclear families, rather than larger extended families and households.

Shifts in household size and composition provide clues to changes in the boundedness of social units and smallholder labor organization, as well as social reproduction and meaning. According to Richard Wilk (1991), household size and form depend on the organization of household labor and the degree to which simultaneous scheduling of tasks requires formation of intermediate-size work groups, which help avoid risks and shortages triggered by bottlenecks in the agricultural calendar. Where household strategies are diversified, agricultural tasks are most likely to involve complicated simultaneous scheduling and larger work groups, and settlements tend to be composed of household clusters that facilitate labor sharing above the nuclear household level. In situations where the domestic agricultural calendar follows a simpler, linear schedule, settlements tend to be composed of nuclear families.

Before the Caste War, then, it is likely that rural communities of all sorts were sufficiently large to permit simpler, linear agricultural schedules, and diversification of agricultural produce was achieved through exchange and local markets. Intermediate-size labor groups could be organized easily among nuclear family households, especially with consanguineous or affinal kin in larger settlements,

THE ARCHAEOLOGY OF PLACE IN EBTÚN, YUCATÁN, MEXICO   **141**

TABLE 7.3. Household change in 1841, 1883, and 1890

Year		n *(Households)*	*Mean*	*Median*	*St. Dev.*
1841	Household size	1,824	3.76	3	3.77
	Generations	1,824	1.77	2	0.45
	Mean age	1,819	22.43	19	11.05
	Ratio Dependents	1,824	0.85		.82
1883	Household size	262	5.39	5	3.36
	Generations	262	2.00	2	.64
	Mean age	262	24.23	21	10.75
	Ratio dependents	262	.75		.71
1890	Household size	352	5.46	5	2.49
	Generations	352	2.13	2	.52
	Mean age	352	22.31	20	9.07
	Ratio dependents	352	.60		.21

Notes: Outliers are present in the distributions, but means, medians, and modes coincide reasonably well. Kruskal-Wallis (nonparametric) comparison of mean ranks (alpha = .05)

House size: $p < .0001$
Generations: $p < .0001$
Mean age: $p < .0027$
Ratio dependents (adults/household): $p < .0236$

to cope with short-term scheduling bottlenecks and shortages. Households of the same patronym group often resided in particular barrios or sections of towns, which facilitated labor sharing. Yet, with the drastic population decline and settlement aggregation during the most violent years of the revolt, local markets were disrupted, and farm produce was often appropriated by rebel Maya and Yucatecan militias (Dumond 1997). These conditions inspired a range of social coping strategies that included remarriages, adoptions, and single adults who moved in with kin (see also Bricker and Hill 2009). Larger households were advantageous for coping with bad year economics, because fewer opportunities for labor sharing and exchange were available in small shrunken communities. Larger household size offered opportunities for subsistence diversification and greater efficiency and flexibility in labor scheduling.[8]

LEADERSHIP AND LANDHOLDING

Changes in the size and household structure of smallholder households and communities had a profound influence on leadership. In the early colonial period,

TABLE 7.4. Comparison of household size among pueblos, ranchos, and haciendas in 1841, 1883, and 1890

Year	Site class	# Households	Mean household size	Mean age	Mean generations
1841	Pueblo	1415	3.76	22.57	1.77
	Rancho	102	3.57	22.40	1.76
	Hacienda	307	3.77	21.79	1.77
1883	Pueblo	221	4.73	24.65	2.02
	Rancho	11	5.57	22.12	1.82
	Hacienda	30	4.33	21.92	1.93
1890	Pueblo	282	**5.53**	22.52	**2.16**
	Rancho	49	**5.61**	20.62	**2.06**
	Hacienda	21	**4.19**	23.46	**1.90**

Notes: Kruskal-Wallis (nonparametric) comparison of mean ranks (alpha = .05)

1841	1883	1890
House size $p < .597$	House size $p < .386$	**House size $p < .031$**
Mean age $p < .0597$	Mean age $p < .208$	Mean age $p < .435$
Generations $p < .597$	Generations $p < .529$	**Generations $p < .042$**

households were grouped into a community (cah) and governed by the República de Indios (town council, cabildo) after the congregación orders were implemented in the sixteenth century. The structure of town governance was based on the batabil, and formal positions in the cabildo included a batab (governor), *escribano* (scribe), *alcaldes, regidores*, and other assorted lower-rank offices (Thompson 1999:19, 49–54). One of the principal functions of the República de Indios was to notarize all transactions involving property within the town boundaries and defend the community's land rights. As a result, continuity of landscape knowledge was tied to the stability of local administration. According to Thompson (1999:283), the batab's term was twenty years (one *katun* within the Maya calendrical system) and was legitimized as hereditary rule within an elite group, and sometimes within a single chibal. The batab and other cabildo offices were chosen from a pool of elite families with privileged access to political office within the town (Restall 1997: 65, 73–78, cf. 61–64).

The República de Indios constituted the crucial interface between the town and all other economic and political institutions of the colony. Therefore, it is not surprising that colonial authorities meddled in local affairs and attempted to limit the power of the batabs from the sixteenth century onward (see Thompson 1999:38–45). Under the Bourbon political reforms, colonial authorities became a significant and interfering presence in rural communities. By the early nineteenth century, the powers of the República de Indios were progressively limited, first with the implementation of the Cortes de Cadiz (1812–14) and most severely after independence (1821), as nonnatives gained control of political positions in local rural government (*ayuntamiento*) (Güemez Pineda 1994, 2005; Rugeley 1997). The República de Indios and native ruling elites forged new factions and alliances with creoles, clergy, and government authorities, especially in the east around Valladolid (Rugeley 1997:94,162).

The nineteenth-century censuses are not the right sorts of documents for tracking changes in village leadership and political organization, but they offer key insights into the composition and size of the pool of elite patronym groups from which local political officials were selected. In 1841, before the onset of the Caste War, the total number of distinct surnames for all male household heads in the study area was 148, but during the aftermath in 1883 and 1890, the number of patronyms had shrunk to 65 and 68 respectively. The distribution and size of the largest patronym groups, measured as the number of male household heads who shared the same surname, also changed between 1841 and 1883. For the 1841 census, it is possible to compare the distribution of male patronyms (number of household heads) among the towns of Ebtún, Kaua, Tekom, and Tixcacalcupul. Table 7.5 shows that households belonging to the largest patronym group could top 16 percent of all households in the community. Yet, a range of several influential patronym groups who shared or competed for leadership positions were situated in each town. The batab was not always a member of the most numerous patronym group, but he was always from one of the larger ones. Further, a simple tally of male and female patronyms by household shows that members of the largest patronym groups intermarried, though people with Spanish surnames tended to marry their distant cousins of the same patronym (table 7.6) (see Thompson 1999:212). Nevertheless, there are exceptions to this tendency. At least one influential patronym group, the Koh from Tixcacalcupul, showed no preferential marriage pattern. It may indicate that the Koh were forging alliances broadly, with as many different patronym groups as possible. Overall in 1841, the recruitment pool for leadership positions was diverse. Individuals could be tapped from six to ten different patronym groups that consisted of more than ten households within each community (table 7.5).

After the Caste War the 1883 census shows that the largest patronym groups of 1841 were still dominant, but a much narrower range of other influential patronym groups remained within each community (table 7.7). In Tekom, the Batun and Tec patronym groups displaced the Cocom and Chulim patronym groups that were more numerous before the Caste War. A shuffling of rank order in the number of households belonging to each patronym group is apparent in Ebtún in 1883. A comparison of tables 7.5 and 7.7 clearly shows that some towns experienced greater continuity in the pool of leaders (Ebtún, Kaua), whereas others underwent more disruption (Tekom, Tixcacalcupul).

TABLE 7.5. The top ten most numerous male surnames (household heads) in 1841

Ebtún	#	%	Kaua	#	%	Tekom	#	%	Tixcacalcupul	#	%
Camal	47	16.97	Tus	58	15.59	Cocom	36	16.22	Canul	34	9.09
Uc	29	10.47	Mis	36	9.86	Chulim	26	11.71	Tun	28	7.49
Dzul	25	9.03	Alcoser†	31	8.33	Batun	24	10.81	Koh*	18	4.81
Un	22	7.94	Canul	28	7.53	Tec	17	7.66	Chan	17	4.55
Noh	20	7.22	Chi	21	5.65	Cauich*	11	4.95	Hoil	15	4.01
Couoh	20	7.22	Che*	19	5.11	May	11	4.95	Alcoser	14	3.74
Huchim	18	6.50	Poot	17	4.57	Ku	10	4.5			
Balam	17	6.14	Ku	16	4.30	Puc	10	4.5			
Cen	12	4.33	May	16	4.30						
Poot*	12	4.33	Xul	16	4.30						
Others	79	19.85	Others	114	30.5	Others	77	34.7	Others	248	66.31
Total	301	19.85		372	100		222	100		374	100

* In 1841 the caciques of each town were Patrisio Poot, Ebtún; Asencio Che, Kaua; Martin Cauich, Tekom; Juan Koh, Tixcacalcupul.

† Alcoser is the only Spanish patronym on this list.

TABLE 7.6. Marriage patterns in 1841

Ebtún M-F	#	Kaua M-F	#	Tekom M-F	#	Tixcacalcupul M-F	#
Camal-Dzul	7	Tuz-Mis	14	Batun-Cocom	7	Tun-Canul	6
Couoh-Dzul	6	Mis-Tuz	12	Cocom-Chulim	6	Canul-Tun	4
Huchim-Camal	6	Alcoser-Alcoser	12	Chulim-Cocom	5	Alcoser-Alcoser	4
Camal-Couoh	5	Tuz-Canul	10	Batun-Chulim	5	Canul-Hoil	3
Dzul-Uc	5	Canul-Tuz	8	Cocom-Chay	5	Canul-Kumul	3
Un-Camal	5	Tuz-Tuz	6			Tun-Hoil	3
Un-Noh	5					Chan-Canul	3
						Hoil-Canul	3
						Hoil-Tun	3
						Hoil-Kumul	3

Note: Alcoser is the only Spanish patronym listed on this table; all others are Maya patronyms.

TABLE 7.7. Most Numerous Male Surnames (household heads) in 1883

Ebtún	#	%	Kaua	#	%	Tekom	#	%	Tixcacalcupul	#	%
Camal	8	22.22	Mis	5	17.24	Batun	13	13.40	Canul	5	10.20
Noh	6	16.67	Poot	4	13.79	Tec	11	11.34	Tun	4	8.16
Balam	3	8.33	Tus	4	13.79	Ku	9	9.28	Fernández	3	6.12
Cen	3	8.33	Ku	3	10.34	Chulim	7	7.22	Hoil	3	6.12
Couoh	3	8.33							May	3	6.12
Dzul	3	8.33							Tec	3	6.12
									Alcoser	2	4.08
Others	10	27.78	Others	13	44.84	Others	57	58.76	Others	26	53.08
	36	100		29	100		97	100		49	100

Note: This census does not identify the names of batabs or other political officials.

In addition, a tally of the incidence of male and female patronyms for each household in 1883 suggests shifts in alliances and factions, and more intermarriage among people belonging to the same patronym group (table 7.8) (see Thompson 1999:206–12). The marriage pattern is undoubtedly the result of fewer choices of potential spouses. Yet, possibly the pattern indicates that the reshuffling of village leadership was accompanied by forging marriage alliances among families of the same patronym, which may have streamlined inheritance and strengthened the wealth and position of some groups.

The censuses make it possible to map the spatial distribution and density of any patronym group for 1841, 1883, and 1890. Although the analysis of these data is not yet complete and an in-depth discussion of population movement is beyond the scope of this brief chapter, a few trends are worth mentioning. First, for all census years, some patronyms (e.g., Batun, Camal) cluster in one or two towns, whereas others (e.g., Canul, Poot) are found in all of them. There is no pattern of increasing compartmentalization of patronym groups in distinct geographic locations as a result of the Caste War. In 1841, the largest patronym groups within each town were widely distributed among haciendas and ranchos of the region. Yet, connectedness was variable. A few influential patronym groups, such as the Noh from Ebtún and the Tec from Tekom, were found in a narrower range of settlements. Also, members of all patronym groups could be found in the city of Valladolid and the parish seats of Uayma and Chichimila.[9] This suggests that the patronym groups that comprised the leadership pool enjoyed broad intraregional connectedness across the study area.

TABLE 7.8. Marriage patterns in 1883

Ebtún M-F	#	Kaua M-F	#	Tekom M-F	#	Tixcacalcupul M-F	#
Camal-Camal	3	Ku-Mis	3	Tec-Cauich	3	Hoil-Tun	2
Balam-Cen	2			Batun-Batun	2	Fernández-Alcoser	2
				Batun-Ku	2	May-Tun	2
				Tec-Batun	2		
				Ku-Chay	2		
				Cauich-Chay	2		

Second, by 1883 the most prominent patronym groups still resided in towns, but a few surnames were widely distributed among rural settlements. For example, households of the Noh and Poot patronym groups, previously among the most numerous from Ebtún, dispersed to reside on a number of haciendas and ranchos by 1890. A process of dispersal to new ranchos, sitios, and haciendas rearranged the relative frequencies of patronym groups in the towns and suggests that village factionalism was resolved through movement in the aftermath of the revolt. Yet, households belonging to specific patronym groups did not reoccupy the same places where they had resided before the Caste War, nor did whole patronym groups up and leave town for the forest in 1890.

Third, movement of patronym groups to new geographic locations was not always accompanied by severing political ties or kin obligations in the parent community. In many cases dispersal to rural settlements and movement to larger towns and the urban center of Valladolid enhanced both the community's and the patronym group's economic potential and political connectedness. Although post–Caste War population movement is exceedingly complex in this region, the towns of Tekom and Tixcacalcupul experienced more movement of patronym groups than Ebtún and Kaua, which led to greater instability in the leadership pool. These landscape shifts set the stage for changes to smallholders' livelihoods that occurred with the push for modernization in the twentieth century.

RECONFIGURING PLACE AFTER THE CASTE WAR

Changing relations between people and place, described above, had a profound influence on the structure of landholding and leadership that emerged out of the Caste War and into the postrevolutionary agrarian reform of the 1930s and 1940s. The migration narratives for individual patronym groups are clearly rooted in post–Caste War experience (see Armstrong-Fumero and Hoil Gutiérrez, this volume) and are further reflected in the development or lack of development of the built environment (Alexander 2012a). As Elizabeth Brumfiel (2003) observed, the construction of social identity is rooted in people's understandings of the past, which are frequently reinforced by interpretations of material remains. In my study area, place-making negotiations that resulted from the tensions of population movement are expressed through variable combinations of written, oral, and material media. The following examples from Tzaab, Bubul, and Chan Kom highlight how place making produces variation in the social reproduction of tangible and intangible heritage.

Tzaab

Yucatán's Caste War resulted in the creation of a new religion centered on the cult of the speaking cross with its own priesthood and religious practices (Bricker 1981; Dumond 1997; Rugeley 1997, 2009; Sullivan 1989). Arguably, the conflict also is the source of a new Maya "cruzob" identity, which traces its roots to the rebels—or *cruzob*—of Noh Cah Santa Cruz, the first seat of the talking cross (Gabbert 2004). The movement created a political divide on the peninsula between communities who supported the rebellion and adopted the new religion and those who did not. The schism is still expressed in the distribution of "dressed" crosses (wooden crosses covered with an embroidered cloth huipil [woman's blouse]) across the landscape (Dumond 1985, 1997:plate 4).

In my study region, all named locales—including unoccupied cenotes, *rejolladas* (sinkholes), and wells—are marked by wooden crosses set in stone footings, called *mojoneras*. These crosses were established in the early colonial period but have become new emblems for signaling the community's relations with the past. Cruzob identity is marked spatially in the region by the distribution of dressed crosses (with a cotton cloth or embroidered huipil spread over the crossbeam) that mark the entrances to communities (figure 7.3). Today, Tixcacalcupul, Tekom, and all of their dependent settlements—including land parcels, wells, cenotes, haciendas, and ranchos—have dressed crosses at settlement entrances. By contrast, the inhabitants of Ebtún, Kaua, Cuncunul, and Chan Kom erect plain crosses at the entrances to their pueblos or dependent communities. The maintenance of dressed crosses for dependent settlements of Tixcacalcupul and Tekom is an important aspect of historical identity that commemorates community experience during the Caste War.

Yet, Tekom and Tixcacalcupul also experienced the greatest disruption to leadership during the mid-nineteenth century. New politicoreligious identities and ideologies, visibly expressed as dressed crosses, clearly tied dependent ranchos, haciendas,

FIGURE 7.3. A shrine at Tzaab.

and sitios to new political authority in the parent towns of Tekom and Tixcacalcupul. The rancho Tzaab is a good example of the material expression of intangible Caste War heritage that also recalls the early colonial period resettlement of patronym groups from pre-Hispanic sites (labcah) to congregación towns (Alexander et al. 2008). A small community of maize farmers (pop. thirty-four, nine households) reestablished itself at the pre-Hispanic site situated around a large, deep cenote in 1841. The settlement was abandoned during the Caste War but was reoccupied in the twentieth century by different patronym groups whose patron saint was Santa Cruz. After Hurricane Gilberto in 1988, they returned to Tixcacalcupul, and at least one family from Tzaab held a leadership position in town in 2006. Families still return to Tzaab on May 2 to celebrate the feast of Santa Cruz. Today they maintain a shrine to Santa Cruz, with elaborately dressed crosses oriented east-west, situated on top of one three-meter-high pre-Hispanic structure (figure 7.3).

Bubul

Migration narratives about how and why new communities were founded in the first half of the twentieth century became enshrined in the ethnographic cannon with Redfield and Villa Rojas's (1934) publication of *Chan Kom*. Yet by the time Chan Kom had become politically independent from its parent community of Ebtún, population movement and dispersal had been ongoing for over fifty years

(Alexander 2006). Between 1890 and 1905, families from Ebtún resettled sixteen ranchos, haciendas, and sitios.[10] To show how post–Caste War dispersal layered additional meanings on the landscape, I situate the founding of Rancho Bubul in a comparative context.

Bubul is a dependency of Ebtún, the most politically stable town in my study region. Material expression of politicoreligious affiliation or dependency is not evident at the site, as it is at Tzaab. Instead, Ebtún's place-making negotiations involving Bubul were conducted with the power of the pen and by linking colonial-era primordial titles to the petitions for *ejido* (collective land grant) lands during the Cardenist agrarian reform. The history of landscape transformation at Bubul diverges sharply from the story of Chan Kom and offers an alternative perspective on the Maya ethnographies produced during Mexico's agrarian reform (1924–40) (Redfield 1941, 1950; Redfield and Villa Rojas 1934; Steggerda 1941; Villa Rojas 1978; see also Armstrong-Fumero 2007, 2013; Castañeda 1996; Re-Cruz 1996; Strickon 1965).

First and foremost, Bubul (like Tzaab) is a cenote located eighteen kilometers northwest of Ebtún (figure 7.4; see also figure 7.1). The name Bubul means half filled with water, which is an apt description since water is found only on one side of the twenty-meter-deep cylindrical depression at the base of a steep vertical limestone wall. Water is only accessible by lowering a jar or bucket on a rope from a wood platform or scaffolding perched on the edge. There is a well located a short distance away from the cenote, known as Txeth. Dense primary and high secondary forest vegetation and large mamey (*Pouteria sapota*) fruit trees are associated with the cenote. The trackway to the cenote is marked by a plain, undressed wooden cross set into a stone base, and the surrounding land is used for milpa cultivation.

Bubul is also an archaeological site consisting of numerous pre-Hispanic structures, the largest of which are five to seven meters high. Architectural features and surface ceramics (slateware) indicate the site dates from AD 900–1200 and likely extends to the conquest. Surface artifacts (ceramics and metal) dating to the twentieth century were scattered on top of one of the pre-Hispanic structures, but generally the ruins are well preserved and have not been looted or stripped of stone for building material. It seems likely that Bubul's inhabitants were resettled in Ebtún under the sixteenth-century congregación orders. The site is a labcah, though it does not appear in the earliest boundary survey in the *Titles of Ebtun* (Roys 1939).

Eighteenth-century documents from the *Titles of Ebtun* show that the lands around Bubul and Txeth had a checkered history of ownership, involving disputes with the batab of Uayma. Patronyms associated with the transfer of the property to Ebtún include Alcocer, Tus, Cime, Kak, Huh, and Kantun (Roys 1939:315). Although the town of Ebtún acquired these tracts from individuals

FIGURE 7.4. The cenote of Bubul.

who had inherited them in the eighteenth century (called *kax cah* [town's forest] in the documents), they became private property afterward (Roys 1939:58, 272). Members of the Un and Couoh patronym groups inherited parts of the tract in 1812 and therefore held legitimate interests in Bubul, along with the town of Ebtún itself.

In 1890 Vicente Un appears to have been the senior household head of a group of twenty people who resided at Bubul. Households consisted of two multifamily groups, headed by men of the Un, Pat, and Noh patronyms and women of the Noh, Camal, and Ydzincab patronyms. They were composed of widowers, married couples, their children, and a widow caring for children whose consanguineous relationship with the family is unclear.[11] Since no members of the Couoh patronym group appear on the list, it appears that the links between place and patronym group were reconfigured in the aftermath of the revolt. The group became full-time residents of Bubul sometime after 1862, since both Vicente Un and his wife Martina Noh appear on Ebtún's 1862 census.[12] The inhabitants remained at Bubul until after 1905, when the rancho is listed as having six houses and forty-six residents.[13] Throughout this period, Bubul's residents were identified as being from Ebtún.

In the years leading up to Mexico's agrarian reform (1924–40), the new municipality of Chan Kom considered Bubul to be part of Ebtún's "unduly large" ejido, yet the town of Cuncunul tried to claim the cenote and surrounding lands as part of their grant (Armstrong-Fumero 2007:139). In 1940 the people of Ebtún challenged Cuncunul's ejido petition and produced a 1798 land title with its boundary survey establishing ownership of Bubul (Armstrong-Fumero, personal communication, 2010, 2013; Roys 1939:272).[14] As the story goes (Alexander et al. 2008:128), a group of outsiders had already built a town hall, houses, and a school, but the Mexican army evicted them, forcing them to leave all their belongings behind, and transported them to Tihosuco (see Leventhal et al. 2012).[15] In the second half of the twentieth century, Bubul was occupied for a stretch of eighteen years by a group of farmers from Ebtún, including members of the Un patronym group. They returned to Ebtún after Hurricane Gilbert in 1988, and Bubul remains the town's forest (kax cah) today.

CHAN KOM

In Yucatán, the relationship between population circulation and culture change were originally understood from within an acculturative framework—Robert Redfield's folk-urban continuum—in which the village of Chan Kom was proposed as the archetypical example of Maya folk culture. *Chan Kom: A Maya Village* (Robert Redfield and Alfonso Villa Rojas 1934) became a touchstone for all subsequent ethnographic studies in Yucatán, as well as one of the principal sources of direct historical analogies for archaeologists. I offer the following comments only as a comparison to the archaeologies of place for Bubul and Tzaab; a complete analysis of Chan Kom's founding and subsequent development is beyond the scope of this chapter.

Redfield and Villa Rojas (1934:34) described the founding of Chan Kom as a response to agricultural necessity, an explanation that is not supported by mine and others' analyses of nineteenth-century demography and agriculture (Alexander 2006; Strickon 1965). It was an agricultural parcel containing a water source (kom) that was farmed by people from Ebtún. By 1918 it had over a hundred people (Redfield and Villa Rojas 1934:25–28). Once the place became permanently inhabited by several pioneer families, a community spirit developed, which led to political independence and local sovereignty from Ebtún, its parent community. Movement to *milperías* and *rancherías* such as Chan Kom was also an important safety valve for peasant communities—a way of resisting the worst exigencies of colonial and postcolonial regimes (Wolf 1957, 1990). Redfield and Villa Rojas predicted constant dispersal and down-the-line expansion of settlement—that Chan Kom would eventually establish *milperío* colonies of its own. Chan Kom's break with its parent community came in 1923 when the population petitioned the government for an ejido grant. Under the leadership of Eustaquio Ceme, Chan Kom grew as it absorbed refugees from Yaxcabá, Kancabdzonot, and Yaxuna who fled the violence of the liberalist and socialist disputes in the region (see figure 7.1).

Although the early history of Chan Kom is similar to Bubul's and Tzaab's, place making at Chan Kom involved a different set of strategies that link the town's origin story and emerging political autonomy to its architecture and infrastructure. Compared to Tzaab and Bubul, Chan Kom's foundational narrative reflects a divergent trajectory of development and the formation of a distinct political identity, which are clearly expressed in in the built environment (Alexander 2012a; Armstrong-Fumero 2013). Residents went on a building spree to commemorate their commitment to modernization, Mexico's 1910 socialist revolution, and the subsequent agrarian reform.

Chan Kom no longer resembles the traditional farming village so carefully documented by Robert Redfield and Alfonso Villa Rojas (Redfield and Villa Rojas 1934; see also Goldkind 1965; Re-Cruz 1996). The success of the community's bid for political autonomy is starkly reflected in the town's buildings and layout. Chan Kom's town center is dominated by a massive administrative building (*palacio municipal*) that faces a modest church with two bell towers across the main plaza. The middle of the plaza contains the cenote or kom, a collective and communal space improved with cemented pathways and retaining walls to permit easy access to the water. The original perishable constructions have been replaced by masonry and cement block buildings constructed in postrevolutionary style. Houses are laid out on a grid plan and are constructed of cement block, some with red tile roofs, and express variation in socioeconomic strata, in contrast to the perishable, pole-and-thatch single-room buildings that were already being replaced with masonry construction during

Redfield and Villa Rojas's time. The principal paved roads lead directly north and south from Chan Kom and connect it to Yucatán's main east-west highway, not to Ebtún. Material expressions of the community's earlier colonial history or Caste War experience are generally absent, as they are in Redfield and Villa Rojas's (1934) ethnography (see Castañeda 1996; Strickon 1965). That is because Chan Kom's claims for political autonomy were not legitimated by its past; rather, they were substantiated by a move toward modernity and progress (Redfield 1950).

FINAL CONSIDERATIONS

It is clear that in the nineteenth and twentieth centuries, Ebtún and related communities were fully engaged in social dynamics that layered new perspectives, meanings, and social memories across a landscape that could hardly be described as static and unchanging. Analysis of nineteenth-century census records clearly shows that relations among space, place, community (cah), patronym group (chibal), and the household (otochnal) were reconfigured to address the demographic, political, and economic challenges of the Caste War and the agrarian reform of the twentieth century.

The dispersed settlement pattern of the early nineteenth century at first became more aggregated in response to Caste War violence. Yet, redispersal of settlement occurred in the last decades of the nineteenth century, which helped to mediate village factionalism caused by population decline and movement among towns. Population circulation reconfigured the size and composition of households. They increased in size and generational depth after the Caste War, and their age structure and ratio of the numbers of dependents were altered.

Nineteenth-century population movements caused shifts in the size and connectedness of prominent patronym groups, and the pool of potential village leaders remained more stable in some towns than in others. In most cases one or two patronym groups became notably dominant after the Caste War, whereas before the revolt leadership positions had been shared among a broader range of patronym groups. Marriage between members of the same patronym group became more common by 1883.

Rural landholdings were in flux in the late nineteenth century. Land parcels, haciendas, and ranchos were abandoned during the most violent years of the Caste War. But by the 1890s new multifamily households had moved away from the towns to form new rural communities. Dispersal to new locations after the Caste War was legitimated through a group's affiliation to a town (cah) that had possessed political jurisdiction over the place, and usually not through claims of prior individual private ownership.

Finally, population movement altered the ways that communities were tied to place, which are manifest in both tangible and intangible expressions of historical memory (Alexander 2012a). Different histories of population movement for Tzaab, Bubul, and Chan Kom clearly influenced the strategies and choices of media (oral tradition, written records, or the material record) employed in the construction of heritage.

This study reveals that in the nineteenth and early twentieth century, social-organizational categories and their relationships to place were reformulated through population movement. It does not demonstrate static continuity of household structure, leadership, or stability of landholding. The landscape forged by Yucatán's Caste War was markedly different from that of the colonial period, and it was remade again in the aftermath of the Mexican Revolution and agrarian reform. It is this process of continual transformation of the relations between people and place—adjusting everyday practice to cope with political and environmental uncertainty—that attests to smallholder resilience in Yucatán.

ACKNOWLEDGMENTS

An earlier version of this paper was presented in the symposium entitled "Archaeology, Ethnohistory, and Ethnoarchaeology of Space: Current Projects and New Directions" at the seventy-seventh annual meeting of the Society for American Archaeology, April 18–22, 2012, Memphis, TN. The archaeological survey and archival research on which this chapter is based were sponsored by a 2006 US Department of Education Fulbright-Hays Faculty Research Abroad fellowship and the College of Arts and Sciences at New Mexico State University. I thank Fernando Armstrong-Fumero and Julio Hoil Gutierrez for their encouragement.

NOTES

1. A *padrón* is a poll, a register of persons in a place who pay taxes.

2. A cenote is a karst solution feature produced when the collapse of the limestone caprock exposes the freshwater aquifer.

3. Nancy Farriss (1984:41) suggests that a nuclear family consisting of a married couple with three surviving children and three dying in infancy is a reasonable estimate of colonial family size and structure. Yet, she also discusses evidence for patrilineal extended families (Farriss 1984:133135) who lived in residential clusters.

4. Archivo General del Estado de Yucatán [AGEY]:

AGEY Fondo Colonial, Ramo Censos y Padrones, Vol. 2, exp. 4, 1811.

AGEY, Poder Ejecutivo, Censos y Padrones Vol. 2, exp. 17, 1841 Ebtún. Padrón general de habitantes del pueblo de Ebtún, partido de Valladolid, con expresión de sexos, edades y ocupaciones, 17 f., caja 1.

AGEY, Poder Ejecutivo, Censos y Padrones Vol. 3, exp. 25, 1841 Pueblo de Kahua (Kaua). Padrón general de habitantes del pueblo de Kahua y su comarca de haciendas, sitios y ranchos del partido de Valladolid, con expresión de sexos, edades y ocupaciones. Kahua, Abril 24, de 1841. Folios 12, caja 2.

AGEY, Poder Ejecutivo, Censos y Padrones, Vol. 1, exp. 6. Pueblo de Cuncunul. Padrón general de habitantes del pueblo de Cuncunul del partido de Valladolid, con expresión de sexos, edades y ocupaciones, Cuncunul, Mayo 1 de 1841, fjs. 10, caja 1.

AGEY, Poder Ejecutivo, Censos y Padrones, Vol. 1, exp. 10. Pueblo de Chichimila. Padrón general del pueblo de Chichimila y su comprensión, partido de Valladolid, con expresión de sexos, edades y ocupaciones. Chichimila, agosto 25 de 1841. Fjs. 42 caja 1.

AGEY, Poder Ejecutivo, Censos y Padrones, Vol. 5, exp. 70. Pueblo de Tixcacalcupul. Padrón general de habitantes del pueblo de Tixcacalcupul y su comprensión de haciendas, sitios y ranchos del partido de Valladolid, con expresión de sexos, edades y ocupaciones. Tixcacalcupul, mayo 5 de 1841, fjs 41 caja 2-BIS

AGEY, Poder Ejecutivo, Censos y Padrones, Vol. 6, exp. 73. Pueblo de Uayma. Padrón general de habitantes del pueblo de Uayma y su comarca de haciendas, sitios y ranchos del partido de Valladolid, con expresión de sexos, edades y ocupaciones, Uayma, mayo 14 de 1841. Fjs 11. Caja 2-BIS

AGEY, Poder ejecutivo, Censos y Padrones, Vol. 7, exp. 59. Pueblo de Tekom. Padrón general de habitantes del pueblo de Tekom y su comarca, partido de Valladolid, con expresión de sexos, edades y ocupaciones. Tekom, mayo 4 de 1841 fjs 15.

AGEY, Fondo Municipios, Libros Valladolid #2, Padrón General de todos los habitantes de este Municipio 1883.

AGEY Población, libros complementarios 1890, Padrón general del municipio de Valladolid.

AGEY Fondo Municipios, Valladolid 1910, caja 16(384), exp. 1, vol. 38, 42 folios.

5. For this analysis I used only the towns of Ebtún, Kaua, Tekom, and Tixcacalcupul. The 1841 census for the town of Cuncunul did not group people according to households, thus prohibiting comparison after the Caste War.

6. It is interesting that the term *cah*—town—is used both for congregación towns and settlements that people were forced to abandon, whereas the term *otochnalob*—householders—is only used for congregación towns. It is possible that otochnal is a purposeful translation of a European concept designed by the friars to encourage political civility and proper

conduct, in the same way that William B. Hanks (2010, 2012) describes the translation and commensuration of concepts such as baptism into Maya as part of conversion and reducción. Thompson (1999:55–80) also describes changes in Maya kin terms and considers its implications for the friars' attempts to regulate household composition and marriage in eighteenth-century Tekanto.

7. My analysis of census information for 1890 covers a smaller jurisdiction than the 1841 and 1883 censuses and includes only the pueblos of Ebtún, Cuncunul, Kaua, Tekom, and Tixcacalcupul and their dependencies.

8. Dispersal is a form of agricultural intensification on the Yucatán Peninsula. Typically it moves household labor closer to the agricultural plot, which provides greater efficiency in agricultural movement (Alexander 2006; see Stone 1996). This pattern raises an intriguing issue. It is possible that the persistence of extended family and multifamily households in the sixteenth century was a response to drastic population decline and the need for larger household and intermediate-size labor groups, which facilitated agricultural diversification (see Alexander 2006).

9. An analysis of post–Caste War urbanization is beyond the scope of this brief chapter.

10. AGEY Ramo Municipios Valladolid, Presidencia, Caja 10, Vol. 26, exp. 6, 1905, Censo de la división topográfica del Partido de Valladolid. It is worth pointing out that land pressure clearly was not the motive for dispersal, given the drastic population loss of the late nineteenth century in this area (see Alexander 2006). Further, the founding of Chan Kom is not a "typical" example of the dispersal process. Rather, the community was founded fairly late in the game (1918) and became independent of Ebtún in 1923–26 following an episode of violent disputes between political liberalists and socialists. It was not established by members of larger and more influential patronym groups in Ebtún.

11. AGEY Población, libros complementarios 1890, Padrón general del municipio de Valladolid.

12. Poder Ejecutivo, Ayuntamiento de Valladolid, Censos y Padrones, Padrón general de los habitantes del municipio de Chichimila, Valladolid (Chichimila, Ebtún, Xocén), 29 abril 1862. Caja 66, Vol. 16, exp. 5.: 2d.

13. Ramo Municipios Valladolid, Presidencia, Censo de la división topográfica del Partido de Valladolid. Caja 10, Vol. 26, exp. 6, 1905.

14. Archivo de la Reforma Agraria Nacional (RAN). Ebtún Dotación 155, Solicitud 20/11/1923, Dictamen 22/12/1930, 5/5/1940 Vecinos de Ebtún a Jefe CAM. The copy of the letter matches word for word Document 180, Certified copy of Acknowledgment for Bubul, in the *Titles of Ebtun* (Roys 1939:272). I thank Fernando Armstrong-Fumero for sharing his notes and observations.

15. This story was related by Ebtún's *comisario ejidal*, Florentino Camal, and his uncle Eleuterio Un Un, while surveying Bubul in 2006.

REFERENCES

Alexander, Rani T. 2006. "Maya Settlement Shifts and Agrarian Ecology in Yucatán, 1800–2000." *Journal of Anthropological Research* 62 (4): 449–70. http://dx.doi.org/10.3998/jar.0521004.0062.401.

Alexander, Rani T. 2012a. "Maya Collapse or Resilience? Lessons from the Spanish Conquest and Yucatan's Caste War." In *The Ancient Maya of Mexico: Reinterpreting the Past of the Northern Maya Lowlands*, ed. G. Braswell, 319–40. London: Equinox Publishing.

Alexander, Rani T. 2012b. "Prohibido Tocar este Cenote: The Archaeological Basis for the Titles of Ebtún." *International Journal of Historical Archaeology* 16 (1): 1–24. http://dx.doi.org/10.1007/s10761-012-0167-0.

Alexander, Rani T., José Diaz Cruz, Adam Kaeding, Ruth Martinez Cervantes, Matthew Punke, and Susan Kepecs. 2008. *La Arqueología histórica en los pueblos de Ebtún, Cuncunul, Kaua, Tekom y Tixcacalcupul, Yucatán, México*. Informe Técnico de campo para la temporada de 2006, presentado al Consejo de Arqueología, Instituto Nacional de Antropología e Historia.

Armstrong-Fumero, Fernando. 2007. *Before There Was Culture Here: Vernacular Discourse on Modernity in Yucatan Mexico*. Stanford: Department of Anthropology, Stanford University.

Armstrong-Fumero, Fernando. 2013. *Elusive Unity: Factionalism and the Limits of Identity Politics in Yucatán, Mexico*. Boulder: University Press of Colorado. http://dx.doi.org/10.5876/9781607322399.

Basso, Keith H. 1996. *Wisdom Sits in Places: Landscape and Language among the Western Apache*. Albuquerque: University of New Mexico Press.

Berdan, Frances F., John K. Chance, Alan R. Sandstrom, Barbara L. Stark, James Taggart, and Emily Umberger, eds. 2008. *Ethnic Identity in Nahua Mesoamerica: The View from Archaeology, Art History, Ethnohistory, and Contemporary Ethnography*. Salt Lake City: University of Utah Press.

Binford, Lewis. 1982. "An Archaeology of Place." *Journal of Anthropological Archaeology* 1 (1): 5–31. http://dx.doi.org/10.1016/0278-4165(82)90006-X.

Bricker, Victoria R. 1981. *The Indian Christ, the Indian King*. Austin: University of Texas Press.

Bricker, Victoria R., and Rebecca Hill. 2009. "Climatic Signatures in Yucatecan Wills and Death Records." *Ethnohistory (Columbus, Ohio)* 56 (2): 227–68. http://dx.doi.org/10.1215/00141801-2008-057.

Brumfiel, Elizabeth M. 2003. "It's a Material World: History, Artifacts, and Anthropology." *Annual Review of Anthropology* 32 (1): 205–23. http://dx.doi.org/10.1146/annurev.anthro.32.061002.093335.

Castañeda, Quetzil. 1996. *In the Museum of Maya Culture: Touring Chichen Itza.* Minneapolis: University of Minnesota Press.

Chance, John. 1996. "Mesoamerica's Ethnographic Past." *Ethnohistory (Columbus, Ohio)* 43 (3): 379–403. http://dx.doi.org/10.2307/483450.

Cline, Howard F. 1947. "Related Studies in Early Nineteenth Century Yucatecan Social History." Microfilm Collection of Manuscripts on Middle American Cultural Anthropology. Chicago: University of Chicago Library.

Dumond, Don E. 1985. "The Talking Crosses of Yucatán: A New Look at their History." *Ethnohistory (Columbus, Ohio)* 32 (4): 291–308. http://dx.doi.org/10.2307/481891.

Dumond, Don E. 1997. *The Machete and the Cross: Campesino Rebellion in Yucatan.* Lincoln: University of Nebraska Press.

Farriss, Nancy M. 1978. "Nucleation versus Dispersal: The Dynamics of Population Movement in Colonial Yucatán." *Hispanic American Historical Review* 58 (2): 187–216. http://dx.doi.org/10.2307/2513085.

Farriss, Nancy M. 1984. *Maya Society under Colonial Rule: The Collective Enterprise of Survival.* Princeton: Princeton University Press.

Fortes, Meyer. 1958. "Introduction." In *The Development Cycle in Domestic Groups*, ed. J. Grady, 1–14. Cambridge: Cambridge University Press.

Gabbert, Wolfgang. 2004. *Becoming Maya: Ethnicity and Social Inequality in Yucatan since 1500.* Tucson: University of Arizona Press.

Goldkind, Victor. 1965. "Social Stratification in the Peasant Community: Redfield's Chan Kom Reinterpreted." *American Anthropologist* 67 (4): 863–84. http://dx.doi.org/10 .1525/aa.1965.67.4.02a00010.

Güemez Pineda, Arturo. 1994. *Liberalismo en Tierras del Caminante, Yucatán, 1812–1840.* Zamora: El Colegio de Michoacán.

Güemez Pineda, Arturo. 2005. *Mayas: Gobierno y tierras frente a la Acometida Liberal en Yucatán, 1812–1847.* Zamora y Mérida: El Colegio de Michoacán, Universidad Autónoma de Yucatán.

Hanks, William B. 2010. *Converting Words: Maya in the Age of the Cross.* Berkeley: University of California Press. http://dx.doi.org/10.1525/california/9780520 257702.001.0001.

Hanks, William F. 2012. "Birth of a Language: The Formation and Spread of Colonial Yucatec Maya." *Journal of Anthropological Research* 68 (4): 449–71. http://dx.doi.org /10.3998/jar.0521004.0068.401.

Holling, C. S., and H. Lance Gunderson. 2002. Resilience and Adaptive Cycles. In *Panarchy: Understanding Transformations in Human and Natural Systems*, ed. L. H. Gunderson and C. S. Holling, 25–62. Washington: Island Press.

Ingold, Tim. 1993. "The Temporality of the Landscape." *World Archaeology* 25 (2): 152–74. http://dx.doi.org/10.1080/00438243.1993.9980235.

Leventhal, Richard, Carlos Chan Espinosa, and Christina Coc. 2012. "The Modern Maya and Recent History." *Expedition* 54 (1): 46–51.

Lightfoot, Kent. 2004. *Indians, Missionaries, and Merchants: The Legacy of Colonial Encounters on the California Frontiers*. Berkeley: University of California Press.

McAnany, Patricia A. 1995. *Living with the Ancestors: Kinship and Kingship in Ancient Maya Society*. Austin: University of Texas Press.

Netting, Robert McC. 1993. *Smallholders, Householders: Farm Families and the Ecology of Intensive Sustainable Agriculture*. Stanford: Stanford University Press.

Netting, Robert McC., Richard R. Wilk, and Eric J. Arnould. 1984. "Introduction." In *Households: Comparative and Historical Studies of the Domestic Group*, ed. R. M. Netting, R.R.W. Wilk, and E. J. Arnould, xiii–xxxviii. Berkeley: University of California Press.

Okoshi Harada, Tsubasa. 2006. Los Canul y Los Canché: Una interpretación del Códice de Calkiní. In *Nuevas perspectivas sobre la geografía política de los Mayas*, ed. T. Okoshi Harada, A. L. Izquierdo, and L. A. Williams-Beck, 29–55. Mexico City.: Instituto de Investigaciones Filológicas, Centro de Estudios, Mayas, Universidad Nacional Autónoma de México.

Okoshi Harada, Tsubasa. 2009. *Códice de Calkiní*. Mexico City: Universidad Nacional Autónoma de México.

Okoshi Harada, Tsubasa. 2011. Ch'ibal y cuuchcabal: Una consideración sobre su función en la organización política de los mayas yucatecos del Posclásico. In *El despliegue del poder entre los Mayas: Nuevos estudios sobre la organización política*, ed. A. L. Izquierdo and de La Cueva, 207–24. Mexico City.: Universidad Nacional Autónoma de México.

Okoshi Harada, Tsubasa, Ana Luisa Izquierdo, and Lorraine Williams-Beck. 2006. *Nuevas perspectivas sobre la geografía política de los Mayas*. Mexico City: Instituto de Investigaciones Filológicas, Centro de Estudios Mayas, Universidad Nacional Autónoma de México.

Quezada, Sergio. 1985. "Encomienda, cabildo y gubernatura indígena en Yucatán, 1541–1583." *Historia Mexicana* 34 (4): 662–84.

Quezada, Sergio. 1993. *Pueblos y caciques Yucatecos, 1550–1580*. Mexico City: El Colegio de México.

Quezada, Sergio. 2014. *Maya Lords and Lordship: The Formation of Colonial Society in Yucatán, 1350–1600*. Trans. T. Rugeley. Norman: University of Oklahoma Press.

Quezada, Sergio, and Tsubasa Okoshi Harada. 2001. *Papeles de los Xiu de Yaxá*. Mexico City: Universidad Nacional Autónoma de México.

Re-Cruz, Alicia. 1996. *The Two Milpas of Chan Kom*. Albany: State University of New York Press.

Redfield, Robert. 1941. *The Folk Culture of Yucatan*. Chicago: University of Chicago Press.

Redfield, Robert. 1950. *A Village that Chose Progress: Chan Kom Revisited*. Chicago: University of Chicago Press.

Redfield, Robert, and Alfonso Villa Rojas. 1934. *Chan Kom: A Maya Village. Volume No. 448*. Washington, DC: Carnegie Institution of Washington Publication.

Reed, Nelson. 2001. *The Caste War of Yucatan*. Rev. ed. Stanford: Stanford University Press.

Restall, Matthew. 1997. *The Maya World: Yucatec Culture and Society 1550–1850*. Stanford: Stanford University Press.

Restall, M. 1998. "The Ties that Bind: Social Cohesion and the Yucatec Maya Family." *Journal of Family History* 23 (4): 355–81. http://dx.doi.org/10.1177/036319909802 300402.

Roys, Ralph L. 1939. *The Titles of Ebtun*. Volume Publication No. 505. Washington, DC: Carnegie Institution of Washington.

Roys, Ralph L. 1943. *The Indian Background of Colonial Yucatan*. Volume Publication No. 548. Washington, DC: Carnegie Institution of Washington.

Roys, Ralph L. 1957. *The Political Geography of the Yucatan Maya*. Volume Publication No. 613. Washington, DC: Carnegie Institution of Washington.

Roys, Ralph L., France V. Scholes, and Eleanor B. Adams. 1940. *Report and Census of the Indians of Cozumel 1570*. Washington, DC: Carnegie Institution of Washington.

Roys, Ralph L., France V. Scholes, Eleanor B. Adams, and Diego Garcia de Palacio. 1959. "Census and Inspection of the Town of Pencuyut, Yucatan, in 1583 by Diego García de Palacio, Oidor of the Audiencia of Guatemala." *Ethnohistory (Columbus, Ohio)* 6 (3): 195–225. http://dx.doi.org/10.2307/480402.

Rubertone, Patricia E. 2008. "Engaging Monuments, Memories, and Archaeology." In *Archaeologies of Placemaking: Monuments, Memories, and Engagement in Native North America*, ed. P. E. Rubertone, 13–33. Walnut Creek, CA: Left Coast Press.

Rugeley, Terry. 1997. *Yucatán's Maya Peasantry and the Origins of the Caste War*. Austin: University of Texas Press.

Rugeley, Terry. 2009. *Rebellion Now and Forever: Mayas, Hispanics and Caste War Violence in Yucatán, 1800–1880*. Stanford: Stanford University Press.

Scarborough, Vernon L., and William R. Burnside. 2010. "Complexity and Sustainability: Perspectives from the Ancient Maya and the Modern Balinese." *American Antiquity* 75 (2): 327–63. http://dx.doi.org/10.7183/0002-7316.75.2.327.

Schachner, Gregson. 2012. *Population Circulation and the Transformation of Ancient Zuni Communities*. Tucson: University of Arizona Press.

Scholes, France V., and Ralph L. Roys. 1948. *The Maya Chontal Indians of Acalán-Tixchel*. Volume Publication No. 560. Washington, DC: Carnegie Institution of Washington.

Smith, Adam T. 2003. *The Political Landscape: Constellations of Authority in Early Complex Polities*. Berkeley: University of California Press.

Steggerda, Morris. 1941. *Maya Indians of Yucatan*. Volume Publication No. 531. Washington, DC: Carnegie Institution of Washington.

Stone, Glenn D. 1996. *Settlement Ecology: The Social and Spatial Organization of Kofyar Agriculture*. Tucson: University of Arizona Press.

Stone, Glenn Davis. 2007. "Agricultural Deskilling and the Spread of Genetically Modified Cotton in Warangal." *Current Anthropology* 48 (1): 67–103. http://dx.doi.org/10.1086 /508689.

Strickon, Arnold. 1965. "Hacienda and Plantation in Yucatan: An Historical-Ecological Consideration of the Folk-Urban Continuum in Yucatan." *América Indígena* 25:35–65.

Sullivan, Paul. 1989. *Unfinished Conversations: Mayas and Foreigners between Two Wars*. Berkeley: University of California Press.

Thompson, Philip C. 1999. *Tekanto: A Maya Town in Colonial Yucatán*. Middle America Research Institute Publication 67. New Orleans: Tulane University.

Villa Rojas, Alfonso. 1978. Los elegidos de Dios: Etnografía de los mayas de Quintana Roo. Mexico City: Instituto Nacional Indígena.

Weeks, John M. 1988. "Residential and Local Group Organization in the Maya Lowlands of Southwestern Campeche, Mexico: The Early Seventeenth Century." In *Household and Community in the Mesoamerican Past*, ed. R. R. Wilk and W. Ashmore, 73–96. Albuquerque: University of New Mexico Press.

Wilk, Richard R. 1991. *Household Ecology: Economic Change and Domestic Life among the Kekchi Maya in Belize*. Tucson: University of Arizona Press.

Wolf, Eric R. 1957. "Closed Corporate Peasant Communities in Mesoamerica and Central Java." *Southwestern Journal of Anthropology* 13 (1): 1–18. http://dx.doi.org/10.1086/sout janth.13.1.3629154.

Wolf, Eric R. 1990. "Distinguished Lecture: Facing Power—Old Insights, New Questions." *American Anthropologist* 92 (3): 586–96. http://dx.doi.org/10.1525/aa.1990.92.3.02a00020.

8

Names, Naming, and Person Reference in Quiahije Chatino

EMILIANA CRUZ

INTRODUCTION

The Chatino language of San Juan Quiahije (Quiahije), Oaxaca, Mexico, is rich with interplay between language and culture in the area of person reference. In this chapter I focus on the discursive use of language and landscape to construct person reference in Quiahije Chatino. The chapter has a large linguistic component, since linguistic analysis contributes to our understanding of how place is constructed and interpreted. Another factor that contributes to this construction and interpretation is the social layering of the community, and the community's relationship with the national project of assimilating indigenous people into Spanish-speaking society. This project of assimilation fits into a broader context of interest, which includes political reordering, patterns of intense Christianization, and linguistic imposition in indigenous communities. One finding in the study is that the people of Quiahije mediate linguistic impositions on their social life by creating their own naming practices through the use of place-names.

Personal names in Quiahije play an important role in the social and cultural life of the community. Every member of the community has a first name, two last names, and a family name that is derived from a place-name. Some community members also have a nickname. The analysis that follows explores how people from Quiahije engage in person reference in their social lives; how speakers verbally associate an

DOI: 10.5876/9781607325727.c008

individual with known properties, such as his or her face, name, social identity, or personality; and how tones function in names borrowed from Spanish. The chapter draws on extended participant observation in the San Juan and Cieneguilla communities, as well as metalinguistic discussions with adult speakers.

I was born in Cieneguilla, a village that is part of the municipality of San Juan Quiahije, but I have lived most of my life outside of the community. My interest in the topic of names came from a desire to learn more about social interaction between native Chatino speakers. In particular, I wanted to better understand the crucial role of personal names in the social lives of the people of San Juan. I am a fluent speaker of Chatino, but fluency is not sufficient to understand face-to-face communication and person reference in the communities of Cieneguilla and San Juan. The focus of this chapter is the set of linguistic and communicative rules that make this interaction successful, such as the rules governing tone of voice and other linguistic choices that are used to avoid uncomfortable social situations. Finally, I include a discussion of the geographic aspect of person reference.

In my research I observed and actively participated in hours of conversations in kitchens (figure 8.1) and public spaces, and took video of narratives in which speakers made reference to various people. Further details regarding the participants, types of conversations, and locations will be provided below.

Throughout the chapter I discuss person reference in interactions in Chatino. Section 1, "The Communities," introduces the community, describes its geographical location, and discusses the ideologies of what I will call "base" and "temporal" home. Section 2, "Ways of Referring to People in San Juan," introduces the construction of person reference in Quiahije. Section 3, "Personal Names," discusses how the people of Quiahije receive their names.

THE COMMUNITIES

The seat (*cabecera*) of San Juan Quiahije has 2,120 inhabitants, while Cieneguilla has 1,330 inhabitants, according to the Mexican Census (2010). Cieneguilla is a separate village (*agencia policía*) within the municipality of San Juan (figure 8.2). The distance between the two communities is about ten kilometers.

Residents of both communities speak the Chatino language. Chatino is one member of the Oto-manguean language stock and belongs to a genetic subgroup within the Zapotecan branch (Campbell 2013; Kaufman 2007). Chatino comprises three varieties: Zenzontepec (ZEN), Tataltepec (TAT), and Eastern Chatino (Campbell 2011; Cruz and Woodbury 2006). Eastern Chatino, in turn, comprises an internally diverse set of varieties spoken in twenty-one communities, including San Juan Quiahije. There are fifteen varieties of Eastern Chatino in all, each with its

FIGURE 8.1. Kitchen interaction. Photo by author.

FIGURE 8.2. Cieneguilla seen from San Juan. Photo by Frida Cruz.

own tone system. Most varieties are monosyllabic, except for Santa María Yolotepec (field notes) and San Marcos Zacatepec (Villard 2007). The Chatino of Quiahije is most notable for its tonal complexity (E. Cruz 2011). Phonetically there are twelve tones, and phonologically there are fourteen tones distinguished at the lexical level (E. Cruz 2011; see also table 8.8 in Appendix 8.A).[1]

Residents of this area consider San Juan to be "the old place," but San Juan is a relatively new municipality in the Chatino region. The place where San Juan would eventually be founded was settled in a wave of migration sparked by evangelization. While scholars have not determined the exact year of the migration, some suggest that it occurred around 200 years ago (Wenceslao Cruz Cortes, personal communication). According to oral tradition, San Juan was founded when a few citizens saw a rooster crowing on top of a hill in San Juan (see figure 8.6: #43). Below the hill there was a pond, where residents claimed to see Saint John appear. This caused people who lived in surrounding areas to move to San Juan. Over time this pond dried up, and the local church now sits at its site (see figure 8.3: #92; Wenceslao Cruz Cortes, personal communication). The people from the surrounding areas who moved to San Juan adopted names related to the new places where they settled (see table 8.9 of Appendix 8.A for examples).

Looking north from the hill where the rooster was found, one can see a flat expanse of land. This was where residents of San Juan raised animals such as cows and chickens. The people of San Juan remember this place as being full of an incredible amount of netleaf oak (*Quercus rugosa*), orchids, ponds, and creeks. They describe it as a wetland. San Juan residents did not have permanent houses in the flat area but would go only to visit their livestock and then return to San Juan.

Cieneguilla was settled in the early 1970s, when the Franciscan friar Edmundo Ávalos Covarrubiasa convinced a group a people to move to the flat land (figure 8.4). The group of San Juan residents included Tomás Cruz (my father), Elucterio Jarquín, Odilón Cortés, and many other families. The people who migrated sought independence from San Juan. Their leaders, especially Tomás, dreamed of having a self-sustaining community. They would be able to have gardens and wells nearby—something Tomás believed would not be possible in San Juan due to the local politics and geographic conditions. (San Juan sits on a high mountain, so there is limited room for gardens and little space to build wells for people to have access to water closer to their homes.)

After forty-five years, the communities of San Juan and Cieneguilla maintain strong family connections but also have political disagreements over state funding. The state government gives funding for projects to San Juan, and San Juan is responsible for distributing the funds. According to the people of Cieneguilla, however, the San Juan municipality is not fair and gives little funding to Cieneguilla.

NAMES, NAMING, AND PERSON REFERENCE IN QUIAHIJE CHATINO 167

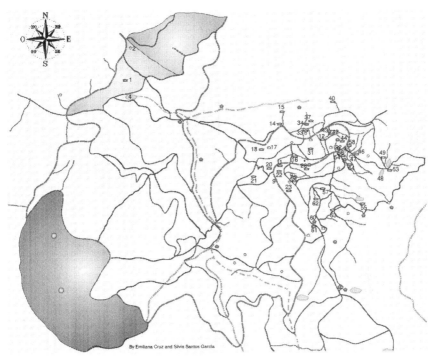

FIGURE 8.3. Map of location-based names.
Meanings of the symbols: ⌂ family with place name, ○ area, ⬭ pond, ⍟ sacred place, ⛲ well, ⌇ trail.

The split between the communities is relatively recent. This is one of the reasons why the people of San Juan and Cieneguilla speak the same variety of Chatino, unlike other Chatino communities, which speak different dialects. When the families who founded Cieneguilla left for the lower land, they continued to consider San Juan as their permanent home, viewing Cieneguilla as a temporary place.

This view of Cieneguilla as temporary is reflected linguistically in what Hilaria Cruz has called the "base" and "temporary" uses of the verb 'to go' (H. Cruz 2008). The verb 'to go' temporary is *tsa^J* 'He/she is going temporary', and the verb 'to go' base is *kya^J* 'He/she is going base'. In discourse, San Juan is always the base. For example, even if someone is born in Cieneguilla, the person still uses *kya^J* to talk about going to San Juan.

The following cases demonstrate some of the uses of the base and temporal versions of "to go."

FIGURE 8.4. The first plane that landed in Cieneguilla (1973). Source unknown.

Case 1. Xna^H 'Josephine', born in Cieneguilla, will go to visit relatives in San Juan. Examples (a–f) refer to Xna^H of Cieneguilla. In the following examples, $Kchi^A_i$ means village in Quiahije Chatino. The * symbol indicates that the sentence is ill formed.

a. Xna^H kwa^F **kya^J** $kchi^E_i$.
       Josephine   that   will go   San Juan (village)
       'Josephine will go (base) to San Juan'.

b.   *Xna^H kwa^F **tsa^J** $kchi^E_i$.
       Josephine   that   will go   San Juan
       'Josephine will go (temporal) to San Juan'.

Case 2. Xna^H is standing in San Juan. She is going back home to Cieneguilla after visiting her relatives in San Juan.

c. Xna^H kwa^F **tsa^J** $nte?^F_i$.[2]
       Josephine   that   will go   Cieneguilla
       'Josephine will go (temporal) to Cieneguilla'.

d.   *Xna^H kwa^F **kya^J** $nte?^F_i$.
       Josephine   that   will go   Cieneguilla
       'Josephine will go (base) to Cieneguilla'.

Case 3. Xna^H is standing in $S?we^F$ 'Juquila', a mestizo commercial town. She is going back to Cieneguilla or San Juan (figure 8.6).

NAMES, NAMING, AND PERSON REFERENCE IN QUIAHIJE CHATINO 169

FIGURE 8.5. Map of San Juan Quiahije and Cieneguilla (Google Earth 2014).

e. Xna^H kwa^F **kya^J** $xi^I\text{-}tyi^A$.
    Josephine   that   will go   hometown
    'Josephine will go (base) to [her] hometown'.

f. *Xna^H kwa^F **tsa^J** $xi^I\text{-}tyi^A$.
    Josephine   that   will go   hometown
    'Josephine will go (temporal) to [her] hometown'.

However, in the common speech of people born in San Juan, San Juan is the base, even for people who have moved elsewhere—for example, the many people from both communities who are migrating to Oaxaca city and the United States. They use the temporal form tsa^J to describe this migration. See the following examples:

g. Xna^H kwa^F **tsa^J** $no^F rte^J$.
    Josephine   that   will go   north
    'Josephine will go (temporal) to the United States (north)'.

h. Xna^H kwa^F **tsa^J** $lo^I\ nt\text{?}a^B$.
    Josephine   that   will go   to guaje
    'Josephine will go (temporal) to Oaxaca City'.[3]

The following examples show the base and temporal form of returning. In example i, Josephine is coming to visit. Example j, Josephine is coming back to her home.

FIGURE 8.6. Map of San Juan Quiahije, Cieneguilla, and Juquila (Google Earth 2014).

i. Xna^H kwa^F $ka^A_{\,;}$ ti^C $ʔa^E$.
    Josephine   that   will come   ADV   later
    'Josephine will come (temporal) later'.

j. Xna^H kwa^F $kya^J_{\,;}$ ti^C $ʔa^E$.
    Josephine   that   will come   ADV   later
    'Josephine will come (base) later'.

My cousin, Lorenzo Cruz, used the above examples to show me the differences between temporal and base forms used to express, for instance, going to San Juan and Cieneguilla. According to him, young people are starting to use base forms for both. Lorenzo is from San Juan and has come to believe the ideology that the "important town" such as San Juan should only be base and not temporal, because the people from Cieneguilla left from San Juan.

WAYS OF REFERRING TO PEOPLE IN SAN JUAN

Some of the common lexemes used in person reference are $neʔ^A\ kwla^A$ 'old person' (respectful); $no^A\text{-}ʔa_{\,;}^{\,E}\ lyuʔ^N$ 'girl'; $no^A\text{-}kyʔyu^E\ lyuʔ^N$ 'boy'; $ʔi_{\,;}^A\text{-}ma^K$ 'deceased person'; $ma^H\text{-}xuʔ^F$ 'old lady' (disrespectful); mba^B 'compadre' (my child's godfather); and lyi^B 'comadre' (godmother). When speakers of any language make reference to objects, persons, or events, they do so in terms of the social and linguistic categories of their communities (Hanks 2007). In Quiahije the kinship terms are inalienable nouns. The possessive kinship terms are the unmarked reference form in the communities of San Juan. Social norms learned through religion, family, local government, and other institutions govern social interaction. For example, in Quiahije it is sometimes the case that when people refer to a member of the community or family, as in $y^2a_{\cdot}^E$ Tyu^B 'Peter's mother', the speaker references some background information. This background knowledge is part of the perspective from which the speaker individuates the referent (Hanks 2007). Research on informal conversation in US English suggests that the simplest way of referring to a person is by first name (Schegloff 1996), but this is not the case with Chatino. There are, however, some similarities in person reference between Yucatecs and Quiahije Chatinos. In both formal and informal conversation in San Juan, the use of personal names is not customary.

During my research, I often participated in conversations in which personal names were the main topic. On one particular day, I was in Cieneguilla with my family, and a woman came to visit my mother. Since we reside outside of the San Juan area, we do not know the name of every person who lives there. I asked the visitor, $^2wq^K$ $niya^K$ na^K $^2wq^K$ ne^{2A} $kwla^A$ 'Miss, what is your name?' I sensed that the question was invasive, but I was not sure why. The visitor did not answer, but instead laughed to herself. When the visitor left, my mother advised me against asking people for their first names, as this is considered invasive: "People get uncomfortable with those types of questions." In this community people prefer the use of kin terms for person reference. Since I reside outside the village, sometimes I embarrass myself by using first names inappropriately to refer to people. In contrast, residents learn the rules that govern the use of names at an early age and therefore avoid the mistakes that I might make. After the incident with the visitor, I became interested in understanding person reference in my community. In the following subsections I will discuss person reference using examples of nicknames and kinship terms.

Nicknames

Nicknames are used only in the absence of the named person. The following examples show various kinds of nicknames. They can be based on verbs, nouns, adjectives, or nominalizations of full sentences. The people in San Juan create nicknames frequently and in different ways. One way of creating nicknames is on the basis of a person's idiosyncrasies. Some people are given nicknames because of their unique physical appearance or for something unusual they once said, as in the following examples.

a.   *Xwa^F*   *ntyku^J*   *tya^E*
        John   eats   corn
        'John the corn eater'
Xwa^F got this name because he ate a lot of corn.

b.   *Xwa^F*   *ktyi̧ʔ^B*
        John   lice
        'Lice John'
Xwa^F got this name because he had lice.

c.   *yʔa̧^{E}*   *ktyi̧ʔ^B*
        mother   lice
        'Mother of lice'
This person got this name because she had a lot of lice.

d.   *Xwa^A*   *ta^F*   *knyi^C*
        John   hunt   bird
        'John the bird hunter'
This person got this name because he was a bird hunter.

e.   *Se^B*   *tso̧^{0}*
        Jose   warm
        'Warm José'
José got this name based on a conversation he had with his lover, which someone overheard.

The following is natural conversation with someone talking about nicknames in San Juan:

Mm^A-mm^F, Wwa^F Ko̧^{H}, Xwa^F Ko̧^{H}. [EC^a: M^A-m^F, ʔo^E ko̧^{H} nga^J ja̧ʔ^{G}no^A ko^B rȩʔ^J a^J]. Xwa^F Ko̧^{H} ne^J rȩʔ^E cha^F lyu^{H}ti^J ku^F. Cha^F tlyu^C ljo^E (ri^H nde^H niya̧^{J}), lyu^H ja̧^{H} xtya̧^{H} cha^F, sa^A ʔa^K ʔwi^K ke^A lye^B ra^K ti^K nsʔwi^J. [EC: na^F nga^E ke^K lye^B ra^K ja̧ʔ^G]. No^A nga^J ke^K lye^B ra^K ja̧ʔ^G na^F ntyʔwi^J jya^C na^F nga^J ja̧ʔ^G-i̧^{H}. [EC: a: ke^F lye^B ra^K]. Ja^A ne^I ja^A ne^I, Xwa^F Ke^A Lye^B ra^K. Na^H-ji̧^{C} xwa^F ke^A lye^B ra^K ʔne^K ra̧ʔ^E ʔo^E ja̧ʔ^H. ʔo^E na^H ji̧^{C} si^K tykwi̧ʔ^K rȩʔ^J cha^F xlya^K Jwa̧^{H} Ke^A Lye^H ra^H ʔne^J rȩʔ^E ʔo^E ja̧ʔ^H [CIEN-2010_02_16-Txt_intv_LBG_BCS-ec-Clip_04.dv]

Translation: Yes, John Pigeon, John Pigeon. [EC: Yes, that nickname means to grind?] They gave him that nickname because he was short. Also, there is One Rock John; he was round like this (rounding arm), he was squat, he looked like a one-pound rock.

TABLE 8.1. Teknonymy

Chatino	Gloss
no^A-xwe^J ʔnya^A	(the little ones) 'my children'
no^A-ʔna^E tʔą^J	(my female sibling) 'my sister'
no^A-kyʔyu^E tʔą^J	(my male sibling) 'my brother'
yʔą^E no^A xwe^J	(children's mother) 'my wife'
sti^A no^A xwe^J	(children's father) 'my husband'
yʔą^E Sa^{A}we^B	'Isabel's mother'
sti^A Sa^{A}we^B	'Isabel's father'
sti^A no^A xwe^J ʔnya^A	(father of my children) 'my husband'
yʔą^A no^A xwe^J ʔnya^A	(mother of my children) 'my wife'
ntę^B ʔįK tʔą^J	(person of my sibling) 'my sibling's spouse'
neʔ^A kla^A ʔnya^A	(my elders) 'my parents'

[EC: What is this one-pound rock?] One-pound rock is the rock that is used for weighing. [EC: ahh, to weigh things.] Yes, yes, John One Pound Rock, they called him One Pound Rock. But if you say it in Spanish, you say Juan One Pound Rock.

TEKNONYMY

In San Juan the use of first names is uncommon when addressing and referring to others. One way this is avoided is by addressing or referring to people using the name of a relative, a pattern known as "teknonymy." For instance, parents in San Juan are referred to using the name of their oldest child. My parents were called by the name of my oldest sibling, yʔą^E La^{H}ya^J 'Hilaria's mom'. In addition, locals use teknonymy in a variety of ways (see table 8.1).

The following are some examples of teknonymy in conversation. A father converses with his son-in-law about his daughter (the wife of the son-in-law). When the father refers to his daughter, he refers to her as 'the mother of the children'. In natural conversation I once saw a woman chasing down a cow. She came upon some young children who were playing and asked to see their mother. When the mother came outside, the two adults had the following conversation:

a. SPEAKER A: ja^A ʔne^A chiʔ^H marka^K ʔnya^K sʔe^A ntʔe^A yʔą^E wa^{A}ldo^{A}me^{F}ro^J kwa^F
    'Please call Waldomero's mother's house'
    SPEAKER B: jo^F ʔwa$_,^K$ niya$_,^K$ tykweʔ^H ʔo^E ka$_,^H$
    'Yes. What do you want me to tell her'

In example a, the speaker refers to the person she needs to contact as 'Waldomero's mother', using the woman's son's name instead of the woman's own name.

KINSHIP TERMS

In San Juan, kinship terms are commonly used to refer to a person. However, they are rarely used to refer to a relative, mainly because the person already has knowledge of the relationship.

Privacy and intimacy play an important role in how people communicate with each other. Thus, people refer to each other differently when they are at home than when they are in public. At home, children address their mother as ma^B 'mom' and their father as tyi^B 'dad'. Outside the home, children avoid directly addressing their parents. Indirect conversation is preferred. The vocative ways parents address their children are ma^H 'dear girl' and tyi^H 'dear boy'. The nonvocative term for referring to children is no^A-xwe^I 'little people, children'. In addition, there are two ways of referring to grandparents (see table 8.2). The first is ma^H $ste\textipa{P}^A$ $\textipa{P}i_;^A$ 'granny of,'[5] a form that is alienable and occurs with the possessive marker $\textipa{P}i_;^A$. The other form, $y\textipa{P}a_;^E$ $ste\textipa{P}^I$ 'grandmother of', is inalienable and is inflected for possessor. Of these forms, the alienable one is informal and the inalienable one is formal.

In conversation there are some restrictions on the use of kinship terms when referring to a close relative—such as a mother, father, or grandfather—in that relative's presence. For example, if I am in a room with my mother, and another person and I are talking about a situation in which my mother is the focus, I would not say, "Then my mother said . . . " Instead, I would use, "Then this old person said . . . " If my mother is not present, I would say, "My mother said." When I am speaking about a person who is not kin, I would say, "The person said," whether or not that person is present.

Compadrazgo 'Co-parenthood'

To refer to their *compadres*, or godparents, people use terms that indicate the *compadrazgo* relation: '$nli^M_;$ 'my *comadre*', and $mban^M$ 'my *compadre*'. This is clearly due to the influence of the Catholic Church. The most important coparenthoods (or godparenthoods) are created in two main events: baptisms and weddings. Since time immemorial, the parents of a couple who wish to marry must sanction the marriage after discussing the relationship between the families. If a pending dispute is discovered, the marriage will not be approved. The reason is that coparenthood is like becoming one family. In San Juan a woman does not take her spouse's patronymic last name; she keeps her last names. I interviewed a woman from San

TABLE 8.2. Consanguinity (kinship terms)

Chatino	Gloss
sti^A	father of
$tyi^H \, ?^J_{\xi}$	father (vocative)
$kwi?C \, ?^E_{\xi}$	baby of
$tyi^H \, jne?^H \, ?^J_{\xi}$	male caregiver of (father role)
$ma^H \, nchi?^H \, ?^J_{\xi}$	female caregiver of (mother role)
$kwi?^H \, ?ya^F$	baby of (whose mother is pregnant)
$cho?^G_{\xi} \, ndyi^G$	youngest child of
$kwi?^H \, kchi?^A$	youngest son of
$t?a^G \, la^H$	sibling of
$ma^H \, ste?^A \, ?^A_{\xi}$	granny of
$y?a_{\xi}^E \, ste?^I$	grandmother of
$tyi^H \, ste?^A \, ?^A_{\xi}$	grandpa of
$sti^A \, ste?^I$	grandfather of
$t?a^G \, sti^A$	uncle/aunt of (maternal and paternal)
$t?a^G \, ste?^A$	cousin of
$y?a_{\xi}^E \, ska_{\xi}^A$	great-grandmother of

Juan who said that her parents did not let her marry the person that she wanted to marry. This was due to some past issues between the two families. The following is her story:

No^A ya$^G_{\xi}$ na?^{H} ji$^C_{\xi}$ Se^B ne?^{J} jla^J Ko^{F}pyo^J ndywi?^{J} re?^{J} i$^H_{\xi}$, ya$^G_{\xi}$ jnya^E ?nya^J ja^H-i^H ja^A ne^I ?o^E na?^{H}-ji$^C_{\xi}$?o^E cha?^{F} no^J y?wi^J wa^G xlya^E-i$^0_{\xi}$. ?o^E ka?^{G} cha?^{F} nty?wi^A lyo$^A_{\xi}$ nty?o^H cha?^{F} nty?i jya^C wa^G nt?a$^J_{\xi}$ chi?^{H} no^A no^A xwe$^J_{\xi}$ nty?i^A jya$^C_{\xi}$. S?we^F s?we$^J_{\xi}$ nty?o^H cha?^{F}. Cha?^{F} no^J nty?ya^B wa^G ja^A tla^I ?wa^G nty?ya^B na?^{H}-ji$^C_{\xi}$ ngya^J cha?^{F} no^J ja^A s?wi^I yja^A ku^{A}ja^A nts?wi^I. na?^{H}-ji$^C_{\xi}$ ka?^{H} ?o^E ykwi?^{A} ky?a$^J_{\xi}$ yja^I cha?^{F} no^J. No^A wjya?^{C} re?^{C} ndiya?^{C} cha?^{F} no^A wjya?^{C} nte^B ndiya?^{C} cha?^{F} ja?^{H}-i$^J_{\xi}$. ?o^E ky?a$^J_{\xi}$?a^E yja^A tla^J nty?ya^E ja?^{H}-i$^K_{\xi}$?o^E ?o^E wa^G re^C nty?a$^J_{\xi}$ yku^J wa^G re^C ja?^{H}-i$^C_{\xi}$ na?^{H} ji$^H_{\xi}$. S?we^F s?we$^H_{\xi}$?o^E nty?o^H cha?^{F} s?we^J s?wi^J wa^G ndiya^A ?o^E maten^H kwa^F ndiya^A wa^F. ?o^E ja^E no^K no^J na?^{H}-ji$^C_{\xi}$. ka?^{G} na?^{H}-ji$^C_{\xi}$ ykwi?^{A} ?o^E ska^J ya?^{J} na?^{H}-ji$^C_{\xi}$. Nde^H ndywi^I ne?^{A} kla^A ?nya^A cha?^{F} no^J na?^{H}-ji$^C_{\xi}$ tsa^J jnya^H ?i$^G_{\xi}$ kwa$^H_{\xi}$ nya^J ntykwi?^{I} ndywi?^{J}. ?a^H s?we^F ra$^F_{\xi}$ ka?^{H} ndywe?^{H} ?o^E wa^C nk?a$^E_{\xi}$ selo^J wa^F pero^A ja^A ja^A-la^I ndiya^B re?$^0_{\xi}$ sa^A ?a^E ti^E. Ka?^{G} ndywi?^{A} tyi ?nya^J ?o^E no^A ngwa^C ma^H ?nya^J ja^E no^0 no^J wa^C ya$^G_{\xi}$ nte?^{B} ja?^{G} no^E ya$^G_{\xi}$ ya$^G_{\xi}$ jnya^K ?nya^J ja?^{H}. Kwna^G nda^F cha?^{F} jya?^{F} cha?^{F} jnya^E re?^{J} jnya^J ?o^E ka?^{G} ?o$^G_{\xi}$ ndo^H ra^E no^K ya$^G_{\xi}$ jnya^E re?^{J} ?nya^J ?o$^G_{\xi}$ ndo$^H_{\xi}$ja?^{H}-i^H. Ka?^{G} ndywe?^{H} ?o^E ja?^{H} na?^{H}-ji$^C_{\xi}$. Nda^F lya^J wa$^J_{\xi}$?nya^J

ʔiJ̧ nteᵦᴮ reᴷ ndyweᵦᴴ sʔaJ̧ ʔoᴱ raᴷ ʔoᴳ jyoᵦᴱ ʔnyaᴱ nkʔaJ̧ tuᶠ-skoᵦᴳ ndoᵦᴴ jaʔᴴ. ʔiᴱ ʔaᴱ-noᴷ waᶜ ntʔoᴱ nteᵦᴮ jaʔᴳ ngyaJ̧ kaʔᴳ noᴬ naʔᴴ-ji̧ᶜ. ʔyaᴳ reʔJ̧ naʔᴴ-ji̧ᶜ, ʔnyiᴱ ykaJ̧ reʔJ̧ ʔnyaJ̧. [CIEN-2008_06_Txt_intv_anonymous-ec-Clip_05.wav]

TRANSLATION: *One day, José and his father, Copyo, came to my parents' house to ask for my hand. I knew José. We went to school together. We were the same age, and we were good friends. He brought lots of tortillas to school. He came from a rich family so he would bring lots of tortillas. He would share his tortillas with my brother and me. Also, he was a good friend of my brother, Martín. One day, José told me, "My parents say that they are going to talk to your parents so we can get married." I said, "Sure, but that guy Marcelo asked for my hand, and he now lives at the house. I do not want to marry him." One day, José and his parents showed up at my house. Since I already told José that I would marry him, I was present in the room while the adults talked. I was ready to go with José and his family. I even had my scarf under my arm so I could go with them straight away. José and his parents left without me. My parents never let me marry him. Later, I had to marry [the man who is now] father of my children.*

The above story shows the importance of creating a new family in marriage. However, stories like this are more common among older generations. Nowadays, young people find ways to get married even without their parents' consent.

Infant baptism is a ritual that was extremely widespread among the people in San Juan, though it is no longer universally practiced, due to the influence of the evangelical church, whose adherents prefer a later baptism ritual. When a child is born to Catholic parents, they seek a married couple to be the godparents of their child. To choose a godparent they use the same strategy as is used in marriage, since they need to make sure there are no past conflicts with the prospective godparents. More recently, people create coparenthood by selecting godparents when children graduate from different stages of school. In these cases, it is not necessary to review the history of the relationship between the families.

DESCRIBING PEOPLE'S IDENTITY

Self-reference in Chatino is a form of identification. The term for a Chatino person is a compound, *neʔᴬ tnyaᴱ*. *Neʔᴬ* means 'person'. The meaning of *tnyaᴱ* is unknown in Quiahije, though other varieties of Chatino would call this 'work'. The following sentences are examples of self-reference and of the lexemes that are used for referring to oneself (table 8.4).

NAMES, NAMING, AND PERSON REFERENCE IN QUIAHIJE CHATINO

TABLE 8.3. Coparenthood

Chatino	Gloss
lyi^B	comadre/comother/godmother
mba^B	compadre/cofather/godfather
$snyi?^A\ tya^J$	godchild of
$snyi?^A\ nt?a^H$	stepchild of

TABLE 8.4. Autonym

Chatino	Gloss
$na?^G\ nga^J\ ne?^A\ t?i^B$	'I am poor'
$na?^G\ nga^J\ ne?^l\ tnya^E$	'I am indigenous' or 'I am Chatino'
$na?^G\ nga^J\ stru^K$	'I am a teacher'
$na?^G\ nga^J\ ne?^A\ tu^F\text{-}ke^A$	'I am of the people of the cave'

TABLE 8.5. Ethnonym

Chatino	Gloss
$ne?^A\ wya^H$	'person from Nopala' (A Chatino town)
$ne?^A\ ta^l$	'mestizo' (lit. 'lard person')
$ne?^A\ xa?^C$	'mestizo' (lit. 'different person' or 'mestizo')
$ne?^A\ kta^E$	'foreigner'
$ne?^A\ pi^H$	'gringos or Europeans' (lit. 'turkey* people')

We now turn to Chatino names for other groups of people. Geographically, San Juan neighbors one mestizo town, Juquila; the rest of the neighboring towns are Chatino villages. Table 8.5 lists names for some of the neighboring people.

PERSONAL NAMES

In addition to the unofficial forms of reference discussed in the previous section, every citizen in San Juan has an official name listed on Catholic Church and government records. In modern Mexico the act of giving a person a name is standard from a legal and cultural perspective, and having a name recognized by the state is considered part of one's social identity. Naming in San Juan takes place upon baptism, which serves as an important cultural rite of passage (Smith-Stark 2000).

Official Names

Every Mexican citizen must be registered with the government when he/she is born. The official name consists of a first name and two last names in Spanish. The parents submit the name of the child, and the civil registry records it. It is important to mention that the practice of naming is changing; some people choose names for their children that they hear in the media or on the Internet, television, or radio. In the last twenty years, there has been a massive migration to the United States, and many children come back home with English names, for example, $Ke^F vi^J$ 'Kevin'.

In addition, in colonial and postcolonial Mexico the government forced people to follow exogenous naming systems in order to identify individuals accurately and to have better control over the population. Currently, every citizen of San Juan has to be registered. Up until a few years ago people had to walk eight hours to register their children, but now the government visits the community to register people. In the following subsections I will discuss in detail the practices of linguistic borrowing names of the people of San Juan. To adequately understand these practices, it is important to note that the Chatino speakers of San Juan were forced by the Catholic Church and Mexican government to speak Spanish. This has led to diverse patterns of linguistic borrowing between Spanish and Chatino.

Names Derived from Spanish

The official first names and last names of the people of San Juan are all derived from Spanish. The first research on the borrowing of proper names in Chatino started with Kitty and Leslie Pride in their dictionary of the Eastern Chatino of Panixtlahuaca, a town neighboring San Juan, where a moderately distinct dialect of Chatino is spoken (Pride and Pride 2004). They made a list of about seventy names that were derived from Spanish. Table 8.6 shows a list of names from Quiahije and Panixtlahuaca that are derived from Spanish.

Traditionally, names in Spanish were taken from saints' days listed on the calendars. These calendars were brought by priests to the village of San Juan during evangelization (Wenceslao Cruz Cortes, personal communication). The pre-Hispanic traditions of naming in San Juan are unknown, though it is possible that Chatinos shared or adopted the practices of nearby Zapotecs and Mixtecs: "In pre-Hispanic times, Mexican people had four names (Horcasitas 1973). The *tonaltoca*, which was from a calendar; *tlalticpactoca*, a name of the period of occurrences; a god's name; and a dignitary's name. The Mayas from Yucatán used a patrilineal and matrilineal last name (Roys 1940). The Zapotecs used a calendar for naming. The Mixtecs used the calendar and at the age of seven got another name" (Caso 1977, quoted in Smith-Stark 2000; translation mine).

NAMES, NAMING, AND PERSON REFERENCE IN QUIAHIJE CHATINO 179

TABLE 8.6. Names derived from Spanish

	Panixtlahuaca	*Quiahije*	*Spanish*
a.	Bla	Me^{H}la^J	Manuela
b.	Be	Nyi^{F}nyo^J	Benigno
c.	Jwasyu	Jwa^{F}syu^J	Bonifacio
d.	Beyu	Be^{H}yu^J	Silverio
e.	Sabe	Sa^{A}we^B	Isabel
f.	Xuwa	Xwa^F	Juan
g.	Laria	La^{H}ya^J	Hilaria
h.	Jeyu	Je^{H}nyo^J	Eugenio
i.	Marku	Mar^{F}ku^J	Marcos

It is difficult to determine whether these practices were part of Chatino customs. Even the Chatino elders do not know their ancestors' naming practices. I am not aware of any person who has a Chatino name based on the practices mentioned in the quote above. All names, to my knowledge, are derived from Spanish.

LAST NAMES

Official last names, as mentioned above, are actually two names: a patronym and a matronym. In San Juan there are few last names. Out of 300 speakers, I found 30 last names. If shared last names indicated a consanguineous relationship, it would seem that everyone was related. However, people regard their last names as imposed by the Catholic Church, so they find ways of distinguishing blood relatives from nonblood relatives despite common patronyms. People with the same patronym can marry one another, so their children end up with the same surname as both patronym and matronym, e.g., Cruz Cruz.

PLACE-NAMES

The family names in Chatino are unofficial names that are based on where one's family lives. Every member of the community has a family name. When a family settles in a particular area of San Juan, it will adopt the name of that location and transmit the name to the next generation of the family. A similar phenomenon was found historically in English, for example, Hill, Overbrook, Woods.

In figure 8.6 one can see that people in San Juan mainly settle around the church (#92). There are many aspects of landscape that are considered for use in informal

180 CRUZ

TABLE 8.7. Distribution of family names and place-names

Item	Numbers in the map
Description	11, 34, 53, 63, 65
Pond	49
Animal	44
River	37, 40
Religion	60
Fluids	61
Trails	22, 54
Plant	1, 16, 42, 55, 64
Well	18, 23, 31, 46
Church	12, 58
Body parts	9, 15, 20, 21, 28, 34, 57, 62

last names, such as place descriptions, ponds, fluids (urine, saliva), animals, rivers, sacred places, plant names, and architectural constructions such as wells and churches, and trails. Table 8.7 lists the distribution of places used in family names in the new settlement of San Juan Quiahije.

LOCATIVES

In Chatino, like many languages of the world, speakers use body parts to talk about location. For example, in English, speakers at times use "the foot of the mountain" to refer to the base of a mountain. An instance of this in Chatino is the following:

a. tu^C $kchi^C$ **$ne\textrm{\textipa{P}}^C$** yka^E $kyji_s^B$ (#2 on map)
    hole   glen   his/her stomach   tree   type
    'Glen of the $kyji_s^B$ tree forest'

In example a, the referent is a glen, which is in the forest of yka^E $kyji_s^B$. This glen is named after a particular tree.

A number of family names use body parts to refer to location. The following examples are of family names referring to places around trees. While the particular trees mentioned in the names often no longer exist, they remain in the memory of the people in San Juan.

b.   *ne?ᴬ*   **so?ᴳ**   *ykaᴬ*   **kya?ᴬ**   (#2 on map)

       people   his/her bottom   tree   his/her foot

       'The family who lives at the bottom of the tree'

c.   *ne?ᴬ*   **t?waᴬ**   *kxį̜ᶜ*   (#20 on map)

       people   his/her mouth   bush

       'People of the edge of the bush/ranch'

d.   *ne?ᴬ*   **so?ᴳ**   *kytyeᶜ*   (#21 on map)

       people   his/her bottom   pine tree

       'People of the bottom of the pine tree'

e.   *ne?ᴬ*   **so?ᴳ**   *ykaᴬ*   *ksuᴵ*   (#62 on map)

       people   his/her bottom   tree   specific tree

       'People of the bottom of *ykaᴬ ksuᴵ*'

The following examples use body parts in conjunction with more permanent locations:

f.   *ne?ᴬ*   *kya?ᴬ*   *yuᴵ*   (#28 on map)

       People   his/her foot   earthy place/hill

       'People of the bottom of the hill'

The next example uses an inset body part to refer to a place. The natural interpretation of the name used would be that the family lives above the anthill. The story told about this place is that in the past it had many anthills, which explains how the family that lives there got their name.

g.   *ne?ᴬ*   *keᴳ*   *tykwa?ᶜ*   (#44 on map)

       People   his/her head   anthill

       'People of the head of the ant hill'

A long time ago, people did not use latrines. When they had to go to the bathroom they went to an empty area, in particular a hill named *lo⁰ nte,ᴵ ky?i,ᶜ* 'poop mountain'. The people who lived in that area were named *ne?ᴬ lo⁰ nte,ᴵ ky?i,ᶜ* 'people of the poop mountain' (#61 on map).

The complete list of place names of San Juan can be found in Appendix 8.A.

CONCLUSION

In this article I explored naming themes of indigenous knowledge by analyzing the connection between the linguistic and physical landscape of San Juan Quiahije municipality. Like many indigenous communities, the speakers of Quiahije Chatino are undergoing a rapid shift away from the indigenous heritage language toward Spanish.

Why, how, and to what extent do elders transmit speech about the land to their communities, which are encountering homogenizing influences? Meandering to and from issues on our journeys, elders offered counternarratives to the dominant one of broader social, economic, and political change: of Mexican state-building, local development initiatives, democracy, migration, and globalization. This was a conscious struggle on their part to articulate the value of the landscape to Chatinos. Place and species names in Chatino languages refer to aspects of the surrounding environment, such as the ecological or cultural uses of the noun in question.

The Quiahije local government is giving new official names for place-names. The assigned names included erroneous Spanish translations of Eastern Chatino lexicons. For example, for $kqya^C tan^B$, Eastern Chatino for 'mountain and oak tree', authorities gave *cerro de manteca*, Spanish for 'mound of lard'. Authorities also borrowed words from Mexico's Catholic heritage, the names of Christian saints, which now appear on official maps and new street signs.

Despite these impositions of nonindigenous personal and place-names, many older means of referencing social life and landscape remain common in the everyday life of Chatino communities. Chatinos name each other not only according to a Spanish-derived system of names set at birth, but also according to the actions they and their families take as members of a Chatino town. Perhaps the most striking difference between the ways of naming is that church and state mandate the first, while the community shapes the other. But it should also be noted that the second way is grounded in a community space; that is, in a particular place and between people in relationships. Those relationships cannot be transplanted. These ways of naming were found to occur in common circumstances, such as when Chatinos select coparents at the church in San Juan, when a woman chases a cow in Cieneguilla, and when Chatinos talk about friends. It is a way of naming rooted in the way the community lives, so it is inseparable from an understanding of Chatino culture.

Appendix 8.A

1. TONES

There are twelve tones in San Juan Quiahije. Table 8.8 provides some examples of words with different lexical and phonetic tones.

TABLE 8.8. Tones

Level tones	Rising tones	Descending tones
$kna^{E[H]}$ 'snake'	$kon^{H[M0]}$ 'I will eat'	$tla^{B[HL]}$ 'night'
$kak^{[0]}$ 'cow'	$sqe̱^{I[MH]}$ 'scorpion'	$kla^{J[ML]}$ 'twenty'
$kna^{C[M]}$ 'theft'	$ko̱^{G[LH]}$ 'tuber'	$tyu^{M[OL]}$ 'dear little'
kna^{A*} 'sandal'	$skwa̱^{L[L0]}$ 'I threw'	
	$si^{F[LM]}$ 'butterfly'	

Note: The letters are the practical representation of the tones: A = [Low], B = [High-Low], C = [Mid], E = [High], F = [Low-Mid], G = [Low-High], H = [Mid-Superhigh], I = [Midhigh], J = [Mid-Low], K = [Superhigh], L = [Low Superhigh], and M = [Superhigh Low].
*This is a toneless tone.

2. PLACE-NAMES

TABLE 8.9. Place-names in San Juan Quiahije

Number	Symbol	Name in Chatino	Gloss
1	▱	$ne?^C yka^E kyji̱^B$	people of the $kyji̱^B$ tree
2	○	$tu^C kchi^C ne?^C yka^E kyji̱^B$	place of the $kyji̱^B$ tree
3	▱	$tyku^E ne?^C yka^E kyji̱^B$	river of a specific tree
4	▱	$s?e̱^A ndwa^B ksio tyku^E kwi^E$	the cross at $tyku^E kwi^E$
5	▱	$tyku^E kwi^E$	pure river
6	▱	$tyku^E ya?^C kwti^E$	river with seven hands
7	⌒	$twe̱^F nda^F na?^A$	trail to $nda^F na?^A$
8	⌣⌢	$twe̱^F xkwa̱^E$	trail to $xkwa̱^E$
9	⌵⌒⌉	$twe̱^F s?we^F$	trail to $s?we^F$
10	⬠	$tyku^E sna^F kchi̱^A$	river snaf $kchi̱^A$
11	▱	$ne?^A lo^A yu^I nk?a^H$	people of the red land
12	▱	$ne?^A ?wa^I la^G$	people of the front of the church

continued on next page

Table 8.9—*continued*

Number	Symbol	Name in Chatino	Gloss
13		*ntę?ᶠ nty?oᴴ tyuᶠ*	place where they make bricks
14		*ne?ᴬ loᴬ ksiᴷ*	people of the cross
15		*ne?ᴬ sǫᴳ kchįᴬ*	people of the bottom of the village
16		*ne?ᴬ ykaᴬ xwaᴳ*	people of the custard apple tree
17		*tykuᴱ ?oᴱ skąᴵ*	well
18		*ne?ᴷ tykuᴱ skąᴵ*	people of well *?oᴱ skąᴵ*
19		*ne?ᴷ sǫᴳ ykaᴬ kya?ᴬ*	people of the bottom of the tree
20		*ne?ᴬ t?waᴬ kxį?c*	people of the edge of the bushes
21		*ne?ᴬ sǫᴳ kytyeᶜ*	people of the bottom of the pine tree
22		*ne?ᴬ twęᶠ s?weᶠ*	people of the trail to Juquila
23		*ne?ᴬ tykuᴱ ky?yaᴶ*	people of the well
24		*tykuᴱ ky?yaᴶ*	well of *ky?yaᴶ*
25		*?oᶠ pątiyǫᴮ*	cemetery
26		*tykuᴱ kya?ᴮ*	above the well
27		*tykuᴱ stę?ᴮ*	curled creek
28		*ne?ᴬ kya?ᴬ yuᴵ*	people of the bottom of the hill
29		*?weᴮ kchįo*	the middle of town
30		*tykuᴱ t?waᴬ laᴳ*	well in front of the church
31		*ne?ᴬ tykuᴱ laᴳ*	people of the well in front of the church
32		*loᴬ kchįᴵ ntę?ᶠ*	on flat land
33		*ne?ᴬ loᴬ kchįᴵ ntę?ᶠ*	people of the flat land
34		*ne?ᴬ jaᴬ keᴵ*	people between rocks
35		*loᴬ ntęᴵ t?waᴬ ykaᴬ xwaᴳ*	edge of custard apple tree mountain
36		*tykuᴱ laᴳ*	church well
37		*ne?ᴬ tykuᴱ swiᴮ*	people of *swiᴮ* river
38		*twęᶠ ntę?ᶠ*	trail to flat land
39		*twęᶠ ngyaᴶ tykuᴱ kwiᴱ*	trail that goes to *kwiᴱ* river
40		*ne?ᴬ tykuᴱ keᴬ xeᶜ*	people of *keᴬ xeᶜ* river
41		*t?waᴬ ykaᴬ ntyaᴵ*	edge of the *ntyaᴵ* tree
42		*ne?ᴬ t?waᴬ ykaᴬ ntyaᴵ*	people of a specific tree

continued on next page

Table 8.9—*continued*

Number	Symbol	Name in Chatino	Gloss
43		ke^G $nt\check{e}^A$	top of the hill
44		$ne\mathcal{P}^A$ ke^G $tykwa\mathcal{P}^C$	people of ant hill
45		twe^F $ngya^J$ $tyku^E$ tsa^J	road that goes to the well-founded well
46		$ne\mathcal{P}^A$ $tyku^E$ tsa^J	people of the well-founded well
47		$tyku^E$ tsa^J	well-founded well
48		$tyku^E$ lo^A $ykwa\mathcal{P}^I$	pond creek
49		$ne\mathcal{P}^A$ $tyku^E$ lo^A $tykwa\mathcal{P}^I$	people of pond creek
50		ke^A $\mathcal{P}o^C$	sacred rock
51		$t\mathcal{P}wa^A$ $nt\check{e}^A$ sti^A $\mathcal{P}o^C$	edge of sacred father mountain
52		twe^F $t\mathcal{P}wa^A$ $nt\check{e}^A$	trail at the edge of the hill
53		$ne\mathcal{P}^A$ tu^C ke^A	people of rock
54		$ne\mathcal{P}^A$ $t\mathcal{P}wa^A$ $nt\check{e}^A$	people of the edge of the hill
55		$ne\mathcal{P}^A$ $s\underset{.}{o}^G$ ki^G	people of the bottom of the bamboo
56		$ykwa\mathcal{P}^A$ $s\mathcal{P}\check{e}^A$ la^E $st\check{e}^J$	pond where our father was born
57		$ne\mathcal{P}^A$ $ne\mathcal{P}^C$ $\mathcal{P}o^F$	people of the cemetery
58		$ne\mathcal{P}^A$ $ch\underset{.}{o}\mathcal{P}^G$ la^G	people behind the church
59		ksi^K loo $\mathcal{P}ya^C$	cross on top of the mountain
60		ksi^K noo $ndwa^B$ loo $nt\check{e}^I$ $ky\mathcal{P}\underset{.}{i}^C$	cross that is on poop mountain
61		$ne\mathcal{P}^A$ loo $nt\check{e}^I$ $ky\mathcal{P}\underset{.}{i}^C$	people of poop mountain
62		$ne\mathcal{P}^A$ $s\underset{.}{o}^G$ yka^A ksu^I	people of the bottom of a specific tree
63		$ne\mathcal{P}^A$ lo^A $\mathcal{P}ya^C$	people of the mountain
64		$ne\mathcal{P}^A$ yka^A ksu^C	people of the avocado tree
65		$ne\mathcal{P}^A$ $ky\mathcal{P}ya^C$ $x\mathcal{P}ya^I$	people of $x\mathcal{P}ya^I$ mountain
66		$t\mathcal{P}wa^A$ $nka\mathcal{P}^A$	edge of leaf
67		$tyku^E$ lo^A yu^C	cascade river
68		$tw\check{e}^F$ si^K keo	trail to flower cross
69		$tyku^E$ $\mathcal{P}ya^C$ $tykw\check{e}\mathcal{P}^E$	$\mathcal{P}ya^C$ $tykw\check{e}\mathcal{P}^E$ river
70		$tyku^E$ $ne\mathcal{P}^C$ ksu^I $lyu\mathcal{P}^H$ ti^J	inside-of-a-small-bag river
71		lo^A $ykwa\mathcal{P}^I$ no^A $ngya^A$ $tyku^E$ $xkw\underset{.}{a}^I$	pond that goes to $xkw\underset{.}{a}^I$ river
72		$nt\check{e}\mathcal{P}^F$ $ndywa^B$ ti^F $kwe\mathcal{P}^G$	flat land where ti^F $kwe\mathcal{P}^G$ sits

continued on next page

Table 8.9—*continued*

Number	Symbol	Name in Chatino	Gloss
73		*tyku^E ne^{7C} ksu^I tlyu^C*	inside of a small bag river
74		*tyku^E t^{7}wa^A ykwa^{7A} nda^F na^{7A}*	edge of pond river
75		*twę^F ngya^J lo^A nk^{7}a^H*	road that goes to red soil
76		*twę^F ngya^J lo^A ^{7}ya^C kwą^C*	road that goes to up high mountain
77		*twę^F ngya^J ke^G kchį^A*	road that goes to the top of the village
78		*twę^F ngya^J s^{7}we^F*	road that goes to Juquila
79		*twę^F ngya^J ky^{7}ya^C kche^{7B}*	road that goes to thorn mountain
80		*twę^F ngya^J tyku^E xkwą^I*	road that goes to *xkwą^I* river
81		*twę^F ngya^J ^{7}we^B kchįo*	road that goes to the middle of the village
82		*ksi^K ^{7}weo kychįo*	cross of the middle of the village
83		*twę^F ngya^J nty^{7}o^H ^{7}o^C cho^{7G} ntę^A*	road that goes around the sacred mountain
84		*ksi^K cho^{7G} ntę^A*	cross that is around the mountain
85		*ksi^K t^{7}wao nka^{7A}*	cross that is at the edge of the leaf
86	○	*lo^F ^{7}ya^C t^{7}wa^A nda^F na^{7A}*	top of the mountain at the edge of *nda^F na^{7A}*
87		*twę^F ngya^J cho^{7G} ki^G*	road that goes around the bamboo
88	○	*nt^{7}ą^A xla^K ^{7}įo no^A xwe^I kche^{7H}*	preschool
89	○	*nt^{7}ą^A xla^K primarya^J*	elementary school
90	○	*nt^{7}ą^A xla^K secundarya^J*	middle school
91	○	*nt^{7}ą^A xla^K ^{7}įo yebo^J*	high school
92		*la^G ^{7}į^A kchį^A Są^A ^{J}wą^J*	San Juan Catholic church
93		*la^G ^{7}į^A ^{7}ermąo^J*	Protestant church
94		*ksi^K ^{7}įo ne^{7A} tu^C ke^A*	cross of the cave people
96		*twę^F ngya^J ke^G ntę^A*	trail that goes to the top of the mountain
97		*twę^F ngya^J ^{7}wa^I ntę^A*	trail that goes to the edge of the mountain
98		*twę^F ngya^J ne^{7C} yka^E xwa^G*	trail that goes inside the custard apple tree
99		*twę^F ne^{7C} yka^E nt^{7}wa^I*	trail that goes inside the *nt^{7}wa^I* tree

Note: The meaning of the symbols are as follows: ▱ family with place-name; ○ area; ▱ pond, ▱ sacred place; ▱ well; ⌣ trail.

NOTES

This research was supported by the National Endowment for the Humanities and the National Science Foundation FN-50126-14. I would also like to thank the following people for their contributions to this project: Isabel Cruz Baltazar, Francisca Cruz, Lorenzo Cruz, Wenceslao Cruz Cortes, and Luisa García Baltazar.

1. I use a practical orthography in this article, rather than International Phonetic Alphabet (IPA), to write Chatino. The consonant phonemes, in practical orthography and IPA, are as follows: bilabial p = [p], b = [nb], m = [m]; apicodental t = [t], d = [nd], ts = [ts], s = [s], n = [n], r =[ɾ], l = [l]; laminoalveolar ty = [ʈ], ny = [ɳ], ly = [ʎ]; alveolopalatal ch = [tʃ], x = [ʃ], y = [j]; Velar k = [k], g = [ng]; labiovelar w = [w]; glottal ʔ = [ʔ], j = [h]. The consonant phonemes, in practical orthography and IPA, are as follows: Oral vowels, as /i/, /u/, /e/, /o/, /a/. The nasalized vowel, as /i̧/, /a̧/, /ȩ/, /o̧/.

2. ntȩʔ[F] means 'flat land' in Quiahije Chatino. The syntax of the examples a through j are acceptable.

3. The place-name Oaxaca comes from the Nahuatl language and means "land of Leucaena leucocephala."

4. 'EC' stands for the name of the interviewer 'Emiliana Cruz.'

5. Here the object of the preposition 'of' is a third person.

REFERENCES

Campbell, Eric. 2011. "Del Proto-Zapotecano al Proto-Chatino." CILLA-VI–11. *Memorias del Congreso de Idiomas Indígenas de Latinoamérica*. Austin: University of Texas, Austin.

Campbell, Eric. 2013. "The Internal Diversification and Subgrouping of Chatino." *International Journal of American Linguistics* 79 (3): 395–420. http://dx.doi.org/10.1086/670924.

Caso, Alfonso. 1977. *Reyes y Reinos de la Mixteca I, II*. México: Fondo de Cultura Económica.

Cruz, Emiliana. 2011. "Phonology, Tone, and the Functions of Tone in San Juan Quiahije Chatino." Ph.D. Diss., University of Texas, Austin.

Cruz, Hilaria. 2008. "Notion of Base in Some Motion Verbs in San Juan Quiahije Chatino." Manuscript, University of Texas, Austin.

Cruz, Hilaria, and Anthony C. Woodbury. 2006. La fonología and tonología comparativa del Chatino: Un Informe de Campo de Zacatepec." In *Las Memorias del Congreso de Idiomas Indígenas de Latinoaméricana-II*. Archive of the Indigenous Languages of Latin America. http://www.ailla.utexas.org/site/cilla2/HCruz_Woodbury_CILLA2_chatino.pdf.

Hanks, William F. 2007. "Person Reference in Yucatec Maya." In *Person Reference in Interaction*, ed. N. J. Enfield and Tonya Stivers, 149–71. Cambridge: Cambridge University Press.

Horcasitas, Fernando. 1973. "Cambio y evolución en la antroponimia náhuatl." *Anales de Antropología* 10: 265–83.

Kaufman, Terrence. 2007. "Proto-Zapotec(an) Reconstructions." Manuscript, University of Pittsburgh.

Mexican Census. 2010. http://www.siegi.oaxaca.gob.mx/app/SIBM/sibm/.

Pride, Kitty, and Leslie Pride. 2004. "Diccionario chatino de la Zona Alta: Panixtlahuaca, Oaxaca y otros pueblos." In *Serie de vocabularios y diccionarios indígenas "Mariano Silva y Aceves" Número 47*. Mexico City: Instituto Lingüístico de Verano, A.C.

Roys, Ralph L. 1940. *Personal Names of the Maya of Yucatan*. Washington, DC: Carnegie Institution of Washington.

Schegloff, E. A. 1996. "Some Practices for Referring to Person in Talk-Interaction: A Partial Sketch of a Systematic." In *Studies in Anaphora*, ed. B. Fox, 437–85. Amsterdam: John Benjamins. http://dx.doi.org/10.1075/tsl.33.14sch.

Smith-Stark, Thomas C. 2000. "Los nombres personales, apellidos, apodos y zoónonimos de Chichicapan." Presentation at the Third ENAH Colloquium, Mexico City, Mexico.

Villard, Stéphanie. 2007. "Los tonos del Chatino de San Marcos Zacatepec." CILLA-IV-07. In *Memorias del Congreso de Idiomas Indígenas de Latinoamérica-III*. Austin: University of Texas, Austin.

9

A Culturescape Built over 5,000 Years, Archaeology, and Vichama Raymi in the Forge of History

WINIFRED CREAMER, JONATHAN HAAS, AND HENRY MARCELO CASTILLO

The Norte Chico region of Peru was home to some of the earliest large-scale monumental mound construction in the Andean region and the New World. The myth of Vichama, collected in this region in 1617, explains human origins and naturalizes status distinctions as well as relating archaeological features of the landscape to local origins. The archaeological record shows the emergence of a system of agriculture, complex economic and social relations, and centralized decision making. The myth of the young gods Vichama and Pachacamac describes the arrival of cultigens and the creation of ruling and working classes. Together, archaeology and myth provide a local context for the region's history, both ancient and recent. The myth's depiction of inequalities of class and gender has enduring resonance, even though it was recorded in the seventeenth century. The myth of Vichama has been adopted as documentation of distinctive regional history and celebrated in community pageantry, helping form a regional identity through which local stakeholders can lay claim to elements of the archaeological heritage that surrounds them.

After presenting a condensed version of the "Myth of Vichama," we sketch the archaeological components of that same landscape at around 2000 BC. Almost 4,000 years later, the myth was published by Henry Marcelo, director of the museum at the Universidad Nacional José Faustino Sánchez Carrión (UNJFSC) in Huacho, Peru. A pageant of the myth was enacted at the Fortress of Paramonga, an imposing archaeological site. The graphic novel format of the publication, the pageant, and

DOI: 10.5876/9781607325727.c009

the well-known, imposing venue were all intended to capture the interest of young people and foster pride in the region's history. The pageant has developed a popular following, stressing the symbolic value of archaeological mounds and monuments as a component of deep cultural continuity across the region, despite the relatively high mobility of the contemporary population.

In presenting the myth and the archaeological associations it describes, we illustrate the value of myth in forging history. The myth of Vichama intimates that agriculture and fishing have an ancient past represented by archaeological settlements. The myth depicts agriculture and fishing as fundamental parts of the regional economy. Young people may not want to follow in their parents' and grandparents' footsteps in these pursuits, but they seek validation from their forebears. Crowds visit an archaeological site to witness reenactment of the myth that reflects rural memory, connecting the current generation to ancient sites as places where they can acknowledge older values without ceding their current lives.

THE REGION

The Norte Chico is a segment of the Peruvian coast consisting of four adjacent valleys, from south to north: Huaura, Supe, Pativilca, and Fortaleza (figure 9.1). This region has long been a zone of natural and cultural transition between the areas further to the north and south. Biologically, the area represents a mixed transitional zone between northern and southern coastal biotic regimes (Dillon et al. 2003). Brian Billman (2001) has also argued that this portion of the coast marked a natural transition between the larger northern coastal valleys with more frequent El Niño events and the smaller southern coastal valleys, where El Niño effects are less frequent. Historically, the label "Norte Chico" itself is indicative of its provincial role as an intermediate sociopolitical zone between the Peruvian capital of Lima on the Central Coast and regional center of Trujillo on the North Coast. Culturally, the Norte Chico was also a frontier zone. During the Late Intermediate Period (AD 1000 to 1400), the enormous Chimú fortification of Paramonga in the northern Fortaleza Valley represented a southern frontier of the empire (Rowe 1946) and stood in opposition to the contemporaneous Chancay fortification of Acaray (Brown Vega 2009; Ruiz Estrada and Domino Torero 1978;) in the southern Huaura Valley.

During the third millennium BC, however, this region was a center of early irrigation agriculture combined with trade between inland farmers and coastal fishermen. The pyramidal structures, sunken courts, and upright stones erected across the region during this period were unique, and they kicked off the development of a distinct and complex coastal culture. Although the connection is distant, it is

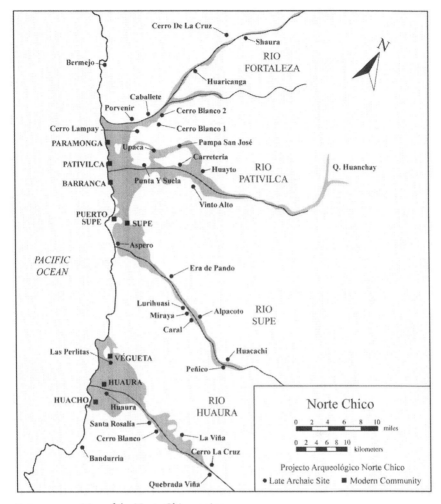

FIGURE 9.1. Map of the Norte Chico region.

possible to see the archaeological sites of the Norte Chico as indicators of a glorious past, which the myth both explains and celebrates.

THE MYTH OF VICHAMA

The myth of Vichama was collected by a Jesuit priest, Father Luis Teruel, living in the Norte Chico in 1617 and was reported by Fray Antonio de la Calancha (1638). A condensed version is as follows:

There were so many *huancas* (upright monoliths) along the coast that Teruel and his assistant (Jesuit Father Pablo Josef de Arriaga) asked about their origin in several towns, and this is what he was told.

At the beginning of the world there was no food for a man and a woman that the god Pachacamac had made. The man died of hunger and only the woman was left, looking for sustenance among the thorns and cactus, and digging up roots, crying piteously to the Sun. Hearing her lament, the Sun came down to console her. He told her to continue pulling the roots, and while she was doing this, the Sun sent his rays and a boy was conceived, who within four days was born, insuring that she would see good fortune and an abundance of food; but the contrary occurred, because the god Pachacamac was indignant that the Sun would favor another. He took the newly born semigod, and disregarding the cries of his mother, he killed his brother and tore him into small pieces. He then sowed the teeth of the dead child and corn [maize] was born (figure 9.2a), whose seeds resembled teeth. He sowed the ribs and bones, and yucas and other fruits of the earth with similar roots were born (figure 9.2b), roots whose roundness has the proportions in length and whiteness of the bones. From the flesh was produced the pepino (*Solanum muricatum*), *pacae* (*Inga feuillei*) (figure 9.2c), and the other fruits and trees, and from that time the people of the coast never suffer the previous kind of extreme hunger.

This did not placate the mother, because in every fruit there was a memory of her son. She asked for either punishment or resolution. The Sun came down, and though he was not powerful enough to go against his son Pachacamac, he consoled the woman, and he asked her for the belly button of the dead child. She showed it to him, and the Sun gave life to the belly button, and out of it grew another son, and he gave the baby to the mother, telling her that his name was Vichama. The child grew up and was a beautiful, strong young man, who, in imitation of his father the Sun, wished to walk the world and see everything grown on the earth. He consulted his mother and departed on his trip, but Pachacamac killed the now aging mother and divided her up into small pieces. When Vichama returned to his homeland, he wanted to see his mother but could not find her, and the chief told him the cruel treatment of his mother.

At that, furious flames came out of his eyes, and from his heart came cries of his feelings. He brought together the people who inhabited these valleys, asking for the bones of his mother, and they knew where they were and they brought them together as they were before, and he gave life to his mother, and in doing so he calmed his sense of revenge. He still wished to destroy the god Pachacamac, but Pachacamac did not want to kill his brother Vichama and, angry with the men, went into the ocean at the site where today his temple is, and the town and valley are called Pachacamac. Vichama, seeing that Pachacamac had escaped, angry that

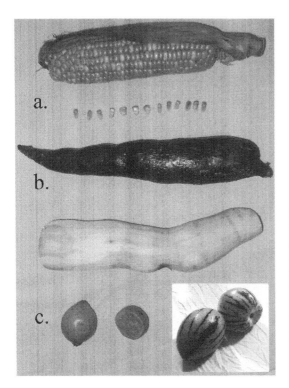

FIGURE 9.2. (a) From the teeth of the murdered child grew maize whose seeds resembled teeth; (b) the ribs and bones yielded yuca and other fruits of the earth with similar roots whose roundness has the proportions in length and whiteness of the bones; (c) from the flesh was produced the pepino, pacae, and the other fruits and trees.

the people had allowed this to happen and that they did not cooperate in punishment of Pachacamac, asked his father the Sun to turn the people into stones.

After having carried out the punishment on the people, the Sun and Vichama repented the actions taken in anger and repented that they could not correct the punishment. The Sun and Vichama wanted to mend the grief they had caused and, determined to give the honor of divinity to the chiefs and leaders, to the nobles and powerful ones, they carried them to the coast and ocean beaches. They left some of them to be adored as shrines (*guacas*) (figure 9.3a) and others they put into the sea, where they are the peninsulas, rocks, and islands (figure 9.3b) and to whom they gave titles of divinity. Every year they were offered sheets of silver, corn beer, and native fruit, with which the converted one would be placated.

Vichama, seeing the shrines and the world without men and the Sun without anyone to worship him, begged his father the Sun to create new men. The Sun sent three eggs, one of gold, another of silver, and the other of copper. From the gold egg came the chiefs, the leaders, and the nobles who were secondary persons and principals, and from the silver egg were engendered the women of these men, and from the copper

FIGURE 9.3. (a) Huanca, or monolith, at Huaricanga, Fortaleza Valley: "Dead chiefs and nobles were carried to the coast and ocean beaches to be adored as shrines [guacas]" (de la Calancha 1638). (b) Headland at the mouth of the Fortaleza River: "Others they put into the sea where they are the peninsulas, rocks, and islands" (de la Calancha 1638).

egg came the people of the lower classes, who were called Mitayos, and their women and families. This conviction was taken as an article of faith by the Indians of Huaura, Supe, Barranca, Aucallama, Huacho, Vegueta, and those who inhabit the coast, and they believed this more than they believed the articles of faith (de la Calancha 1638).

The myth of Vichama explains the origin of men and women, domesticated plants, social classes, the rocky coastline, and veneration of monoliths. In the myth domesticated plants first grew from the bones and teeth of a child murdered by Pachacamac. Peninsulas, rocks, islands, and monoliths represent the remains of chiefs and leaders murdered by the Sun and Vichama, while social classes of men and women emerged from three eggs sent by the Sun in reparation. In his account of the myth of Vichama, de la Calancha stressed that the people of the region, supposedly converted to Christianity, believed in the myth more fervently than they believed in the tenets of their new faith. The myth built on familiar local tradition and had been repeated over generations. Archaeological data provides evidence that an agricultural society with hierarchical leadership similar to that described in the myth may be more than 4,000 years old in this region, suggesting the myth articulates long-standing relationships between man and the environment.

THE ARCHAEOLOGY OF MYTH

Myths are sometimes absorbed into national consciousness, such as the cactus, eagle, and snake of the Aztec origin myth that appear on the flag of Mexico. Archaeological finds, too, suggest connections between current populations and the ancient past and have contributed to revitalization of the myth of Vichama.

FIGURE 9.4. Figurine of a woman with white paint streaked on her cheeks, and a figure of the sun inscribed on the back of her head from the site of Huaricanga, Fortaleza Valley, Peru.

In 2007, excavations at the Late Archaic site of Huaricanga in the Fortaleza Valley turned up a small (four centimeters tall) clay figurine of a woman (figure 9.4) associated with a temple dating to the middle of the third millennium BC. While clay figurines have been found at other sites in the Norte Chico (see Shady 2004), this one had attributes that seemed in their own tenuous way to link the archaeological record of the distant past to the historical record of the seventeenth century.

The figurine is a woman who appears to have tears flowing from her eyes, and on her back in the center of her long hair is a clear symbol of the sun. Although the original significance of this person is hidden in prehistoric memory, the woman brings to mind a key figure, the mother of Vichama, whose tears brought the Sun to save her. A symbol of all mothers, she was reborn in the myth through the efforts of her devoted son. The myth may be seen as a universal message of a compassionate god. The crying woman may also be interpreted as referencing an ongoing belief system, a symbol such as La Llorona or the Virgin Mary rather than a relic of an unknown, irrelevant past. Finds like this one can alter public perception of sites and artifacts as having a real connection to present-day residents based on individual or even imagined themes.[1] The image of the "crying woman" figurine subsequently appeared on posters and other publicity associated with the Vichama pageant. This convergence of a third millennium BC figurine, a seventeenth-century myth, and a contemporary celebration is an especially eloquent testament to the often convoluted trajectories through which diverse elements of archaeological heritage are made intelligible to stakeholders today.

NORTE CHICO ARCHAEOLOGY

This convergence of archaeological remains, myth, and contemporary identity offers some especially rich possibilities for narrating the longer history of human interactions with the environment of the Norte Chico. Beginning in the third millennium BC, the Andean region underwent a deep and lasting cultural transformation that not only distinguished it from other parts of the Americas but ultimately led to the florescence of one of the world's six independently developed civilizations. For over a thousand years, the Norte Chico region served as the focal point or "crucible" for the development of the earliest expressions of Andean civilization (Haas and Creamer 2006). Work in recent years has discovered thirty major ceremonial and residential centers in the four valleys of the Norte Chico, all occupied in the time between 3000 and 1800 BC. (Creamer et al. 2007; Creamer et al. 2013; Haas et al. 2004; Shady 2004; Shady and Leyva 2003d; Shady et al. 2001) (figure 9.1).

Archaeological research over the course of the past fifteen years has demonstrated that a distinctly Andean pattern of economy, society, and ceremonial architecture emerged in the Norte Chico region in the first centuries of the third millennium BC. (See Haas and Creamer 2004, 2012; Haas et al. 2013; Shady and Leyva 2003a, b, c, d). Elements of this societal framework are employed in the myth of Vichama. The body parts of the first son yield corn and other crops that are still the economic engine of the coastal valleys. Marine resources come from the "peninsulas, rocks and islands" of the coast. The description of monoliths, or huancas, as the remains of errant chiefs and nobles blurs the boundary between man and nature, where punishment can be harsh and the social order as timeless as the rocky coastline.

PLANT CULTIVATION

Norte Chico occupation from 3000 to 1800 BCE is marked by a number of characteristics that differentiate it from the preceding pattern of smaller settlements and mobile groups of hunters, foragers, and fishermen. One of the greatest distinctions of the occupants of these early sites is that they were economically dependent on irrigation-based agriculture and domesticated plants (Haas et al. 2013). Analysis of pollen, phytoliths, starch grains, coprolites, and macrobotanical remains has shown the presence of maize, cotton, gourds, beans, pacae (a legume), lucuma (a fruit), avocado, *chile*, squash, guava, and achira (purple arrowroot) (Alarcon 2005; Haas and Creamer 2004, 2006; Huaman et al. 2005; Shady 2003d, 2006; Vergel 2009; Zechenter 1988). As with people elsewhere in Peru (Dillehay et al. 2007), the residents of the Norte Chico were moving from harvesting natural resources to producing their own harvest. The transition to an agriculturally based economy happened relatively quickly in the Norte Chico region, as the local residents adopted

A CULTURESCAPE BUILT OVER 5,000 YEARS, ARCHAEOLOGY, AND VICHAMA RAYMI **197**

a comprehensive suite of domesticated plants in the course of only several hundred years. Most or all of these plants were independently brought under human control elsewhere (see Dillehay et al. 2007; Piperno and Pearsall 1998), but a fully sedentary, agriculturally dependent economy emerged very rapidly and early in the Norte Chico itself. The people of the Norte Chico took advantage of small-scale experimentation or tinkering with plant domestication in other areas and then brought them together in an interconnected regional economy (Haas 2001; Haas and Creamer 2004, 2006, 2012; Haas et al. 2013).

MARINE RESOURCES

Crucial to the growth of society during the Late Archaic period was exploitation of marine resources. Although there is ample evidence of plant cultivation, the protein requirements of Late Archaic people living on the coast were met with marine resources of fish and shellfish. Excavations at sites from a few to more than twenty kilometers from the coast reveal large quantities of fish bone in midden and in coprolites, and few or no remains of terrestrial fauna. Twenty species of shellfish have been identified at each site tested (Creamer et al. 2011). Although bone from some large fish was recovered, the vast majority of fish bone comes from small species such as anchovy and sardine. The widespread presence of fish and shellfish remains, as well as of net fragments, indicates that a portion of the population of each site was involved in obtaining marine foods, whether directly traveling to and from the coast or by means of exchange.

MONOLITHS—*HUANCAS*

Coupled with the transition to an agricultural economy was an explosion in the occupation of large sites and the construction of monumental architecture in the Norte Chico region in the third millennium BC. The thirty early sites recorded in surveys of the four Norte Chico valleys are all quite extensive, ranging from 10 to over 100 hectares in area, and have monumental communal architecture. Each of the sites has from one to seven terraced platform mounds that range from 3,000 to over 100,000 cubic meters in volume. The large majority have at least one and up to four sunken circular courts fifteen to forty-five meters in diameter (figure 9.5). In addition to the consistent plan of the mounds, the circular courts also show strong patterning, centered on the atrium of the adjacent mound with a stairway leading from the atrium to the base of the mound and then to the floor of the circular court. There is commonly an opening on the opposite side of the circular court that leads into the public space beyond. Upright stone huancas are associated with many of

FIGURE 9.5. Photo of the mounds, circular courts, and U-shaped layout at Caballete, Fortaleza Valley, Peru.

the circular courts. These stones range from one to three meters in height and cluster between 0.75 and 1.00 meters across. The largest of these weighs several tons and required a significant workforce to transport them from their quarry (Authier 2005) to the site and then to lift them into position (figure 9.3a). While the use of huancas is common throughout the Norte Chico, they appear to have different roles at different sites. At Caral and Chupacigarro Grande, huancas were used to mark the openings into circular courts. At Caballete and Pampa San José, the entire diameter of the court was outlined in huancas. There are also isolated huancas at many sites that stand as independent features (see Shady 2004).

Later sites with similar terraced platform mounds, sunken courts, and monolithic stones are found to the north and south on the coast, as well as to the east in the highlands, and all of these can be traced back historically to Norte Chico antecedents. Such platform mounds with associated sunken courts, for example, appear at Initial Period (1800–1000 BC) sites such as Sechin Alto and Pampa de las Llamas-Moxeke in the Casma Valley (S. Pozorski and T. Pozorski 1986, 1987, 1990; T. Pozorski and S. Pozorski 2000) to the north and Cardal in the Lurin Valley to the south (Burger 1995; Burger and Salazar-Burger 1991). The same pattern is also a dominant element in the site layout of the Early Horizon (1000 to 200 BC) highland center of Chavín de Huantar (Burger 1995; Lumbreras 1970, 2007) to the northeast of the Norte Chico region as well as at the contemporary site of Chiripa in the southern highlands (Hastorf 1999). Terraced platform mounds and sunken courts are an integral part of the Andean architectural landscape up until the time of the Inca Empire. Overall, the historical continuity of public architecture appears to indicate that the beginnings of a distinctive Andean pattern of ceremonialism and associated ideology can be traced back to the third millennium occupation of the Norte Chico.

SOCIAL STRATIFICATION

The Norte Chico also appears to mark the beginnings of a stratified, centralized political organization in the Andean region. The people who occupied and used these sites appear to have been socially ranked. Based on her excavations at Caral, Shady and colleagues (Blanco Flores 2006; Noel 2004; Shady and Leyva 2003a, 2003c, 2005:183–84) have asserted the presence of at least two and perhaps as many as four separate social classes based on architectural differences. Similar patterns of distinct architectural differences are found at other sites in the region (Haas and Creamer 2006; Rubio Ruiz 2007), where complexes of large formal residential units with well-plastered stone walls and floors are juxtaposed with much smaller wattle-and-daub residential structures. The formal construction of platform mounds by itself indicates a centralized organization (Haas and Creamer 2006). These monumental mounds are not simply piles of stone and dirt but carefully engineered with large formally shaped and plastered retaining walls; fill of stone-filled fiber bags, or *shicra*; and a consistent plan from one mound to the next. The outside surfaces of the mounds were coated with fine clay of varying colors—shades of pink, red, white, yellow, and beige. The U-shaped site layout aligns a raised atrium with a sunken circular court (figure 9.5). Rooms with restricted access lay behind the atrium and off to the sides.

The combination of carefully engineered construction of the mound and court complexes, the monumentality of these structures, the ubiquity of monolithic huancas, and the formal layout of site architecture around a central court is highly indicative of centralized organization and direction (Billman 1999, 2002; Feldman 1980, 1987; Haas and Creamer 2004, 2006; Moore 1996; Moseley 1975, 1985; Shady and Leyva 2003a, 2003c, 2003d, 2005; cf. Vega Centeno 2005, 2007). Altogether, the transformation of culture in the third millennium BC involved significant numbers of people living in residential-ceremonial centers, centralized organization of labor for monument construction, organized religion as manifested in prescribed canons of public ceremonial architecture and the use of huancas, and distinct differences in social ranking or classes (Haas et al. 2005; Shady 2004).

At the end of the Late Archaic, after 1,200 continuous years of building, remodeling, and using these numerous platform mound/court sites, the Norte Chico cultural landscape began to change and its preeminent role in the Andean region declined (Sandweiss et al. 2009). A few smaller Late Archaic sites continued to be occupied after 1800 BC, but most were abandoned, and new sites were built in the subsequent Initial Period (1800–1200 BC). Following the Initial Period, and for the ensuing 2,500 years, the Norte Chico appears to have played a role mostly as a frontier zone between much larger and more powerful polities to the north and south. There are no major cities, political or religious centers, or royal cemeteries. Indeed, the monumental architecture of the numerous Late Archaic sites was the largest-scale construction ever to appear in the Norte Chico.

Just as ceremonies carried out on platform mounds and in sunken courts served to materialize the political and ideological organization of the Late Archaic (see DeMarrais et al. 1996), these monumental constructions also materialized power and ideology for subsequent generations (Earle 2001; Moore 1996). Mounds were originally designed to be seen by people coming into the valleys from different directions, and they still stand in salutation to visitors entering the valleys by paths, roads, and highways (Rutherford 2008). These monuments loom from open *quebradas*: broad, dry alluvial fans reaching back into the foothills bordering the valley bottoms. There are also indications that these large early sites were recognized as exceptional places in later time periods. There was remodeling and reuse of some Late Archaic sites during the Early Horizon (1000 to 200 BC) and the Middle Horizon (AD 600 to 1000). Circular courts were intentionally selected as cemetery locations (Haas and Creamer n.d.). Today, a number of these sites are the focus of "magic" and local mythology. Empty bottles of alcohol-based "elixirs" are discarded on a hillside overlooking one Late Archaic site amid candles, coca leaves, and a heap of skulls retrieved from looted burials. A black candle in the form of a female torso, stuck with pins, was among items left behind. Overall, the selective reuse of these early sites and their physical prominence on the Norte Chico landscape over more than 4,500 years points to a lasting place in the cultural memory of the region. This association is an indirect one. Most visitors could probably say very little about the age or history of a mound site, yet many visitors would agree that an unspecified "power" or "spirit" is associated with archaeological sites where large structures can still be seen. We argue that this is a materialization of power as transmitted from one generation to the next.

FORWARD TO THE PRESENT, VICHAMA RAYMI

Revival of the myth of Vichama began in 2002. After a presentation on the myth at a conference in Paramonga during the Fiestas Patrias national holiday in July 2002 by Arturo Ruiz Estrada (1979; Ruiz Estrada and Haas n.d.), regional authorities became interested in sharing the story with a public audience. A popular version of the myth, described as an "epic prose poem," was written by Henry Marcelo Castillo (2002), director of the museum at UNJFSC in Huacho, Peru, assisted by students in the Department of Communication Science. The work was part of a project called "Recovery of Cultural and Natural Patrimony as Sustainable Ecotourism for Regional Development." Popularization of the myth was intended to help strengthen regional identity in an area of considerable population mobility.

The following July, a pageant called Vichama Raymi was held. The pageant presented the myth of Vichama with a cast of costumed participants, music, and folkloric dance groups in a historic setting, the Fortress of Paramonga. Visitors began arriving around 1:00 PM, taking advantage of booths selling food and crafts. Regional dance groups began performing traditional dances from the highlands of Ancash, source of most recent migrants. Shortly after 4:00 PM the pageant began on the summit of the fortress, with the principal characters announced by a large sound system. The highlight of the pageant is the return of Vichama from his travels to seek restoration of his mother and the repopulation of the world (figure 9.6). The event was enthusiastically adopted by people of the region, who seem to accept the myth as a way to renew their connection to the landscape. Those involved include individuals whose families no longer farm and city dwellers who seek a sense of connection with the region. Others are among the thousands of migrants from the highlands to the coast who are creating new traditions of belonging.

ARCHAEOLOGY, ETHNOHISTORY, LANDSCAPE, AND CULTURESCAPE

The myth of Vichama demonstrates the value of ethnohistory in linking the ancient past to the present day with documentary accounts. In this case we suggest that the myth collected by de la Calancha from the Norte Chico region conveys an awareness of the ancient past that endured for many centuries. Bringing the myth to public attention in association with recent archaeological research further expanded the impact of the document. The tale of Vichama reminds us that archaeological features are still present on the landscape as reminders of people of the past. In the myth, huancas are literally people from the past, though they may be viewed differently today. Further, the myth is a focus of regional solidarity, bringing people together to witness a pageant that reenacts the initial peopling of the coast and reaffirms the long-term importance of agriculture and the sea. This reenactment of myth has proved successful in highlighting solidarity in a region where many today see themselves as newcomers and seek a sense of belonging.

FIGURE 9.6. The triumphant return of Vichama, highlight of the pageant held at the Fortress of Paramonga, Peru (2006).

NOTE

1. There is a negative side to the adoption of archaeological sites or artifacts as contemporary icons such as looting to find "lucky" objects, or the use of an archaeological site for contemporary ceremonies such as a *pago* (Au: Possible to translate?) or as a shrine (cf. Haas and Creamer n.d.).

REFERENCES

Alarcon, Carmela. 2005. "Preceramic Diet during the Late Archaic Period in the Norte Chico Region of Peru." Paper presented at the 70th Annual Meeting of the Society for American Archaeology, Salt Lake City.

Authier, Martin. 2005. "Where Do Huancas Come From? Preceramic Megaliths of the Norte Chico." Unpublished undergraduate thesis, Department of Anthropology, Tulane University, New Orleans.

Billman, Brian. 1999. "Reconstructing Prehistoric Political Economies and Cycles of Political Power in the Moche Valley, Peru." In *Settlement Pattern Studies in the Americas:*

Fifty Years since Virú, ed. Brian Billman and Gary Feinman, 131–59. Washington, DC: Smithsonian Institution Press.

Billman, Brian. 2001. "Understanding the Timing and Tempo of the Evolution of Political Centralization on the Central Andean Coastline and Beyond." In *From Leaders to Rulers*, ed. Jonathan Haas, 177–204. New York: Kluwer Academic/Plenum Publishers. http://dx.doi.org/10.1007/978-1-4615-1297-4_9.

Billman, Brian. 2002. "Irrigation and the Origins of the Southern Moche State on the North Coast of Peru." *Latin American Antiquity* 13 (4): 371–400. http://dx.doi.org/10 .2307/972222.

Blanco Flores, Luis. 2006. "Estudios de unidades residenciales en el Subsector I2 de Caral, Valle de Supe—Perú." Unpublished licenciatura thesis, Universidad Nacional Mayor de San Marcos, Lima, Peru.

Brown Vega, Margaret. 2009. "Prehispanic Warfare during the Early Horizon and Late Intermediate Period in the Huaura Valley, Perú." *Current Anthropology* 50 (2): 255–66. http://dx.doi.org/10.1086/597084.

Burger, Richard. 1995. *Chavín and the Origins of Andean Archaeology*. 2nd ed. London: Thames and Hudson.

Burger, Richard, and Lucy Salazar-Burger. 1991. "The Second Season of Excavations at the Initial Period Center of Cardal, Peru." *Journal of Field Archaeology* 18 (3): 275–96.

Creamer, Winifred, Jonathan Haas, Edward Jakaitis III, and Jesus Holguin. 2011. "Far from the Shore: Comparison of Marine Invertebrates in Midden Deposits from Two Sites in the Norte Chico Region, Peru." *Journal of Island and Coastal Archaeology* 6 (2): 176–95. http://dx.doi.org/10.1080/15564894.2011.582071.

Creamer, Winifred, Alvaro Ruiz, and Jonathan Haas. 2007. *Archaeological Investigation of Late Archaic (3000–1800 BC) in the Pativilca Valley, Peru. Fieldiana, New Series (40)*. Chicago: Field Museum of Natural History.

Creamer, Winifred, Alvaro Ruiz, and Jonathan Haas. 2013. *Archaeological Investigation of Late Archaic Sites (3000–1800 BC) in the Fortaleza Valley, Peru. Fieldiana: Anthropology, New Series (44)*. Chicago: Field Museum of Natural History.

de la Calancha, Antonio. 1638. *Crónica moralizada del Orden de San Augustín en el Perú, con sucesos egenplares en esta monarquia*. Barcelona: Pedro Lacavalleria.

DeMarrais, Elizabeth, Luis Jaime Castillo, and Timothy Earle. 1996. "Ideology, Materialization and Power Strategies." *Current Anthropology* 37 (1): 15–31. http://dx.doi .org/10.1086/204472.

Dillehay, Tom D., Jack Rossen, Thomas C. Andres, and David E. Williams. 2007. "Preceramic Adoption of Peanut, Squash, and Cotton in Northern Peru." *Science* 316 (5833): 1890–93. http://dx.doi.org/10.1126/science.1141395.

Dillon, Michael O., Miyuki Nakazawa, and Segundo Leiva Gonzales. 2003. "The Lomas Formations of Coastal Peru: Composition and Biogeographic History." In *El Niño in Peru: Biology and Culture over 10,000 Years*, ed. Jonathan Haas and Michael Dillon, 1–9. *Fieldiana, Botany*, New Series (43). Chicago: Field Museum of Natural History.

Earle, Timothy. 2001. "Institutionalization of Chiefdoms: Why Landscapes are Built." In *From Leaders to Rulers*, ed. Jonathan Haas, 105–24. New York: Kluwer Academic / Plenum Publishers. http://dx.doi.org/10.1007/978-1-4615-1297-4_6.

Feldman, Robert A. 1980. "Aspero, Peru: Architecture, Subsistence Economy, and Other Artifacts of a Preceramic Chiefdom." PhD diss., Anthropology Department, Harvard University, Cambridge, MA.

Feldman, Robert A. 1987. "Architectural Evidence for the Development of Nonegalitarian Social Systems in Coastal Peru." In *The Origins and Development of the Andean State*, ed. Jonathan Haas, Shelia Pozorski, and Thomas Pozorski, 9–14. Cambridge: Cambridge University Press.

Haas, Jonathan. 2001. "Cultural Evolution and Political Centralization." In *From Leaders to Rulers*, ed. Jonathan Haas, 3–18. New York: Kluwer Academic / Plenum Publishers. http://dx.doi.org/10.1007/978-1-4615-1297-4_1.

Haas, Jonathan, and Winifred Creamer. 2004. "Cultural Transformations in the Central Andean Late Archaic." In *Andean Archaeology*, ed. H. Silverman, 35–50. Malden, MA: Blackwell Publishing.

Haas, Jonathan, and Winifred Creamer. 2006. "Crucible of Andean Civilization: The Peruvian Coast from 3000 to 1800 B.C." *Current Anthropology* 47 (5): 745–75. http://dx.doi.org/10.1086/506281.

Haas, Jonathan, and Winifred Creamer. 2012. "Why Do People Build Monuments: The Platform Mounds of the Late Archaic Norte Chico." In *Early New World Monumentality*, ed. Richard Burger and Robert Rosensweig, 289–312. Gainesville: University of Florida Press. http://dx.doi.org/10.5744/florida/9780813038087.003.0011.

Haas, Jonathan, and Winifred Creamer. n.d. "Reuse of Late Archaic (3000–1800 BC) Monumental Sites in the Norte Chico Region of Peru." Paper presented at the symposium, Archaeologies of Intrusiveness, 75th annual meeting of the Society for American Archaeology, St. Louis, MO, April 14–18, 2010.

Haas, Jonathan, Winifred Creamer, Luis Huaman Mesia, David Goldstein, Karl Reinhard, Cindy Vergel, and Alvaro Ruiz. 2013. "Evidence for Maize (*Zea mays*) in the Late Archaic (3000–1800 BC) in the Norte Chico Region of Peru." (PNAS) *Proceedings of the National Academy of Sciences of the United States of America* 110 (13): 4945–49. http://www.pnas.org/content/early/2013/02/28/1219425110.full.pdf+html. http://dx.doi.org/10.1073/pnas.1219425110.

Haas, Jonathan, Winifred Creamer, and Alvaro Ruiz. 2004. "Dating the Late Archaic Occupation of the Norte Chico Region in Peru." *Nature* 432 (7020): 1020–23. http://dx.doi.org/10.1038/nature03146.

Haas, Jonathan, Winifred Creamer, and Alvaro Ruiz. 2005. "Power and the Emergence of Complex Societies in the Peruvian Preceramic." In *Foundations of Power in the Ancient Andes*, ed. Kevin Vaughn, Dennis Ogburn, and Christina Conlee, 37–52. Archeological Papers of the American Anthropological Association, Number 14. Arlington: American Anthropological Association.

Hastorf, Christine, ed. 1999. *Early Settlement at Chiripa, Bolivia: Research of the Taraco Archaeological Project*. Berkeley: University of California Press.

Huaman, Luis, Karen Ventura, Erika Paulino, and Liliana Zegarra. 2005. "Palynological and Botanical Studies from the Proyecto Arqueológico Norte Chico, Peru." Paper presented at the 70th annual meeting of the Society for American Archaeology, Salt Lake City.

Lumbreras, Luis. 1970. *Los templos de Chavín*. Lima: Corporación Peruana de Santa.

Lumbreras, Luis. 2007. *Chavín: Excavaciones arqueológicas*. Vol. 1. Lima: Universidad Alas Peruanas.

Marcelo Castillo, Henry. 2002. *Vichama y la morada de los Dioses del Fuego Sagrado*. Biblioteca Nacional del Perú 2008-08355. Huacho, Peru: Museo Arqueológico Universidad Nacional José Faustino Sanchez Carrion.

Moore, Jerry D. 1996. *Architecture and Power in the Ancient Andes: The Archaeology of Public Buildings*. Cambridge: Cambridge University Press. http://dx.doi.org/10.1017/CBO9780511521201.

Moseley, Michael E. 1975. *Maritime Foundations of Andean Civilization*. Menlo Park: Cummings.

Moseley, Michael E. 1985. "The Exploration and Explanation of Early Monumental Architecture in the Andes." In *Early Ceremonial Architecture in the Andes*, ed. Christopher Donnan, 29–58. Washington, DC: Dumbarton Oaks Research Library and Collection.

Noel, Arturo. 2004. "Investigación arqueológica en un módulo arquitectónico del Sector A de Caral, Valle de Supe." Unpublished licenciatura thesis, Universidad Nacional Mayor de San Marcos, Lima.

Piperno, Delores, and Deborah Pearsall. 1998. *The Origins of Agriculture in the Lowland Neotropics*. San Diego: Academic Press.

Pozorski, Shelia, and Thomas Pozorski. 1986. "Recent Excavations at Pampa de las Llamas-Moxeke, a Complex Initial Period Site in Peru." *Journal of Field Archaeology* 13 (4): 381–401.

Pozorski, Shelia, and Thomas Pozorski. 1987. *Early Settlement and Subsistence in the Casma Valley, Peru.* Iowa City: University of Iowa Press.

Pozorski, Shelia, and Thomas Pozorski. 1990. "Reexamining the Critical Preceramic/Ceramic Period Transition: New Data from Coastal Peru." *American Anthropologist* 92 (2): 481–91. http://dx.doi.org/10.1525/aa.1990.92.2.02a00160.

Pozorski, Thomas, and Shelia Pozorski. 2000. "Una reevaluación del desarrollo de la sociedad compleja durante el Precerámico Tardío en base a las fechados radiocarbónicos y a las investigaciones arqueológicas en el Valle de Casma." In *El Periodo Arcaico en el Perú: Hacia una definición de los orígenes*, ed. Peter Kaulicke, 171–86. Lima: Pontificia Universidad Católica del Perú.

Rowe, John H. 1946. "Inca Culture at the Time of the Spanish Conquest." In *Handbook of South American Indians*, vol. 2, ed. Julian H. Steward, 183–330. Washington, DC: Smithsonian Institution, Bureau of American Ethnology.

Rubio Ruiz, Alvaro. 2007. "Proyecto de investigación arqueológica en el Norte Chico: Excavaciones en Caballete, Valle de Fortaleza, Perú—2006." Final report submitted to the Instituto Nacional de Cultura, Lima.

Ruiz Estrada, Arturo. 1979. Notas para la historia de Végueta. Ahora, V (1035).

Ruiz Estrada, Arturo, and Jonathan Haas. n.d. "The Myth of Vichama and the Archaeology of the Norte Chico." Unpublished manuscript in possession of the authors.

Ruiz Estrada, Arturo, and Manuel Domino Torero. 1978. *Acaray: Fortaleza Yunga del Valle de Huaura.* Huacho, Perú: Comité de Educación de la Cooperativa de Ahorro y Crédito "San Bartolomé."

Rutherford, Allen. 2008. "Space and Landscape in the Norte Chico Region, Peru: An Analysis of Socio-Political Organization through Monumental Architecture." MA thesis, Anthropology Department, Northern Illinois University.

Sandweiss, Daniel H., Ruth Shady Solis, Michael E. Moseley, David Keefer, and Charles Ortloff. 2009. "Environmental Change and Economic Development in Coastal Peru between 5,800 and 3,600 Years Ago." *Proceedings of the National Academy of Sciences of the United States of America* 106 (5): 1359–63. http://dx.doi.org/10.1073/pnas.0812645106.

Shady, Ruth. 2004. *Caral: La ciudad del fuego sagrado.* Lima: Centura.

Shady, Ruth. 2006. "Caral-Supe and the North-Central Area of Peru: The History of Maize in the Land Where Civilization Came into Being." In *Histories of Maize: Multidisciplinary Approaches to the Prehistory, Linguistics, Biogeography, Domestication, and Evolution of Maize*, ed. John Staller, Robert Tykot, and Bruce Benz, 381–402. San Diego: Academic Press. http://dx.doi.org/10.1016/B978-012369364-8/50280-1.

Shady, Ruth, Jonathan Haas, and Winifred Creamer. 2001. "Dating Caral, a Preceramic Site in the Supe Valley on the Central Coast of Peru." *Science* 292 (5517): 723–76. http://dx.doi.org/10.1126/science.1059519.

Shady, Ruth, and Carlos Leyva, eds. 2003a. "El sustento económico del surgimiento de la civilización en el Perú." In *La ciudad sagrada del Caral-Supe: Los orígenes de la civilización andina y la formación del estado prístino en el antiguo Perú*, ed. Ruth Shady and Carlos Leyva, 101–6. Lima: Instituto Nacional de Cultura.

Shady, Ruth, and Carlos Leyva, eds. 2003b. *La ciudad sagrada de Caral-Supe: Los orígenes de la Civilización Andina y la formación del estado prístino en el antiguo Perú*. Lima: Instituto Nacional de Cultura.

Shady, Ruth, and Carlos Leyva, eds. 2003c. "Los orígenes de la civilización y la formación del estado en el Perú: las evidencias arqueológicas de Caral-Supe." In *La ciudad sagrada del Caral-Supe: Los orígenes de la civilización andina y la formación del estado prístino en el antiguo Perú*, ed. Ruth Shady and Carlos Leyva, 93–100. Lima: Instituto Nacional de Cultura.

Shady, Ruth, and Carlos Leyva, eds. 2003d. "Sustento socioeconómico del estado prístino de Supe-Perú: Las evidencias de Caral-Supe." In *La ciudad sagrada del Caral-Supe: Los orígenes de la civilización andina y la formación del estado prístino en el antiguo Perú*, ed. Ruth Shady and Carlos Leyva, 107–22. Lima: Instituto Nacional de Cultura.

Shady, Ruth, and Carlos Leyva, eds. 2005. *Ritual and Architecture in a Context of Emergent Complexity: A Perspective from Cerro Lampay, a Late Archaic Site in the Central Andes*. PhD diss., University of Arizona, Tucson. Ann Arbor, MI: University Microfilms.

Vega-Centeno Sara-Lafosse, Rafael. 2005. *Ritual and Architecture in a Context of Emergent Complexity: A Perspective from Cerro Lampay, a Late Archaic Site in the Central Andes*. PhD diss., University of Arizona, Tucson. Ann Arbor, MI: University Microfilms.

Vega-Centeno Sara-Lafosse, Rafael. 2007. "Construction, Labor Organization, and Feasting during the Late Archaic Period in the Central Andes." *Journal of Anthropological Archaeology* 26 (2): 150–71. http://dx.doi.org/10.1016/j.jaa.2006.07.002.

Vergel, Cindy Nathali Rodríguez. 2009. "Análisis biológico de coprolitos: Visión multidisciplinaria para la caracterización de la dieta y salud en el precerámico tardío en el centro arqueológico de Huaricanga, Lima." Licenciatura thesis in Biology, Facultad de Ciencias y Filosofía, Universidad Peruana Cayetano Heredia, Lima.

Zechenter, Elzbieta. 1988. "Subsistence Strategies in the Supe Valley of the Peruvian Central Coast during the Complex Preceramic and Initial Periods." PhD diss., Anthropology Department, University of California, Los Angeles. Ann Arbor: University Microfilms.

10

Interpreting Long-Term Human-Environment Interaction in Amazonia

ANNA C. ROOSEVELT

This chapter seeks to combine a retrospective analysis of archaeology in Amazonia with a reflection on how scholarly agendas evolved to dovetail with the interests and perspectives of living Amazonian peoples. In mid-twentieth-century scientific approaches, Amazonia was seen by pioneering social anthropologists and archaeologists as a wilderness that limited human adaptation to a unitary tropical forest culture of camps and villages relying on slash-and-burn cultivation and foraging. Although these scholars did not conceive of the possibility of indigenous impacts on the forest, the cultural geographers of that time did, based on cultural features of soil and topography that they observed. In the later twentieth century, ethnographers also recognized in Amazonia evidence of cultural effects on habitats, in the course of research on surviving indigenous land management systems and the cultural concepts behind them. At the same time, research in the approaches of "New Archaeology" revealed evidence of not just one indigenous tropical forest culture but a wide variety of chronologically and regionally distinctive indigenous human cultures and landscape adaptations through prehistory and history that had significant effects on the habitat even to today. Throughout this whole period, researchers' approaches tended to bifurcate into those who used deductive scientific hypotheses and empirical tests of them on the one hand and those who used description and analysis of native views and knowledge on the other, approaches not always compatible with each other.

Native Amazonians, as informants and as assistants in research studies, have made their own observations about and interpretive insights into both ancient and

DOI: 10.5876/9781607325727.c010

modern human-environment interactions, via traditional cultural approaches that embody deeper and broader memories and understandings of these relationships than do the Western ones. In their more integrative cultural systems of ancient landscapes, acute and fundamental scientific knowledge is interwoven with emotional states and symbolic concepts into a rich tapestry of a widely shared Great Tradition of Amazonian mythic and historical cosmology. These traditions explain the creation of the world, the origins of human societies, and the relationship of human societies with their environments through time and space. With such expansive knowledge and concepts, Amazonians have maintained high levels of sustainability and a high quality of habitat and human health over more than 13,000 years. However, the domination by European populations from the outside has marginalized Amazonian people politically, geographically, and economically and has significantly damaged their physical and mythological environments, as well. In the future, by taking a more sovereign role, Amazonian communities can contribute further to the preservation of their cultures and habitats as both project directors and contractors in research based on more holistic, nuanced, and practical views of Amazonian landscapes through time and space. Their participation as sovereign stakeholders could also help secure their rights to both territories and lifestyles and lead to fairer, more effective, and more productive sociopolitical, judicial, and environmental management there in the future.

A THEORETICAL JOURNEY IN AMAZONIA: ENVIRONMENTAL LIMITATION THEORIES ON HUMAN OCCUPATION OF THE AMAZON RAINFOREST

In the mid-twentieth century, in approaches of the first generation of scientific anthropologists and archaeologists to the question of indigenous land use in Amazonia, the environment was seen as an unalterable given that limited or even forcibly directed human affairs. As such, the character of the environment was assumed and thus not investigated by researchers at the time. The overall environmental determinism theory seemed so logical that it was used more to explain the archaeological record than to be tested by that record. Human adaptation to the Amazon environment was seen as more or less unitary and unchanging through time: an archetypal "tropical forest culture." So, human subsistence and land-management patterns in Amazonia were not treated as archaeological problems but as givens. Similarly, the behavior of indigenous populations through time had expected characteristics for scholars. People were assumed to have adapted to habitat by migrating from one place to another, rather than by developing new ways to use resources in place and cultural methods to maintain connections to communities in other regions. Scholars nevertheless recognized major variations in the environment over space, and these were incorporated into their statements about regional differences in tropical forest culture and changes through time as populations migrated through Amazonia (Lathrap 1970; Meggers 1972; Steward 1949). Generally, anthropologists contrasted the resource productivity of the major alluvial floodplain regions to the resource poverty of the uplands away from large rivers. Such differences were considered the causes for contrasts in population size and density and in cultural complexity between regions. But this approach—often called cultural ecology after the concept developed by cultural anthropologist Julian Steward—only saw causality from environment to humans, not the other way around. Thus, people in resource-rich areas could develop denser settlement and more complex cultures, and people who moved out of those areas into poorer areas were considered to have been diminished in population and cultural complexity because of the lesser resource availability there.

THE GAIA HYPOTHESIS

In the natural sciences, however, field researchers had recognized for a long time that both animals and plants could have strong effects on their habitats and each other. Different levels of population density of deer, for example, were known to have very different effects on forest vegetation and thus on other animals, and even plant species distributions were recognized to have influenced other plants in the community, as when certain tree species, such as Black walnut, change soil chemistry around them in ways inimical to other plant species. In the late twentieth century, the Gaia Hypothesis built such insights into a comprehensive scheme that has gained popularity and even general scientific acceptance. First articulated in the mid-twentieth century, it contributed the insight that the larger community of biota has a strong effect on the global characteristics of the earth and its atmosphere, over and above the effects of particular chemical and physical processes (Lovelock 2000).

After a period of criticism, refinement, and testing, the tenets of the Gaia Hypothesis have been integrated into many disciplines. Its practical implications for human ecology are that the entire community of life-forms are essential in the development and maintenance of physical and chemical systems on earth and in the atmosphere. Thus, disrupting life-forms on a massive scale through uncontrolled industrial impacts could lead to significant deterioration of the earth's ability to sustain life. In its early application in Amazonia, particularly, scientists studying environmental water budgets showed that more than half of the tropical forest region's moisture at any particular time was tied up in the vegetation of the forest mass (figure 10.1) (Salati and Marques 1984; Salati and Vose 1986). When the forest was removed, these scientists showed, much of the original moisture became

FIGURE 10.1. Tropical forest at Taperinha.

unavailable, and the sudden direct exposure of the ground to sun and wind led to further losses. Thus, not only was the forest an important factor in stability and recycling of moisture in Amazonian climate, but its removal could threaten the integrity of the entire biophysical system.

Perhaps such research eventually made anthropologists more aware of the possibility that the Amazon rainforest might not have been a purely natural unilinear causative force upon indigenous human cultures as much as a complex natural community that had long interacted with human communities, resulting in continuing change, mutual influence, and adaptation in both communities. In any case, scientists' first conscious awareness of the possibility that there had been a more complex, multilinear, and mutualistic relationship between humans and Amazonian habitats during prehistory came not so much directly from theoretical insights but from problem-oriented empirical findings that they made as a result of applying methodological innovations from North America to the region.

THE "NEW ARCHAEOLOGY" IN AMAZONIA

A new generation of archaeologists began looking at Amazonian sites, sequences, and regions in the 1970s and 1980s, many of them influenced by contacts with founders of the "New Archaeology" (Binford and Binford 1969), such as Stuart

Struever, Jane Buikstra, and Howard Winters, in my case. Developments in North American archaeological theory and method motivated its practitioners to pursue problem-oriented research in interdisciplinary paleodietary, paleoenvironmental, and bioarchaeological fields, as well as settlement analysis, among other directions. The "New" approach by American archaeologists continued and developed Steward's environmental determinism/cultural ecology. But in doing so, it also brought more recognition of the fact of systematic cultural change through time, especially in response to change in demographic parameters. By implication, if there had been a series of different cultural solutions to humans' need to engage with their environments, then the characteristics of a particular environment could not have been as limiting to demographic and cultural development as originally thought by Steward.

Applied to Amazonia, such research soon furnished evidence that there had been—not just one but—many chronologically and regionally distinct prehistoric human cultures and settlement arrangements and that their sequence of development was unexpectedly long and complex, going back at least 13,000 calendar years (e.g., Roosevelt 2000, 2014). So, whereas the early Paleo-Indians chose to move about seasonally, collecting a broad spectrum of natural plant and animal species as they moved, early Holocene foragers chose to settle down along rivers and wetlands and subsist by intensifying use of certain local fish and shellfish (figure 10.2). Subsequently, so-called Formative Amazonians added various domestic crops to their subsistence mix and spread out widely but thinly in most regions. In only a few places did the early agriculturalists group into large dense concentrations of population. Populous later prehistoric complex cultures narrowed and intensified resource use, specializing in mass collection of aquatic resources and cultivation of plant staples, while their country cousins in the hinterlands maintained a broader spectrum of resources for their support. Thus, by implication a current people's relationship with their habitat was not necessarily the same as that of their predecessors nor even of their neighbors (Roosevelt 1989, 2014). Since there had been changes through time, one could not necessarily "project" today's ethnographic patterns into the deep past. One had to investigate specifically the patterns of different periods as well as different places to reveal the patterns of similarity and difference.

NATIVE AMAZONIANS' AGENCY IN THE RELATIONSHIP WITH THEIR HABITATS

More or less at the same time as these developments in archaeological method and theory in Amazonia, several ethnobotanists and ecological anthropologists

FIGURE 10.2. Floodplain and floodplain forest, Monte Alegre.

began to look more closely at the details of landscape management by living Native Amazonians through ethnographic research (Anderson et al. 1991; Balee 1999; Posey and Balee 1989; Posey 2002; Smith 1999). Insightful early research by cultural geographers in Amazonia already had revealed instances of widespread purposeful alterations of the habitat by certain prehistoric communities. These alterations involved such things as large raised field systems in wetlands and large anthropic earth deposits on uplands (Denevan 1966; Smith 1980; Sternberg 1975). The abovementioned ethnographic and economic botany studies of the 1970s and 1980s found further evidence of significant, purposeful human effects on the botany and soils of their habitats and recovered important new information on indigenous savants' interpretation of habitat in terms of regional ritual systems and cosmologies. Not only were living Amazonian Indians visibly impacting their environments, but they were doing so in both purposeful and in unconscious ways, leaving their virtual "footprints" in the forests. For example, some people had created vast cultural forests dominated by certain useful palms. Others had made a series of clearings in order to encourage the proliferation of plants useful in their medicine or technology systems. Recognition of these dynamic processes enriched understanding of the relationship of people to their habitats, but attention to the role of cosmology and myth in the relationship was rare (Balee 1999).

ARCHAEOLOGISTS COME TO RECOGNIZE THE DYNAMISM
OF THE HUMAN-ENVIRONMENT RELATIONSHIP

Continuing archaeological research in Amazonia in the 1990s and first decade of the twenty-first century also encountered evidence of prehistoric indigenous landscape management strategies that altered habitats, in some cases with far-reaching effects that still today influence the nature and quality of environmental resources and condition people's attitudes and approaches to them. Evident from this continuing research were interesting contrasts among contemporary but different patterns of prehistoric settlements within a community in terms of people's choices of resources to use and management of their landscape as a whole. Archaeologists interested in issues of environment and subsistence had to develop collaborations with local savants as well as with academic natural scientists, in order to identify species and explore their properties and significance. These collaborations exposed further contrasts in different prehistoric groups' approaches to and interpretations of landscape, in addition to the continuities (e.g., Heckenberger 2004; Piperno and Pearsall 1998; Roosevelt 1991, 2000, 1994).

In the background behind this research, general archaeological theory continued to develop in new directions, some of them inspired by early debates between "New Archaeologists" influenced by environmental determinism and other archaeologists influenced by "Postmodern" thinking that privileged a view of the human past where human agency was unfettered by any systematic influence from environments. Many of the archaeologists practicing in Amazonia subsequently adopted elements from both paradigms in their approaches and also maintained relationships of communication and collaboration across anthropological subfields and national boundaries. Both the American Anthropological Association and the Society for American Archaeology welcomed these kinds of cross-paradigm relationships by providing places and times for discussion and publication about them. Archeologists themselves organized formal interdisciplinary discussions of these issues with the help of sponsorship of natural history museums, universities, and foundations (Neves et al. 2010; Roosevelt 1994; Visigalli and Roosevelt 2010). One result of these interactions was the integration of the new archaeological evidence of prehistoric cultural complexity and change into social anthropologists' interpretations of the ethnographic present. Another of the results of these processes of interaction was the further development of archaeologists' analysis of archaeological iconography and style in the context of their growing familiarity with the conceptual iconography and interpretive art styles of living Amazonians (e.g., Roosevelt 1991). Thus, Amazonian archaeology benefited from the addition of conceptual studies of aesthetic and ideological patterns to the more utilitarian materialistic study of empirical food and demographic patterns.

EXAMPLES FROM THE LOWER AMAZON

Once archaeologists working in Amazonia became interested in recovering biological objects from sites, such a wealth of specimens turned up that they have only just begun to be identified and interpreted. Nearly all sites that have been explored with directed recovery techniques have produced an abundance of ecofactual as well as cultural materials. These materials in the discrete components of archaeological sites furnish a partial picture of an ancient human landscape at different points in time because during each phase of occupation people brought to the sites many kinds of environmental materials from the wider areas of their catchments, and ecofacts also entered site-deposits through natural processes. People presumably did not utilize and bring back specimens of all the possible species available to them, but archaeological sites nonetheless usually yield large numbers of diverse specimens of bone, shell, macroplant parts, pollen, phytolith, leaf scale, or other microscopic components, often identifiable at least to genus and often to species (with the exception of pollen, which may be only identifiable to family or subfamily). Some items are adventitious inclusions in sites, such as parts of insects from the soil fauna or weeds, but these, too, can reflect features of human activities and their habitats. The available species at any point in time and people's choices from the available species are illuminating both for understanding the nature of the environments in their catchment areas and of their sense of the importance and utility of different plants, animals, and materials, whether from practical considerations or from considerations deriving from their ideas about human ecology, society, and the supernatural.

CONTRASTING HUMAN APPROACHES TO BIOTA AND CATCHMENTS IN A REGION OVER TIME AND SPACE

The differences and similarities between the biological remains in different time components of ancient human sites and in archaeological sites of the same time period in different parts of a region were revealing (Roosevelt 2000).

The prehistoric community at Santarem on the south bank of the Lower Amazon in Brazil had maintained a dense, diverse, high canopy forest and broad faunal diversity in its environs in the Formative period around the beginning of the first millennium BCE. In the local region Formative pottery is decorated with simple incised geometric designs. In the gray-brown-stained, charcoal-flecked soil layers of that site, we found the remains of a diverse group of large and medium fleshy fish and a few smaller mammals, such as large rodents. There also were specimens of tasty, succulent fruits and berries along with the faunal remains. The structure of the wood charcoal and isotopic chemistry of the dated carbonized plant remains fell in ranges of reference studies in closed-canopy tropical forests. According to our excavations, the soils in the perimeter of the living areas of the early period lacked the artifacts and earth structures we found in intensively occupied areas but were also magnetized by burning and stained and mottled a light gray-brown from soot and charcoal. We've interpreted these latter areas as the agroforestry sites where people maintained or planted desirable trees in open patches that they created for planting of cultigens, through selective clearing and burning of vegetation.

Later on, between about AD 1200 and 1500 in late prehistory, the human occupation of the Santarem site became much larger and more crowded. Our analysis of the charcoal showed that the effects of this later occupation turned the closed-canopy hardwood tropical forest habitat that existed in the Formative cultural period into a more simplified one dominated by more open-grain, fast-growing trees and shrubs and more open areas of crops and orchards. The community's faunal-collection activities and plant-cultivation systems also had been simplified by this time. The great majority of fish eaten daily were now very small: between anchovy-sardine-size to trout-size catfishes and characins, and among the carbonized plants were more remains of the common, coarse but productive cultivated Cocosoid palm fruit genera such as *Astrocaryum* and *Attalea*. Larger fish such as the Formative people dined on now only occurred in the deposits of the remains of ceremonial feasts, adjacent to people's house mounds. The foods consumed at feasts include remains from more succulent and delicate fruits, such as the cultivated water palm *Euterpe* (acai) and the domesticate *Bactris gasipaes* (pupunha), and the large fleshy fish the Formatives appreciated, though no longer the small mammals. Thus, in this later time people's resource base seems to have been partitioned, with high-volume everyday food production focused on smaller and bonier but more abundant and resilient populations of food fishes and common palms, and the rarer, more difficult to catch or produce species and succulent, delicate fruits used only for food in ceremonial occasions, identified by funerary remains and the making and use of fine ritual art objects.

Late prehistoric Santarem residential neighborhoods were composed of regular rows of small house mounds next to ceremonial facilities and large, low platforms, where cremations and ritual caches of fine art objects were placed in formal ceremonies. The density and size of the human population in these neighborhoods were so great that people's meter-thick, charcoal-black refuse deposits literally blanket the entire four square kilometers of the late prehistoric site. In Brazil these black cultural soil deposits are called black Indian soils. We know from contact period accounts that these deep dark deposits rich in artifacts and ecofacts were used by Indians for intensive infield cultivation of field crops and orchards, and most are still used this way by Brazilian country people (figure 10.3). In this way the Amazonians developed a way to efficiently reap further harvests from the refuse produced by the

FIGURE 10.3. Santarem period cultural black soil site, Alter do Chao.

consumption of prior harvests and foraging in the past. Such anthropic soil deposits have been widely found throughout the Lower and Middle Amazon, both along floodplains and away from them, and are a testament to indigenous Amazonians' ability to make a good living in the forest without using it up. That the Amazonian forests were never cleared on a wide scale by indigenous people seems quite firmly established by the results of paleoecological research, which give overwhelming evidence of prehistoric biological assemblages whose characteristics fall well within the range of current forests, not of savannas.

The approach of the Santarem community to its habitat and subsistence would presumably have been responsive to changes in the cultural role of the site as it evolved from a large, independent Formative village to a large and wealthy cultural center in its region toward the end of the prehistoric period. The choices probably also reflected the large size and density of population of the later settlement, which stood along major transportation routes between different cultural and ecological regions. Its location was the junction of several large, productive resource biomes at the intersection of the mainstream Amazon and the Tapajos River, a large tributary coming from the Brazilian shield and limestone areas: the upland forests, extensive cultivable floodplains, and major fisheries.

This late prehistoric Santarem site was the center for the classic style of the Incised and Punctate Horizon, which extended for hundreds of kilometers along the Amazon banks east and west of the Tapajos river mouth (Stenborg 2004). This style's iconography emphasized raptorial birds and carnivores and well-ornamented men and women. Females are most common in the art by far, but the males hold special objects, such as rattles and bags, seemingly related to shamans' roles. The relationship of communities in the larger region seems to have been partly conditioned by the threat of raiding, in addition to intense cultural and ecological exchange, for many of the closely culturally related communities near Santarem felt the need to take defensive locations along the high riverbanks, despite the inconveniences these must have entailed, such as distance to water, fisheries, and floodplain planting fields. People in many regions of Amazonia developed their own versions of the Incised and Punctate Horizon and other cultural horizons, and it seems, based on the evidence for defensive works, that these entities may have competed as well as participated in shared cultural styles with each other.

CONTRASTING APPROACHES TO HABITAT BETWEEN DIFFERENT SITES OF PREHISTORIC CULTURES AND DIFFERENT PERIODS OF OCCUPATION AT SITES: MONTE ALEGRE

Different kinds of ancient communities within the same cultural sphere also sometimes had different approaches to the development and exploitation of their habitats in the Amazon. In contrast to the Santarem center site and the many other large, complex, concentrated occupations along the Amazon banks both upstream and down, during this entire period of later prehistory a small settlement at Cavern of the Painted Rock—a large cave-rock-shelter in the wooded, rocky hinterland hills of Monte Alegre on the other side of the Amazon river (figure 10.4)—maintained a very diverse habitat around it, with deep, tall forest on both hills and adjacent lakes and wetlands and some clearings for orchards and field crops. In addition, its take of collected-managed plants and collected or hunted animals was dominated by much larger species and larger individuals of species than those at Santarem at the time, and the species representation in their take was much more diverse than at Santarem. It included larger faunal species, such as crocodilians and deer, which have not yet been identified among the many remains of fauna at the Santarem site. Plants used at the cave site included many species of fruits, such as wild cashews, that seem to have been absent in the environs of the large settlement at Santarem, as well as cultivated plants, such as maize, palms, and tree fruits also enjoyed at Santarem. Like the contemporary cliff villages near Santarem, however, this hinterland community seems to have sensed a threat of raiding, for it maintained a sturdy post-and-thatch wall across the entrance of the cave at this time.

This cave is also the site of one of the first documented human occupations in the Amazon (figure 10.5). In the millennium between about 13,000 and 10,000 years ago (calendar years), we find Paleo-Indians living both in the floodplains and interior

FIGURE 10.4. Cavern of the Painted Rock, Monte Alegre.

forests in the Lower Amazon (Roosevelt et al. 1996; Roosevelt et al. 2009). They seem to move around a lot but return repeatedly to the same campsites for hundreds of years, sometimes staying for many months. The Paleo-Indians created large polychrome painting compositions on the rocks and caves of Monte Alegre, opposite Santarem, representing both people and animals and important heavenly bodies such as the sun, which they aligned to mark seasonal events like winter solstice sunset (Davis 2014). The paintings also include geometric designs, some of which may have served as notational devices. Monte Alegre is not the only region with extensive rock art; other site complexes occur in many parts of the Amazon and in eastern and southern Brazil outside the basin. The large numerous paintings constitute a lasting imprint of the cultures of the first colonists on the Amazon landscape.

Only a few living sites of the period have been identified as yet, so we only know about their resource use at certain times of year. In the late rainy season and early dry season, Monte Alegre Paleo-Indians living at the cave focused their attention on groves of rugged, fertile upland palm trees (genera *Attalea* and *Astrocaryum*), whose fruits and seeds are rich in fat, vitamins, and carbohydrates, and also certain common and prolific tree beans (*Hymenaea* genus of the Fabaceae family) in the hill forests, whose fruits are rich in fat, vitamins, starch, and protein. They also spent a lot of time in the floodplain lakes below the rocky hills to get fish, turtles,

FIGURE 10.5. Cavern of the Painted Rock strata with Paleo-Indian camp layer at the bottom and late prehistoric Santarem period house at the top.

and shellfish, which they laboriously lugged up to the cave, a half hour walk uphill. Our fine-screening of the archaeological cave's stratified sediments revealed that most of the fish bones are from small species of characins and catfishes (just like the ones that were prominent in the late prehistoric domestic food at Santarem center thousands of years later on), with a few exceptions of large fishes more than a meter long. There are few mammals in their food remains, though, other than a small number of medium-size rodents. Perhaps because of their more mobile lifestyle, the Paleo-Indians were not there long enough each year to exploit the great breadth of resources that the later Santarem culture inhabitants of the cave sampled. To judge from the distribution of their distinctive projectile point types, Paleo-Indians roamed in much larger catchments than the late prehistoric people, reaching deep into the fast rivers of upland interfluvial areas south of the Santarem municipality in the middle Xingu River drainage. In contrast, the late Santarem period people's culture never extended far inland from the main Amazonian floodplains, though it reached long distances along it. In the southern interfluves that they penetrated, the Paleo-Indians would have found both diverse lithic raw materials and the huge fishes that migrate between the fast tributary streams and the Amazon main floodplains.

Already during this earliest-known human occupation period, Paleo-Indians seem to be actively managing their habitat. My and other's results suggest that some cutting and burning were being done in the forest to encourage concentrations of the Cocosoid palms, which proliferate under human disturbance, often sprouting more vigorously when cut to the ground or burnt, outcompeting less aggressive reproducers among the trees. The fruits of such palms were the single most abundant plant remains in the Paleo-Indian deposits at the site, and their stable carbon isotope ratios indicate that they had grown not in the shade of the understory but in clearings cut in the tall forest that still clothed the hills at the time. The Paleo-Indians cached large heavy cutting and chopping tools flaked from tough, resilient stone in the cave, presumably for that purpose. It is also evident that these Paleo-Indians were thrifty with their food resources. Not a single example of the carbonized palm fruits that we excavated in the cave had escaped being laboriously cracked open to get out its fatty inner kernel.

TAPERINHA

Amazonian people don't seem to have settled down in year-round settlements until after most regions had been reached by the Paleo-Indians' descendants: the Archaic people. Permanent settlements occur only in a few regions at first, starting around 6,000 to 7,000 years ago in the middle Archaic period. We found one of their sites at Taperinha, nor far downriver from Santarem, where richly wooded uplands abut extensive creeks, rivers, and wetlands (figure 10.6.) (Roosevelt 1995). Paleo-Indians had roamed there periodically, leaving behind a few projectile points, but to maintain themselves longer in one place, the people of the subsequent pottery Archaic culture focused on a more monotonous diet of shellfish and those small fish that can be harvested intensively locally and won't quickly run out or migrate away for good. The early people's garbage heaps are really full of their remains and not much else. In only a few Amazonian regions that we know of did people settle down in this way, usually where wooded upland creeks and rivers debouched into especially productive muddy river backwaters or estuaries. It's easy to dig shellfish in the soft mud there and, though Amazonian people mostly gave up the shellfish for horticultural plants in the Formative period, mentioned above, almost all riverside communities have kept their focus on small fish for their everyday protein food. The best way to get these tiny fishes nowadays is to net them in small streams or capture them in baskets behind dams in the dry season when the main rivers are low.

The people of the Taperinha culture were the first to create pottery vessels, which they used for cooking, presumably, the fish and shellfish that predominate in their middens. Only a few of the sherds are decorated, with simple geometric incised and

FIGURE 10.6. Cultural and natural palimpsest: Taperinha Plantation.

punctate designs. Their imagery is poorly understood because of the small sample and small pieces, but the patterns continue to be used in later Amazonian pottery, and in it they represent hair, weavings, and basketry. The Archaic people also built mounds, as did later Amazonians, by heaping up empty shells and other garbage, and they ate different food during ceremonies. For example, small turtles are common in sandy areas around the mound where burials were placed but they are not common in the shell-midden remains.

During the Santarem period in late prehistory, when the paramount chiefdoms warred for cultural and natural resources, people clustered their houses densely all along the high cliffs that loom above Taperinha, apparently for defensive purposes, as mentioned above. The thick black cultural soils and orchards that accrued around houses remain among the most important agricultural resources in the area still today.

MARAJÓ

The low-lying major estuarine regions at the mouth of the Amazon, almost a thousand kilometers downstream from Santarem, was the birthplace of the magnificent Amazonian Polychrome Ceramic Horizon more than a thousand years ago. Large

FIGURE 10.7. Cultural forest on Monte Carmelo mound group, Marajó Island.

villages of the Polychrome culture on Marajó Island were built atop large mounds in the middle of the seasonally flooding plains. The ancient villages had groups of large thatched dwellings built on top of wide, flat artificial mounds, with anthropic black soil deposits, orchards, and urn cemeteries between individual house mounds (figure 10.7). Village mound platforms vary in height from less than a meter to ten meters or more, which is much higher than necessary to avoid the seasonal floodwaters. Thus, either or both defense and status may have motivated the creation of these monumental constructions

Here on Marajó, people continued the ancient reliance on small fish as a staple protein source, complemented with pods of the legume tree *Inga*, the common Cocosoid palm fruits, and various herbaceous plants, probably planted and cultivated on the black soil areas. Large, succulent fishes, some of them from one to three meters long, and special cultivated water-palm fruits, such as acai, were used only for ceremonial feasts, held in the open areas of the mound sites (Roosevelt 1991). Around the mounds today acai will only grow if you water it, so it seems likely that the Marajoarans indeed were planting and tending palms of this species.

The large ceremonial dishes and funerary urns and ritual items from the feasts are absolutely covered in the sinuous polychrome designs for which the cultural horizon is named. This, perhaps the most important of the Amazon-wide ancient art styles, was still spreading upstream across the region when Europeans arrived, so missionaries were able to learn from the Omagua elite female artists that their polychrome style represented the skin patterns of the Great Anaconda, creator and ruler of the universe and shaman leader of the fearsome Amazon women who invented sorcery and the ritual arts (Roosevelt 2013). This mythic iconography is one of the strongest links between Amazonians over space and time.

THE SUPRAREGIONAL AMAZONIAN COSMOLOGY

Today, the heritage of the Polychrome Ceramic Horizon is an important nexus from which archaeologists can bring the findings of generations of research on interactions between humans and the environment into a dialog with the cultures and identities of living Amazonian peoples. Among the many modern Amazonian cultures descended from the Polychrome Horizon culture, worship of the great supernatural anaconda female shaman continues, serving to integrate the body of indigenous scientific knowledge of the environment with people's ideas about proper social organization, cosmological origins, and the nature of the supernatural powers (Roosevelt 2013).

The modern supraregional cosmology is centered upon a creation myth in which Anaconda Woman is carved from the trunk of a fruit tree by her father, the Old Shaman, and the Sun wins her for his wife in challenges of his skill and resourcefulness. In the course of a series of confusing events, the Sun creates fish and manioc, and Woman Shaman creates magic and the arts and fashions the Milky Way galaxy, which is the supernatural Amazon. She fills this part of the Amazon with the life-giving and protecting milk from her breasts. By following the shamanic rituals that she invented, including the taking of the hallucinogenic drugs that flow from the supernatural river as milky sap through certain plants, humans can learn from and appeal to the supernaturals in support of human interests. The anthropomorphic spirit twin animals that each person is thought to have are enlisted by ritualists to intercede with the supernatural "masters" or "mistresses" of the animals on behalf of human souls and their access to life-giving knowledge and resources. The spirit people's bodies, as seen in trances, are said to be covered with the bright designs of the anaconda's skin patterns. Modern women shaman paint these patterns on people's bodies and on artifacts as prayers to the spirits for help and protection. The spiritually potent beings and things described in the creation myths also bear significant scientific information about the structure and function of human societies and the natural environment. For example, the stories of the interaction of Woman Shaman and the Sun actually follows the interaction of the heavenly bodies, as Amazonians understand them (Davis 2014). Similarly, beliefs about the relationships of spirit animals and plants express knowledge of not only the appearance but also the social behavior, reproduction, and ecology of the biota (Roosevelt 2013). So, the mythic

Great Anaconda is represented as female, following knowledge of the larger size and social dominance of female anacondas. She also is cast as a dangerous cannibal, for female anacondas do eat other anacondas, including the smaller males, who cluster about females during mating. In relation to human society, she is the spirit animal espoused by leading women in the matrilineal/matrilocal communities of the Shipibo, where women are considered to own the family house, where they were born, and where mature women lead the society's only initiation ceremonies, which are for girls, not boys.

Important elements of this immaterial cosmology can be traced back into Amazonian prehistory, through the material remains of ancient cultures, mentioned above. With their rock art, the Paleo-Indians had created solar observatories to watch the movements of the sun and constellations (Davis 2014). Men, women, and children were all involved in rituals at the sites, for we find their handprints marked within some designs. Some constellations and comets are personified as humans or animals, and sometimes their reproductive status is marked, as in the images of breeding plumes shown on a heron icon. Later on, some Formative art styles depict animals with human stance, limbs, and accoutrements; these appear to represent beings such as the ethnographic supernatural "masters" and "mistresses" of the animals. Santarem art also depicts men and women with their spirit animals mounted on their heads and shoulders, as well as the images of male shaman shaking rattles, mentioned above. These dynamic images represent people going through the process of communicating and traveling to be with supernaturals in the other world.

In Polychrome art, both ancient and modern, the patterns of the anaconda's skin dominate the style just as Woman Shaman, the Great Anaconda, is thought to dominate the other world. On Marajó her image is a prominent effigy, and elements of her creation story are referenced in ceremonial objects, such as small ritual cups shaped as breasts. Depictions of her include references to shamanic procedures, such as rattling (figurines representing her body may contain rattlers), whistling or blowing, containing a spirit in her belly, or wearing a shaman's shirt (Roosevelt 1991).

There are interesting changes as well as the continuities in ritual Amazonian art and presumably the cosmologies behind it as different societies develop and change through time in different spaces. For example, animals from the waters or underground, now considered Woman Shaman's sphere, predominate in the art of Marajó and its successors among the matrilineal Shipibo and Omagua, whereas animals of the land and sky, the Sun's sphere, dominate Santarem art. Yet, even among very different current Amazonian societies, such as the small, patrilineal village societies of the northwest Amazon and the populous matrilineal societies of the upper

Amazon, the basic cosmology is essentially similar, despite the myriad of local particularities. Both the Shipibo and the Tukanoans recognize and worship Woman Shaman as their creator, and both employ very similar customs and rituals to link their societies to the supernatural powers.

How is it that through such a long time span and such diversity of culture and environmental interaction, Amazonians preserved basic outlines of a cosmology? Part of the explanation may be that their cosmology is based on an understanding of the universe, the Amazon basin, and the skies that has not changed much through the millennia of human occupation (Roosevelt 2014). Another explanation is that a cosmology first formed by the Paleo-Indians has been passed down to today because of the continuous settlement in the basin from the beginning. Each new culture that archaeologists recognize shows clear links to earlier ones, and such links can often be traced over wide areas of the basin.

If we can judge from modern customs, ancient Amazonians would have visited other communities to take part in their rituals and would have invited outsiders to their own. In this way local versions of myths that developed would have a chance of influencing other ones. Communities' current myths about their origin often link their region with one of the other important cultural regions of Amazonia, showing that people recognize a mythic-historical landscape much larger than that where they now live and much older than the era in which they live. For example, northwest Amazon peoples who retain the Polychrome Horizon style claim that the Great Anaconda brought their ancestors up in her belly from Marajó Island at the mouth of the Amazon where a woman ruled. Mythic-historical narratives communicated in formal ceremonial enactments and accoutrements, in the iconography of the communal house as well as in informal storytelling, are themselves an important medium of transmission for the cosmology today. For example, modern shamans who have never made or seen a type of prehistoric object, such as the atlatl, are nonetheless perfectly able to recognize pictures of them because of descriptions encoded in mythological accounts. (I observed this phenomenon of ancient knowledge preserved by myths rather than by actual objects in 2005 when discussing pictures of prehistoric objects with shaman and chiefs who had gathered in Santarem for a Brazilian government workshop before they took on the job of being the teachers for their communities.) Also important in communicating cosmological concepts over time and space would have been the material representations of the ideas in ancient and modern Amazonian art. Ancient objects retrieved by later people from deposits of earlier cultures are sometimes found placed reverently in the later cultures' ceremonial deposits (Roosevelt 1991). Today, also, some Amazonians learn about ancient cultural ideas and knowledge through archaeologists' books and presentations, and vice versa.

CHANGES IN THE AUTONOMY OF AMAZONIAN COMMUNITIES
VIS-À-VIS RESOURCES AFTER EUROPEAN CONQUEST

Huge changes have taken place at Santarem and its environs and Marajó since the European conquest of the Amazon and their incorporation as provincial municipalities in the modern nation-state. In this situation of lesser local autonomy, new patterns of human-environment interaction have changed the approaches to the landscapes around occupation sites. The environment around Santarem—now a much larger and more urbanized settlement—has become even more depauperate in diverse life forms than in late prehistory. With the much larger modern population, the addition of large transient visitor populations, rampant illegal gold-mining upstream, few cheap local fuel sources, a large interregional market, and the introduction of domestic animal pasturing, what was fast-growing secondary forest in later prehistory has now diminished to open savanna woodland over much of the land around the city. The loss of forest is associated with a loss of rainfall in both Santarem and Monte Alegre, close by across the river. As a result, at Santarem larger forest and river faunas and the diverse, succulent wild and domestic Amazonian fruits have become expensive to obtain because they are no longer available in the thinly vegetated, ravaged environment around the city. Ordinary people cannot afford these foods or the petroleum-based fuels of the modern economy, with the result that their general nutrition and health are not good, and their fuel scavenging has further reduced the woody vegetation around the city, which otherwise could furnish them with valuable dietary supplements in the form of fruits, herbs, and small faunas. In the overgrazed, overburned cattle pastures on the upland areas around Santarem and Monte Alegre, the *Attalea* palms so appreciated by the Paleo-Indians are flourishing, but the cattle grazing there are the primary beneficiaries.

In the Monte Alegre hills, the human population seems to have diminished since later prehistory. No one has lived at or near the cave site since the conquest, we know from the cave radiocarbon dates and cultural remains, though there is now a village of dispersed houses and gardens down the hill on the floodplain at the lakes, as there was in later prehistory, and its inhabitants regularly come into the hills to hunt, gather, or pasture animals. A wide range of fruits and fish continue to be easily available to the lakeside villagers, both from the hill forests and from the floodplains, their gardens, and their corrals. Deer and other sizeable game still can be caught in the hills, despite the creation of much pasture for the cattle economy and despite hunting now being illegal there. Although the population in the Monte Alegre hills lacks a nearby clinic for treatment of ailments, people's health is quite robust, for they continue to support themselves with local cultivated, collected, and hunted foods without undue effort into advanced old age. And there is still more than enough forest around to supply their fuel needs.

The general Amazonian pattern of using the abundant smaller fishes for daily food continues in the Lower Amazon today, and many riverside communities earn cash by selling their surplus catches. But the larger species can be had mainly in city restaurants for tourists or elites or in the outer hinterlands, such as the Monte Alegre hills, where the population is low enough and isolated enough that people can get still the larger fish for themselves. The industrial fishing industry in both municipalities of Santarem and Monte Alegre is causing big problems for local people now because the large mechanized boats can easily overfish, using refrigerators to preserve the large catches for sale in the city markets. Despite the existence of laws on the books that protect local communities' resources from outsiders' use without permission, enforcement is nonexistent.

On Marajó, the ancient forest has been removed over much of the eastern part of the island, and cattle herds have replaced the flourishing population centers of the ancient mound-building societies. Indigenous languages, religion, and social organization have been effaced for the most part on Marajó. Both new migrants and families with local roots now live in small villages and towns, and scattered tenant ranchers serve the ranchers who own most of the anthropic pastures. The land in much of the Amazon was distributed as huge baronies to the generals who led the defeat of the final uprising against the Portuguese, and Marajó was divided into large ranches. Conversion of so much land to grassland must have diminished rainfall, and overgrazing and trampling by herds has muddied Marajó rivers and lakes. However, many indigenous skills continue to be held: pottery making, artisanal fishing and foraging, and cultivation of fruit trees and native crops, which continue to be important in people's diets.

Something that stands out about recent change through time in Amazonia is the contrast between Euro-American and indigenous attitudes toward settlement mobility in regard to resources. Some archaeologists, colonial administrators, missionaries, and development aid specialists tend to feel that permanent settlement is the preferable pattern. Certainly it fits an environment in which most land is privately owned, as it is today. Archaeologists tend to think it was an important evolutionary advance to produce enough food locally with agriculture to stop having to forage over a lot of territory to get enough to eat. Missionaries and colonial administrators felt that it was more civilized, organized, and Christian to produce food with domestic animals and plants, and it was certainly more convenient for them when the Indians they were trying to control stayed in one place near colonial centers. Modern development experts don't approve of shifting cultivation and hunting, which they assume harms the land and wastes people's time traveling to dispersed fields and hunting sites. However, shifting settlement has been one of the ways that Amazonians have managed their environments without permanently reducing their economic productivity.

For example, indigenous Amazonians who have been interviewed seem to give a high value to what social anthropologists refer to as trekking (e.g., Politis 2007). Listening to what Amazonian people have said about it over the years makes the trek seem a combination rest cure, second honeymoon, hiking-and-swimming vacation to the cabin for the children, going fishing with dad and mom, tourist trip to commune with the wilderness, gourmet picnicking, and special expedition to gather valued resources to bring home. People do not complain about having to go on trek. They look forward to it. Trekking means getting away from it all, being away from noise and smoke and chatter of the village or town. It means the family and its special friends and affiliates can be together. The water at trekking sites is cleaner, and the beach is less crowded. The kids get to snack on especially delicious unusual fruits and bite-sized faunas you can catch with your hands. Participants can get together for dam-fishing picnics on small streams and eat as much as they can hold of delectable smoked fish, then collapse in their hammocks and sleep peacefully in the quiet of the currently uninhabited forest.

Spiritual reasons for trekking also have been articulated by Amazonians. For example, the Nukak of the northwest Amazon in Colombia told anthropologist Gustavo Politis that they like to go deep into the heart of their territory to special long-standing groves of domesticated palms such as pupunha because they believe that their ancestors established those, and they can commune with their spirits there (Politis 2007). Away from crowded settlements and their unsanitary conditions, there's less exposure to infectious disease, a pattern that might be interpreted as spiritually safer, since evil spirits are thought by Amazonians to be a cause of illness. In addition, the faraway places have culturally special foods and materials not available at current horticultural villages, and people appreciate and seek these out between harvests. Many ethnographers have written that Tukanoans and Arawakans in the northwest Amazon schedule their important initiation dances with the fruiting time of special groves of trees with a mythological relation to the creation time when the ancestral lines of humans were born. Such ancient groves have been identified over large areas of the Amazon and stand as witnesses to the long-term management of vegetation by indigenous people. As such, they are not only a seasonal resource but also an important tangible cultural ecological property for future generations. That seasonal and periodic changes of settlement are good for the environment as well as good for people is unarguable. Game animals and faunas helpful for pollination or other services come back in greater numbers in the now-quiet settlement. Secondary vegetation containing nutrients for future harvests can grow back in gardens and fields left fallow when people spend time away.

Trekking in the forests has become an unavailable luxury, though, for many people in the Santarem-Monte Alegre region because of the rise of industrialized and globalized soybean farming to the south and north. In league with a Brazilian government port-administration company, the US Cargill Company has developed a truly enormous facility at Santarem to load soybeans onto large transport craft from as far away as Europe. The Brazilian company CDP bulldozed large areas of the archaeological mounds in Santarem to create the port for this trade, and the remaining deposit is being heavily polluted by illegal dumping of dangerous chemicals used in mechanized loading operations. To feed the international shipping trade, very large areas of ancient cultural forests in the south of Para State have been deforested for permanent farms to grow the beans to be exported from Santarem. Established by outsiders with sweetheart loans from Cargill or the Brazilian government, these farms are not being managed in a sustainable way. The widespread clearing and exposure of land to weather lead to drought and nutrient deficiencies, and with time it reverts to pasture for the cattle herds that replace the former local Indian communities, who have withdrawn further south ahead of the bulldozers.

At the mouth of the Amazon, on the tidal rivers of Marajó and the other delta islands, local people both feed themselves and their families and make money making floodplain forest products such as the valuable water palm acai. The local family concerns work sustainably, living on fish and forest products and both harvesting and regenerating the groves. Their sites are literally covered with dense anthropic acai groves (figure 10.8). In contrast, foreign companies usually destroy these ancestral groves as they harvest the trees, limiting future production in those spaces.

Finally, perhaps the most harmful change since the conquest was the forced acculturation that people along the Amazon mainstream underwent during the first two centuries of missionization and that continues still today. This process separated people both from their conceptual cosmology and from their social organization, neither of which suited the Christian religion and Western notions of proper social organization that conquerors forced on them. This deculturation process did not, however, separate people from their deep knowledge of their habitats and basic artisanal skills, which continue quite intact. And, despite statements to the contrary (Fraser et al. 2014), Amazonian Indians have not disappeared. Indigenous people who still speak their traditional languages and carry out their ceremonies and art traditions still dominate populations in the hinterlands of Amazonia. However, this situation will not remain for long, because indigenous lands and cultures are not in practice being protected from forced dispossession by Amazonian countries, despite all the laws that provide for maintaining them on their ancient lands.

FIGURE 10.8. Anthropic acai grove, Marajó Island.

NATIVE AMAZONIANS, RESEARCH, AND REPARATIONS

Native Amazonians, incorporated into projects both as informants and as assistants and participating in debate as members of conferences, have contributed further observations and interpretive insights of their own about both ancient and modern relationships of people to their habitats (Neves et al. 2010; Posey 2002; Visigalli and Roosevelt 2010). Whether they are Native Americans or rural nationals of mixed heritage and geographic origins, these people from the Amazonian regions being studied by anthropologists turn out to have their own range of research interests relating to cultural development and landscape management.

The following are some of the thoughts that indigenous community members have articulated to me. Some leaders of Cayapo communities in the southern Amazon drainage have expressed interest in studying examples of ancient Marajó art, which they regard as the work of their ancestors. They also express strong interest in the possibility of archaeological excavation of their ancestral sites and the maintenance of museum collections of special prehistoric art objects in the local community, rather than in national museums. When we retrieved from gold miners a huge, jewel-like crystal projectile point that had been removed from the area (figure 10.9), the Cayapo living at the find-site requested that it be returned to be kept in their ritual men's house (Roosevelt et al. 2009). At present, Cayapo chiefs of communities in the middle Xingu interior south of Santarem

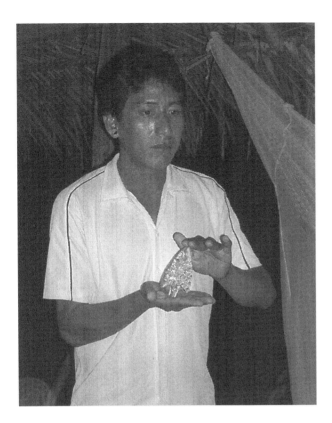

FIGURE 10.9. Paleo-Indian quartz crystal point curated by a Cayapo community, middle Xingu.

and Altamira still make gorgeous museum-quality ritual paraphernalia and ornaments of semiprecious materials, such as mother-of-pearl ceremonial tiaras, that they like to sell to visitors.

The Curuaia community a little further north on the Curua River in the middle Xingu in the direction toward Santarem also sees anthropological research as a validation of their cultural histories. When we invited Curuaia leaders to recruit adolescents from their community to take our intensive field-training course in environmental archaeology in the future, the leaders expressed the wish to learn the archaeological techniques and evidence themselves. They were especially interested in our archaeological evidence for long-term intensive occupation of the region by indigenous groups. They felt that the information was ammunition for being more assertive in maintaining their independence, holding onto their land, and being more involved in negotiations when companies or government agencies wanted to implement large projects locally. When Brazilian nationals try to deny that the Curuaia have always been there, as they are wont to do, the community now can use the archaeological evidence to prove their long-term presence in the landscape.

The surviving people of the ancient Polychrome Horizon have been especially engaged with researchers in the past. For example, the Shipibo communities of the Ucayali drainage in lowland Peru have long collaborated with social anthropologists and archaeologists, giving help to their research and at the same time learning about their past culture from sources they get access to through exchanges with the scholars (Lathrap 1970; Roosevelt 2013; Weber 1975). Some Shipibo leaders have even come to US cities to go over museum collections from their culture, and they keep in touch with anthropologists through the Internet. Important results that some ethnographers have had through interviews with Shipibo artists on the subject of the symbolic and spiritual meaning of iconography suggest that further work with other living descendants of the ancient Polychrome Horizon in, for example, French Guiana, would be useful. Polychrome-descendant people have already given important testimony about their understanding of the ritual and ecological meaning of animal images, and their interpretations of specific images on the ancient pots from nearby archaeological sites promise to be illuminating in the future. As mentioned above, Shipibo say that their large female effigy beer pots represent the Great Anaconda, who created the heavens. This Shipibo belief is just one example of the stories with which Amazonian Indians integrate the great tradition of their cosmology with their acute observation and understanding of the natural world and their societies.

Rio Negro Tukanoans and Arawakans, also descendants of the Polychrome Horizon, have been collecting, interpreting, and publishing with scholars their research relating archaeological features such as petroglyphs with their current mythology, cosmology, and landscape ecology (Cabalzar 2010; Roosevelt 2013). Their take on the iconography of the Great Anaconda, whose image they portray on their longhouse, is parallel to that articulated to ethnographers by modern Shipibo. Northwest Amazon people's concepts integrate their expert knowledge of social life and the anthropic environment into a complex and vivid legendary landscape populated with ancestral animal-human characters. For them, the Amazon mainstream is the Great Anaconda, who they believe carried them up to the Rio Negro from Marajó Island, where they say the Woman Shaman ruled before she was defeated and fled with her minions to the otherworld in the sky. They point to the Paleo-Indian petroglyphs on rock outcrops as the marks they made in the course of their escape. Shamans say that they can obtain her precious, life-protecting milk from the sap of the sinuous, mottled-bark *Banisteriopsis caapi* vine, her magical plant species. Not surprisingly, the patterns of the anaconda's skin has become a pan-Amazonian symbol of solidarity in the northwest Amazon and beyond (Jean Jackson in Roosevelt 1994).

I can envision in the future a conference of indigenous Polychrome Horizon–descendant groups from all over the Amazon with researchers from all over the world, to pursue further study of this cultural tradition and discussion of its broader significance in the memorializing of historic landscapes and the interpreting of Amazon ecology. To record and explore further the range of traditional concepts connecting particular species of plants and animals with ancestral deities and social and ritual practices would be a great advance. People's current understanding and practices in regard to the anthropic dark earths of the Amazon would also be illuminating. But even just collecting a registry of all known cultivated trees, vines, shrubs, and herbs, all recognized animal species, and their characteristics and linkages within the ecosystem and the mythic cosmos would go far in clarifying the details of ancient indigenous management and ritual systems.

Today, Native Amazonian communities have the option to contribute to research more assertively as both project directors and contractors, and their concepts of the integration between humans and spiritual ancestors could contribute to an even more holistic and nuanced approach to the study of humanized landscapes through time and space. Such pursuits might lead to an entirely different approach from all past scholarly ones, not envisioned by anthropologists. In any case, the communities' active participation in research on their regions could give important incentives and pressures for the acceptance of more assertive leadership from indigenous people and communities in the face of the growing power of governments and outside companies to intervene in locales without the permission of their inhabitants. It's clear that recent industrial-scale, globalized systems of land use in the Amazon have been unsustainable economically and destructive both ecologically and culturally. But it's also clear that Amazonia is a durable land of great natural resources and can certainly continue to both support its populations and produce abundant wealth. By their dynamic cultural sequence, native Amazonians have given ample proof of their ability to devise ingenious new ways of resource management and lifeways over time, all the while keeping very much alive their regional cosmology. Their long-lived prehistoric societies and the evident continuity in their culture sequences are a testament to their success. And they have done these things without destroying the region's fundamental resource base. One might even say that they had enriched the soil as well as the forest's diversity of useful species and at the same time built one of the great cultural traditions of the world. Therefore, in addition to their unassailable human right to a strong role in decision making about this region, their patrimony, they bring an unbeatable record of effective and innovative land management and cultural development, a contribution that is sorely needed now.

REFERENCES

Anderson, Anthony B., Peter Herman May, and Michael J. Balick. 1991. *The Subsidy from Nature: Palm Forests, Peasantry, and Development on an Amazon Frontier.* New York: Columbia University Press.

Balee, William. 1999. *Footprints in the Forest: Ka'apoor Ethnobotany—The Historical Ecology of Plant Utilization by an Amazonia People.* New York: Columbia University Press.

Binford, Sally R., and Lewis R. Binford. 1969. *New Perspectives in Archaeology.* Chicago: Aldine.

Cabalzar, Aloisius. 2010. "Petroglifos e concepções sociospaciais dos povos indígenas no Alto Rio Negro: Entre a origem e os dias de hoje." Paper presented in the II Encontro Internacional de Arqueología Amazônica, Manaus, Amazonas, Brazil.

Davis, Christopher S. 2014. "Archaeoastronomy of Terminal Pleistocene Rock Art on the Amazon River at Monte Alegre, Para, Brazil." PhD diss., Anthropology, University of Illinois, Chicago.

Denevan, William M. 1966. *The Aboriginal Cultural Geography of the Llanos de Mojos of Bolivia.* Berkeley: University of California Press.

Fraser, James A., Melissa Leach, and James Fairhead. 2014. "Anthropogenic Dark Earths in the Landscapes of Upper Guinea, West Africa: Intentional or Inevitable?" *Annals of the Association of American Geographers* 20 (10): 1–17.

Heckenberger, Michael J. 2004. *The Ecology of Power: Culture, Place, and Personhood in the Southern Amazon, AD 1000–2000.* New York: Routledge.

Lathrap, Donald. 1970. *The Upper Amazon.* New York: Praeger.

Lovelock, James. 2000. *Gaia: A New Look at Life on Earth.* Oxford: Oxford University Press.

Meggers, Betty J. 1972. *Prehistoric America.* Chicago: Aldine.

Neves, Eduardo, et al., organizers. 2010. *O II Encontro Internacional de Arqueología Amazônica.* Final Program, September 12–17, Manaus, BR.

Piperno, Dolores R., and Deborah M. Pearsall. 1998. *The Origins of Agriculture in the Lowland Neotropics.* Bingley: Emerald Publishing Group.

Politis, Gustavo. 2007. *Nukak: Ethnoarchaeology of an Amazonian People.* Walnut Creek: Left Coast Press.

Posey, Darrell A. 2002. *Cayapo Ethnoecology and Culture.* London: Routledge.

Posey, Darrell A., and William Balee, eds. 1989. *Resource Management in Amazonia: Indigenous and Folk Strategies. Advances in Economic Botany.* Vol. 9, 30–62. New York: New York Botanical Garden.

Roosevelt, Anna C. 1989. "Resource Management in Amazonia before the Conquest: Beyond Ethnographic Projection." In *Resource Management in Amazonia: Indigenous and Folk Strategies*, ed. Darrell A. Posey and W. Balee, 30–62. Advances in Economic Botany, vol. 9. New York: New York Botanical Garden.

Roosevelt, Anna C. 1991. *Moundbuilders of the Amazon: Geophysical Archaeology on Marajó Island, Brazil*. San Diego: Academic Press.

Roosevelt, Anna C., ed. 1994. *Amazonian Indians from Prehistory to the Present: Anthropological Perspectives*. Tucson: University of Arizona Press.

Roosevelt, Anna C. 1995. "Early Pottery in the Amazon: Twenty Years of Scholarly Obscurity." In *The Emergence of Pottery: Technology and Innovation in Ancient Societies*, ed. William Barnett and John Hoopes, 115–31. Washington, DC: Smithsonian Institution.

Roosevelt, Anna C. 2000. "The Lower Amazon, a Dynamic Human Habitat." In *Imperfect Balance: Landscape Transformations in the Precolumbian Americas*, ed. David L. Lentz, 455–92. New York: Columbia University Press. http://dx.doi.org/10.7312/lent11156-018.

Roosevelt, Anna C. 2013. "The Great Anaconda and Woman Shaman: A Dangerous and Powerful Ancestral Spirit from Creation Time to Today." Presentation at The Conference for the Exhibition: Les Habitants de l'Eau. Autres Histoires de Guyane, Aquarium Tropical de la Porte Dorée, Paris, May 4.

Roosevelt, Anna C. 2014. "The Amazon and the Anthropocene: 13,000 Years of Human Influence in a Tropical Forest." *Anthropocene* 4 (December): 67–87.

Roosevelt, Anna C., M. Lima da Costa, Lopes Machado, M. Michab, N. Mercier, H. Valladas, J. Feathers, W. Barnett, M. Imazio da Silveira, A. Hernderson, et al. 1996. "Paleoindian Cave Dwellers in the Amazon: The Peopling of the Americas." *Science* 272 (5260): 373–84. http://dx.doi.org/10.1126/science.272.5260.373.

Roosevelt, Anna C., John E. Douglas, Anderson Marcio Amaral, Marua Imazio da Silveira, Carlos Palheta Barbosa, Maura Barreto, Wanderley Silva da Souza, and Linda J. Brown. 2009. "Early Hunter-Gatherers in the Terra-Firme Rainforest: Stemmed Projectile Points from the Curua Goldmines." *Amazonica* 1 (2): 442–83.

Salati, Eneas, and J. Marques. 1984. "Climatology of the Amazon Region." In *The Amazon: Limnology and Landscape Ecology of a Mighty Tropical River and its Basin*, ed. Harold Sioli, 85–126. The Hague, W.: Junk. http://dx.doi.org/10.1007/978-94-009-6542-3_4.

Salati, Eneas, and Peter B. Vose. 1986. "The Water Cycle in Tropical Forests, with Special Reference to the Amazon." *Studies in Environmental Science* 26:623–48. http://dx.doi.org/10.1016/S0166-1116(08)71812-0.

Smith, Nigel. 1980. "Anthrosoils and Human Carrying Capacity in the Amazon." *Annals of the Association of American Geographers* 70 (4): 553–66. http://dx.doi.org/10.1111/j.1467-8306.1980.tb01332.x.

Smith, Nigel. 1999. *The Amazon River Forest: A Natural History of Plants, Animals, and People*. Oxford: Oxford.

Stenborg, Per, ed. 2004. *In Pursuit of a Past Amazon: Archaeological Researches in the Brazilian Guyana and in the Amazon Region*. By Curt Nimuendajú. A Posthumous Work Compiled and Translated by Stig Rydén and Per Stenborg. Goteborg: Etnologiska Studier.

Sternberg, Hilgard O'Reilly. 1975. *The Amazon River of Brazil*. Wiesbaden, DE: Franz Steiner.

Steward, Julian H. 1949. "South American Cultures: An Interpretive Summary." In *Comparative Ethnology of South American Indians: Handbook of South American Indians*, vol. 5, ed. Julian H. Steward, Washington, DC: Smithsonian Institution.

Visigalli, Egle Barone, and Anna C. Roosevelt, eds. 2010. *Amaz'hommes: Sciences de'homme et sciences de la nature en Amazonia*. Cayenne, French Guiana: Ibis Rouge.

Weber, Ron. 1975. "Caimito: An Analysis of Prehistoric Culture in the Central Ucayali, Eastern Peru." PhD diss., Department of Anthropology, University of Illinois, Urbana Champaign.

Contributors

RANI T. ALEXANDER
New Mexico State University

FERNANDO ARMSTRONG-FUMERO
Smith College

HANNAH BECKER
Smith College

MINETTE CHURCH
University of Colorado, Colorado Springs

BONNIE CLARK
University of Denver

CHIP COLWELL
Denver Museum of Nature and Science

WINIFRED CREAMER
Northern Illinois University

EMILIANA CRUZ
University of Massachusetts at Amherst

CONTRIBUTORS

T. J. FERGUSON
University of Arizona

JULIO HOIL GUTIERREZ
Universidad del Oriente

JONATHAN HAAS
Field Museum

SAUL L. HEDQUIST
University of Arizona

MAREN P. HOPKINS
Anthropological Research, LLC

STUART B. KOYIYUMPTEWA
Hopi Cultural Preservation Office

CHRISTINE KRAY
Rochester Institute of Technology

HENRY MARCELO CASTILLO
Universidad Nacional José Faustino Sánchez Carrión

ANNA C. ROOSEVELT
University of Illinois at Chicago

JASON YAEGER
University of Texas at San Antonio

KEIKO YONEDA
CIESAS Golfo

Index

acai, 217, 224, 231
agrarian reform, 8, 13, 26–27, 153–54
agriculture, 8, 11, 19, 23–24, 71, 82, 101, 152, 161, 189–90, 201, 205, 229, 236; early irrigation, 190; early mechanized, 71; irrigation-based, 196; swidden, 24; traditional, 5, 9
Altamira, 233
Alter do Chao, 218
Amache, 9, 13, 79–95
Amache internees, 85, 89–90, 92
Amazon Frontier, 236
Amazonia, 12, 209–17, 219–21, 223, 225, 227–31, 233, 235–38
Amazonian archaeology, 215
Amazonian Peoples, 209–10, 213–14, 217, 222–23, 225–27, 229–32, 234–37
Amazon women, 225, 227
Anaconda Woman, 225
ancestors, 21, 33, 52, 55–56, 70, 93–94, 101, 139, 159, 179, 227, 230, 232
ancient agroforestry, 217
Ancient Maya, 22, 157, 160
Ancient Zuni, 160
Andean Archaeology, 203–4
Andean Civilization, 196, 199, 204–5
Andean highlands, 198, 201

Andean Late Archaic, 204
Andean region, 189, 196, 199–200
Anderson, Anthony, 214, 236
Andes, 205
Anthropocene, 237
anthropogenic dark earths, 235–36
Anthropological Archaeology, 157, 206
Anthropology, 14, 16, 31, 50–51, 74–76, 88, 94–96, 157, 161, 202–4, 236, 238
Apache, 48, 51, 93–94, 157
Arawakans, 230, 234
Archaeoastronomy, 236
archaeobotanical analysis, 94
archaeology, 14, 16, 79, 88, 90, 95–96, 189, 191, 193, 195, 197, 199, 201, 203, 205–7
Archaic People (Amazonia), 222–23
Armillas, Pedro, 129
Astrocaryum, 217, 220
Attalea, 217, 220, 228

Balee, William, 236
Basso, Keith, 48, 93–94, 132, 157
batab, 8, 17, 134–36, 142–43, 145, 149
Belize, 53, 57–58, 60, 72, 74–76, 161
Belize City, 61, 73–74
Bender, Barbara, 39, 48, 92, 94

BEPCO (Belize Estate and Produce Company), 55–56, 60, 65–68, 70–71, 73–74, 76–77
Binford, Lewis R., 132, 157, 212, 236
Black Mesa, 46; Mine, 40; Project, 39–42, 49
black soil areas, 224
Blue Creek (Belize), 57
Bolivia, 205, 236
Bonfil Batalla, Guillermo, 22–23, 30
Bourbon reforms, 24
Bricker, Victoria, 131, 141, 147, 157
British buccaneers, 57
British Honduras, 53, 59–60, 66, 70, 75–77
Bubul, 134, 147–52, 154, 156
Buikstra, Jane, 213
Burger, Richard, 198, 203–4

Caballete, 198, 206
Cabalzar, Aloisius, 234, 236
cah (Yucatan), 133, 135–36, 142, 150–51, 153
Calancha, Antonio de la, 191, 194, 201, 203
California, 34, 75, 81–82, 84, 95–96, 207
Calkiní, 159
Camal, Florentino, 156
Caral and Chupacigarro Grande (Peru), 198
Cargill Company, 231
Carrasco, David, 102–3, 110–11, 117, 124–25, 127, 129–30
Caste War of Yucatán, 9–10, 17, 25–26, 55–56, 58, 76, 131–33, 137, 139–40, 143, 145–49, 153–55, 160
catfishes, 217, 221
Cayapo, 232–33, 236
Cayo District, 73–74
CDP (Brazilian company), 231
cenote, 8, 133, 135, 147–52, 154, 157
census, 8, 139, 143, 145, 151, 155, 160
Central America, 59
Central Andes, 206–7
Central Coast (Peru), 206
Chaco Canyon, 50
Chan Kom, 31
Chanmul, 18–24, 27, 29
Chan Santa Cruz, 25
characins, 217, 221
Chatino Language: base verb, 170; Eastern, 164, 182; temporal verb, 167
Chatino languages, 10, 23, 163–64, 167, 171, 173, 175–80, 182–88
Chatino region, 166

Chatinos (Chatino speaking people), 171, 178, 182
Chavín, 198, 203, 205
Ch'ibal, 8, 133, 135–36, 139, 153, 159
Chichanhá, 56–58
Chichén Itzá, 18–22, 29, 131–32
Chichicapán, 188
Chichimec, 101, 111
Chichimilá, 145, 155–56
chicle, 65, 67, 73
Chicomoztoc, 129–30
Chilam Balam, 24
chinampas, 98, 102, 112–14, 116–18, 123–25
Chiripa, 198, 205
Cholollan, 109, 111
Cholula, 109, 111
Ch'ortí, 31
Christianity, 16, 137, 163, 182, 194, 229, 231
Chupacigarro Grande, 198
Cibola, 51
Cieneguilla (Oaxaca, Mexico), 10, 13, 164–71, 182
circular courts, 197–98, 200
Closed Corporate Peasant Communities in Mesoamerica and Central Java, 161
Coastal Peru, 203–6
Cocom family, 16
cocosoid palms, 222, 224
Códice Chimalpopoca, 127
collaborations, 9, 21, 56, 90, 215
collective identities, 7–9, 11
collective memory, 4–5, 11–12, 23–26, 137
Colombia, 230
colonialism, 10, 16, 23, 30–31, 53–55, 58, 60, 65, 67–71, 74–75, 97, 102, 105, 152, 158–59; Spanish, 10, 16, 18, 24, 75, 97–98, 102, 104, 133, 135, 139, 182, 206
colonial Mexico, 98, 101, 119
colonial period (Latin America), 9, 26, 100, 105, 133, 135–36, 141, 147, 154
Colonial Yucatán, 158, 160–61
Colonization of Belize, 74
Colorado Plateau, 42
Colorado River, 43–45, 49
compadrazgo, 174
Conlin, Eleanor, 94
conquest, 16, 74, 101–2, 106, 122, 149, 228, 231, 236
cosmology, 12, 49, 214, 226–27, 234
creation myths, 29, 189, 210, 225

INDEX 243

Creole mahogany workers, 64, 73
Cuauhtinchan, 103, 109, 127–30
Cuauhtitlan, 111, 127
Cuba, 126
Cuchcabal, 136
cultural complexity, 211, 215
Cultural continuity, 3, 5, 11, 97, 131–32, 190
cultural forest, 214, 224, 231
cultural geography, 4, 42, 209, 214; Amazonia, 209, 214
cultural heritage, 5–7, 9, 11, 13, 30, 53, 79; intangible, 5–8, 12–13, 15, 22, 27–30, 34, 53, 56, 69, 72, 94, 132, 147
cultural heritage objects, 16, 19, 21–22, 29
cultural heritage sites, 4, 11, 18, 81, 92
culture, 4, 7–8, 48–50, 157, 163, 199, 204, 210, 220, 225, 227, 231, 234, 236
Cuncunul, 24, 26, 133–35, 147, 151, 155–57
Cupul, 135
Cupul polity, 134
Curuaia, 233
Curua River, 233

Davis, Christopher, 220, 225–26, 236
Denevan, William, 214, 236
descendant communities, 6, 8, 29, 132
Dine (Navajo) People, 40, 50–51
dispersal, 8
Douglas, Mary, 67
Dumond, Don, 73

Ebtún, 8, 10, 24, 26, 31, 131, 133–37, 139, 141, 143–53, 155–57, 159–61
Edo period, 89
ejido (Mexico), 19–23, 27–29, 149
El Niño effects, 190, 204
Elsie Clews Parsons, 51
encomienda, 159
Environmental Limitation Theories (Amazonia), 210
ethnoarchaeology, 95, 154, 236
ethnography, 34, 46, 51, 116; Amazonia, 214; interviews, 40, 61, 67–68, 72, 234
ethnohistory, 30, 50, 76, 131, 154, 157–58, 160, 201
Euro-American attitudes towards settlement (Amazonia), 229
European conquest of Amazonia, 228
European pathogens, 135
euterpe, 217

factionalism, 30, 157
families, nuclear, 117, 139–40, 154
family names, 163, 179–80
Farriss, Nancy, 25, 30, 132, 135–36, 154, 158
feasting, 206
Fewkes, Jesse Walter, 35, 44, 49
figurines, 195, 226
foragers, early Holocene, 213
forest, 53, 57–58, 61–62, 65, 133, 135, 209, 211–12, 214, 218, 220, 222, 228, 230, 236; closed-canopy tropical, 216; fast-growing secondary, 228; floodplain, 214; high canopy, 216; mature, 58; northwestern, 53; tall, 219, 222
Formative Amazonians, 213
Fortaleza, 190, 206
French Guiana, 234, 238

Gaia Hypothesis, 211, 236
garden, 9, 80, 83–85, 87–89, 91, 93–95, 98, 103, 161, 166, 228, 230
garden features, 83, 85, 87
Glen Canyon, 43, 45; National Recreation Area, 34, 39, 41–43, 46, 50
Granada (Colorado), 80–81, 83–84, 88–89, 94–96
Grand Canyon, 35, 49
Great Anaconda, 225–27, 234
Great Anaconda and Woman Shaman, 237
Great Depression, 55, 68, 70, 72
guacas, 193–94
Guatemala, 6, 14, 57, 60, 65, 160

haciendas, 139–40, 142, 145–47, 149, 153, 155, 161
hallucinogenic drugs, 225
Hanks, William B., 137, 156
Harvey, David, 4, 14
Heckenberger, Michael, 215, 236
heritage management, 4–5, 8, 22, 28, 48
historical archaeology, 96, 157
Hodder, Ian, 11, 14
Holocene foragers in Amazonia, 213
Honduras Land Titles Acts, 58, 64
Hopi, 8–9, 33–51; ancestors, 35, 37, 39, 41, 43–45, 47, 49, 51; Cultural Preservation Office, 33–34, 37, 39–42, 45, 49–51; Hisatsinom, 35; history, 35, 37, 41–43, 45–46, 49; homviikya, 36–37; Hoopoq'yaqam, 35, 49; Màasaw, 35; Mesas, 34–35, 39–40, 45; Motisinom, 35; oral tradition, 48; Palatkwapi (ancient location),

244 INDEX

35, 44; Pisisvayu (Colorado River), 44, 49; place-names, 42, 47; Reservation, 36, 39–41, 46; Sipapuni, 35; Tiyo (oral tradition), 44–45, 50; Toko'navi (Navajo Mountain), 43–45; traditional cultural properties, 37, 49; Tribe, 8, 13, 33–34, 36–37, 39–40, 42, 49–50; Tuuwanasavi, 35; Wupatki (ancient settlement), 45

Hopis, Rattlesnake Clan, 43, 46

Hopi Tribal Council, 39

Hopitutskwa, 33, 35–37, 40, 43, 46, 50–51

households, 3, 26, 112, 116–17, 119, 132–33, 135–37, 139–43, 145–46, 148, 151, 153, 155, 159, 161

houses, 10, 62, 66, 68, 97–98, 100, 103–6, 108–18, 120, 124–27, 135–36, 151–52, 176, 223, 232

house sites, 27, 119

Houston, James D., 85, 95

huancas, 192, 194, 196–98, 201

Huaura, 190, 194, 206

Huitzilopochtli, 101

Hulmal, 24–25

Human Carrying Capacity, 237

Human Rights, 14

Hurricane Gilbert, 148, 151

Hymenaea genus, 220

Icaiché Maya, 58–60, 68, 73

ICC. *See* Indian Claims Commission

iconography, 215, 225, 227, 234

Inca Empire, 199, 206

INDEMAYA (Yucatan, Mexico), 20

Indian Claims Commission (ICC), 36–37, 50

indigenous attitudes towards mobility (Amazonia), 229

indigenous house plans, 99, 101, 103, 105, 107, 109, 111, 113, 115, 117, 119, 121, 123, 125, 127

Inga feuillei, 192

inheritance, 10–11, 97, 104

Instituto Nacional de Antropologia e Historia, Mexico (INAH), 16, 18–22, 27–28, 31, 128–29

internment camps, 9, 13, 81, 90, 92

Irrigation, 203

Issei, 82, 85, 90

Itzpapalotl, 129–30

Iximché, 6, 14

Japanese American Internment, 79, 81, 83, 85, 87, 89–91, 93, 95–96

Japanese American National Museum (JANM), 92

Japanese Americans, 9, 79–82, 87, 96

Joseph, Gilbert M., 17, 31

Juquila, 168, 170, 177, 184, 186

Kachinas, 49

Kancabdzonot, 24–25, 152

Kaua, 26, 133, 135, 138, 143–47, 155–57

Kekchi Maya, 161

Kellogg, Barbara, 105, 117, 124, 127

Kirchhoff, Paul, 103, 128

Kiva, 51

knowledge, 3, 5, 8, 23, 26, 39, 53, 55, 87, 90, 174, 179, 225, 227, 231

Kuwanwisiwma, Leigh, 35, 37, 39, 49–51

Lacandon Maya, 60–61, 64–65

Lake Powell, 42, 44

Lake Texcoco, 101, 106

landforms, natural, 41–42

landholding, 133, 137, 141, 146, 154

land management, 34; prehistoric Amazonia, 209, 235

landscape: agricultural, 15, 102; anthropogenic, 13; archaeological, 46; architectural, 199; carceral, 79; coastal, 12; cultural, 33, 37, 39, 42–43, 80–81, 200; historic, 235; historical, 8, 12

landscape ecology, 234, 237

landscape knowledge, 22, 26–27, 142

landscape management, 214, 232

landscape memory, 23, 53–57, 59, 61, 63, 65, 67, 69–73, 75, 77

land tenure, 5, 9–10, 23, 45, 53, 72, 97–98, 100–101, 103–4, 118, 135

land title, 10–11, 26, 97, 151

Las Llamas-Moxeke, 198, 205

last names, shared, 163, 174, 178–80

Late Archaic (Peru), 195, 197, 199–200, 202–4, 206–7

late twentieth-century archaeology in Amazonia, 215

Lathrap, Donald, 211, 234, 236

Latin alphabet, 98

Latin America, 6, 187

Latour, Bruno, 7, 14

Lefebvre, Henri, 4, 14

Leventhal, Richard M., 56, 151, 159

Levi-Strauss, Calude, 126–27

liberalismo, 158

linguistics, 206

Little Colorado River, 35, 45
Lockhart, James, 103–5, 111, 118, 123–26, 128
London, 14, 58, 66, 74–77, 157, 203, 236
Los Angeles, California, 83, 92
Lovelock, James, 211, 236
Lower Amazon, 216, 220, 229, 237
lowland neotropics, 205, 236
Lurin Valley, 198

maize, 25, 192–93, 196, 204, 206, 219; beer, 193; dough, 70; gruels, 70; kernels, 62; referred to as corn, 61, 69–70, 72, 102, 116–17, 172, 192, 196; seeds, 61; soaking, 62, 64
Maní (Yucatan, Mexico), 16–18, 20, 22
Manzanar (California, USA), 85, 90, 95
Marajó, 223–24, 226, 228–29, 231
Marajó art, 232
Marajó Island, 224, 227, 232, 234, 237
marine resources, 196–97
marriage patterns, 143–46
masters and mistresses of the animals (Amazonia), 225
matrilineal, 178, 226
Maya, 14, 16, 21, 24–25, 30, 55–58, 60–61, 64–66, 73–74, 132–33, 136, 156, 158–61, 178, 188
Maya calendrical system, 142
Maya Collapse, 157
Maya-language colonial documents, 133–34
Meggers, Betty, 211, 236
Mérida, 16, 20, 29, 158
Meskell, Lynn, 93, 95
Mexicas, 16, 101–3, 123
Mexico, 8–10, 19, 22, 30–31, 57, 59, 97–98, 101–2, 104, 126–31, 157, 159, 161, 163, 187–88; basin of, 101, 123
Mexico City, 29, 31, 97–98, 102, 117–18, 120, 129
Mexico-Tenochtitlan, 98, 100–103, 106, 118, 123
Mexico-Tlatelolco, 101
Michoacán, 158
mid-twentieth archaeology, Amazonia, 210–11
Milky Way, 225
Mixteca, 187
Mixtecs, 178
Moche Valley, 202
Mohave Generating Station, 40
Monte Alegre, 214, 219–20, 228–29, 236
Monte Carmelo, 224
monumental architecture, 197, 200, 206
monuments, 16–17, 20, 29, 160, 190

Moundbuilders, 237
mounds, 197–200, 223–24
Muchukux, 25–26, 29
Museo Yucateco, 15–16
myth, 12, 189–91, 194–96, 200–201, 214, 227
mythic-historical narratives, 227

Nahua Peoples (Mexico), 10, 97, 100–101, 116, 118–19, 157
National Environmental Policy Act, 40
National Historic Preservation Act (NHPA), 33–34, 37–38, 46; Section 106, 38, 40–41; Section 110, 38, 42
National Park Service (NPS), 42–43
National Register of Historic Places. See NRHP
native alcaldes (Belize / British Honduras), 59
Native American Graves Protection and Repatriation Act (NAGPRA), 6
Native Americans, 6, 127, 160, 232
Navajo Reservation, 40
Neves, Edouardo, 215, 232, 236
New Age, 11
New Archaeology, 4, 209, 212, 215
Nikkei, 87, 96
Noh Cah Santa Cruz, 147
Norá, Pierre, 4, 14
Norte Chico region of Peru, 11–12, 189–91, 195–204, 206
North America, 212
NRHP (National Register of Historic Places), 33, 38–42
Nukak people, 230, 236

Oaxaca, 163, 188
Oaxaca City, 169
Office of Surface Mining, 40
Old Spider Woman, 45
Omagua, 224, 226; female artists, 224
Oncised and Punctate Horizon, 218–19
Ono, Gary, 92–93, 96
O'Odham, 51
Oraibi Wash, 40
oral narrative, 23, 30, 61, 65–66, 69
Orange Walk (Belize), 66, 68–70, 73–75
orchards, 217, 219, 223–24
Oto-manguean languages, 164

Pachacamac, 189, 192–94
Painted Rock, 219–21

246 INDEX

Paleo-Indians (Amazonia), 213, 219–22, 226–27, 233–34, 237
Palm Forests, 236
Pampa de las Llamas-Moxeke, 198, 205
Panbá, 139
Panixtlahuaca, 178–79, 188
Paramonga, 189–90, 200–202
Pativilca, 190
patriclans, 136, 139
patrilineal, 126, 154, 178
patronym groups, 131, 133, 135–36, 139, 141, 143, 145–46, 148, 151, 153, 156
Pearl Harbor, 81–82
Pearsall, Deborah, 197, 205, 215, 236
Pencuyut, 160
Peón, Juan, 16–17
person reference, 10, 163–64, 170–71, 177, 188
Perú, 11, 189, 195–96, 198, 201–7
Petén, 59, 61–62, 64
pictographic documents, 97, 105, 122, 125
Piperno, Delores, 197, 205, 215, 236
Pisté, 21
place-names, 23, 93, 163, 179–80, 182–83, 186
platforms, 197–200, 204, 217
political centralization, 204
pollen data, 61–62
Polychrome Ceramic Horizon (Amazonia), 223–25, 227, 234
population, 24–25, 116, 123, 133, 137, 152–53, 158, 194, 197, 211, 213, 218, 228–29, 231, 235
Posey, Darrell A., 214, 232, 236–37
postmodernism, 215
poststructuralism, 14, 30
private property, 4, 33, 35, 55, 58, 100, 103, 105, 150
Proto-Chatino, 187
Proto-Zapotec, 188
Puebla, state of, 103, 128
Puerto Rico, 126
pupunha, 217, 230

Qa'toya, 45–46
Quetzalcoatl, 51
Quiahije Chatino, 163, 166–69, 171, 173, 175, 177, 179, 181, 183, 187
Quintana Roo, 161

Rainbow Bridge National Monument, 42–43, 50
Rancho Bubul, 149
Redfield, Robert, 148–49, 151–53, 160

Reed, Nelson, 56–57, 76, 131, 133, 160
Restall, Matthew, 16, 31, 135–36, 142, 160
Río Bravo, 73
Rio Negro, 234
ritual, 6, 12, 111, 124, 129, 176, 207, 226–27, 232, 234
Roosevelt, Anna C., 12, 209–10, 212–16, 218, 220, 222, 224–28, 230, 232, 234, 236–38
Roys, Ralph L., 24, 31, 132–37, 139, 149–51, 156, 160–61, 178, 188

Salati, Eneas, 211, 237
San José Nuevo, 68–69, 73
San José Palmar, 68–69, 72–73, 76
San José Viejo, 55
San José Yalbac, 55–57, 61, 68, 71
San Juan Amanalco, 120
San Juan Amanaldo, 108
San Juan Moyotlan, 98, 120–21
San Juan Necaltitlan, 121
San Juan Quiahije, 10, 12, 163–64, 169–70, 180–81, 183, 187
San Juan Tlatilco, 121
San Juan Xihuitonco, 120
San Juan Yopico, 121
San Marcos Zacatepec, 166, 188
San Pablo Teocaltitlan, 112, 120
San Pablo Zoquipan, 98, 125
San Pedro Belize, 56, 58–62, 64–65, 70, 73–75
San Pedro Maya, 56, 58–59, 63, 75–76
San Pedro Siris, 56, 60, 62–63, 76
San Pedro Valley (Arizona, USA), 49
San Pedro Yalbac, 61
San Sebastián Ahuatonco, 121
San Sebastián Atzacualco, 98
San Sebastián Tzacualco, 98, 114, 121–22
San Sebastián Zacatla, 122
Santa Barbara, 95
Santa Cruz Maya, 57–58
Santa María Cuepopan, 98, 121
Santa María Yolotepec, 166
Santarem, 216–17, 219, 221–23, 227–29, 231–33
Santarem art, 226
Secakuku, Alph, 35, 44, 51
Second Mesa, Hopi, 36–37, 51
Seinan neighborhood of Los Angeles, 82
settlement aggregation, 133, 137, 141
settlement patterns, 15, 17, 19, 21, 23, 25, 27, 29, 31, 202
Shady, Ruth, 195–96, 198–99, 206–7

INDEX **247**

shellfish, 197, 213, 221–22
Shipibo people, 226, 234
Sierra Tarahumara, 52
site plans, 98, 100, 102, 104–6, 108–9, 112–14,
    116–20
smallholders, 132–33, 139–40, 146, 159
Smith, Nigel, 214, 237
Snake Dance (Hopi Religion), 44, 48
soil, 21, 29, 65, 67, 69, 71–72, 82, 87, 93, 102, 209,
    214, 217, 235
soil chemistry, 80, 87–88
Soja, Edward, 4, 14
space: domestic, 112, 119; household, 10, 97, 100,
    116; public, 83, 89, 164, 197; social, 67
spirit animal, 225–26
stakeholders, 4–5, 7, 9, 12–13, 15, 18, 195
Stenborg, Per, 218, 238
Sternberg, Hilgard, 214, 238
Steward, Julian H., 206, 238
subsistence, 4, 10, 22, 26–28, 55, 63, 132, 205, 215,
    218
sun, 29, 110, 192–95, 212, 220, 225–26
Supe, 190, 194, 203, 205
swidden, 58, 66

Talaswaima, Leonard, 45, 51
Talking Crosses, 158
Tapajos River, 218
Taperinha, 212, 222–23
Tekantó, 136, 156, 161
Tekom, 24–26, 133, 135, 143–48, 155–57
Tenayocan, 110
Tenochtitlán, 16, 101, 117, 123, 127
Teopan, 98, 125
Tepanecs, 101
territoriality, 8–10, 15, 22–24
territories, 7, 11, 27, 35–37, 46–47, 58, 97, 103, 105,
    111, 136, 210, 229–30
Teruel, Father Luis, 192
Texcoco, 101, 123
Tezozomoc, 123
Ticul, 16
Tihosuco, 25, 151
Titles of Ebtun, 24, 31, 133–34, 137, 149, 156–57,
    160
Tixcacalcupul, 24, 133, 135, 143–48, 155–57
tiyo, 44–45, 50
Tlachcuiltitlan, 121
Tlacopán, 101, 127

Tlatelolco, 101, 123, 127
Tlatilco, 112
Tlaxcala, 103, 129
tones, 164, 183
tourism, 5, 21, 90, 229
traditional cultural properties, 33–34, 37–42, 46,
    49, 51; general description, 38
Triple Alliance, 101, 127
Tukanoans, 226, 230
turtles, 220, 223
Tutul Xiu, 16–18
Tzaab, 133–34, 147–49, 151–52, 154

Uayma, 145, 149, 155
Ucayali River, 234
UNESCO, 5
United States, 6, 9, 11, 37, 50, 65–66, 79, 81, 87, 89,
    169, 178, 204, 206
urn cemeteries, 224
US Highway 160, 39, 41–42, 49

Valladolid (City in Yucatan, Mexico), 131, 143,
    145–46, 155–56
Veracruz, 112, 116, 119, 129
Vichama Raymi, myth of, 11, 189–97, 199–203,
    205–7
Villa Rojas, Alfonso, 132, 134, 148–49, 152–53, 161
Visigalli, Egle, 215, 232, 238

walls, 16, 92, 106, 109–10, 125, 152, 199
Wauchope, Robert, 127
Weber, Ron, 234, 238
Wilk, Richard R., 133, 139–40, 159, 161
Wolf, Eric, 152, 161
Woman Shaman, 225–26, 234, 237
Woodbury, Anthony C., 164, 187
World Heritage sites, 13
World War II, 79, 82, 93
WRA (War Relocation Authority), 80–82

Xcalakdzonot, 26, 30
Xingu River, 221, 232–33
Xiu family, 16
Xocén, 156
Xochimilco, 98, 110, 125

Yalbac Hills, 9, 53, 55–56, 58–61, 64–65, 67,
    70–74
Yalbac Hills Maya, 9, 53, 61, 63–64, 69, 72

248   INDEX

Yaotl, Diego, 106, 108
Yaotl, Gabriel, 106, 108, 124
Yaxá, 159
Yaxcabá, 152
Yaxuná, 152
Ydzincab patronyms, 151
Yolngu, 48
Yucatán, 10, 12, 14–21, 23, 25, 30–31, 59, 70, 72, 74–76, 131–37, 139, 151, 153–55, 157–61

Yucatán Peninsula, 16, 18, 27, 57, 156
Yukatek (Yucatec) Maya, 8–9, 13, 24, 26–30, 53, 55–56, 61, 70, 72–73, 158, 188

Zapotecan branch, 164
Zapotecs, 178
Zongolica, 112, 116, 119, 126, 129
Zuni, 48, 51